Clinical Simulations as Signature Pedagogy

Clinical Simulations as Signature Pedagogy

Educator Preparation Across the Disciplines

Edited by

Benjamin Dotger
Kelly Chandler-Olcott

HARVARD EDUCATION PRESS
Cambridge, MA

Paperback ISBN 978-1-68253-705-3

Library of Congress Cataloging-in-Publication Data is on file.

Published by Harvard Education Press,
an imprint of the Harvard Education Publishing Group

Harvard Education Press
8 Story Street
Cambridge, MA 02138

Cover Design: Endpaper Studio
Cover Image: Ajwad Creative/DigitalVision Vectors via Getty Images

The typefaces in this book are Myriad Pro and Sabon LT.

To Dr. Sharon Dotger, for being a friend, colleague, and conceptual sounding board for clinical simulations for fifteen years

To the six teacher candidates in Ben's first simulation course, for engaging sincerely in the process and offering honest, energizing feedback

Contents

SECTION I: BACKGROUND AND CONCEPTUAL UNDERPINNINGS **1**

1. CLINICAL SIMULATIONS IN EDUCATOR PREPARATION 1
Benjamin Dotger and Kelly Chandler-Olcott

2. THE CONCEPTUAL UNDERPINNINGS OF CLINICAL SIMULATIONS 15
Benjamin Dotger

SECTION II: PROGRAM-SPECIFIC USES OF SIMULATIONS **31**

3. SIMULATIONS IN SECONDARY MATHEMATICS TEACHER EDUCATION: THE ROLE OF DEBRIEFINGS IN PROVIDING OPPORTUNITIES TO DEVELOP KNOWLEDGE FOR TEACHING 31
Duane T. Graysay and Joanna O. Masingila

4. "HOW CAN SHE PARTICIPATE?" EXAMINING INCLUSION IN PHYSICAL EDUCATION THROUGH SIMULATION 53
Michael L. Norris, Luis Columna, and Benjamin Dotger

5. DESIGNING SIMULATIONS FOR BUILDING SCIENTIFIC EXPLANATIONS WITH ELEMENTARY TEACHER CANDIDATES 67
Sharon Dotger and Benjamin Dotger

6. USING NESTED SIMULATIONS TO ASSESS SCHOOL COUNSELOR LEARNING 83
Sharon L. Bruner and Melissa M. Luke

7. USING SIMULATIONS TO PREPARE SCHOOL LEADERS TO CONDUCT DIFFICULT CONVERSATIONS 103
Joseph Shedd, Leela J. George, and Diane Canino-Rispoli

SECTION III: CROSS-PROGRAM PERSPECTIVES ON CLINICAL SIMULATIONS **127**

8. A CROSS-PROGRAM ANALYSIS OF DISABILITY, DIFFERENCE, AND INCLUSION IN MULTIPLE SIMULATIONS FOR EDUCATOR CANDIDATES **127**
Christine Ashby and Megan E. Cartier

9. COLLABORATING TO SUPPORT THE DESIGN, IMPLEMENTATION, AND INVESTIGATION OF CLINICAL SIMULATIONS **153**
Kelly Chandler-Olcott

Notes 171

Acknowledgments 187

About the Editors and Contributors 189

Index 195

SECTION I
BACKGROUND AND CONCEPTUAL UNDERPINNINGS

CHAPTER 1

Clinical Simulations in Educator Preparation

BENJAMIN DOTGER AND KELLY CHANDLER-OLCOTT

As a new assistant professor in 2006, Ben taught Study of Teaching, an introductory education foundations course for undergraduates in the School of Education (SOE) at Syracuse University, where we both work. Each week, the course included two class sessions on campus and three hours of field placement in a local K–12 school. During class discussion of an article on teacher engagement with families, one of the course topics, Ben asked candidates about their experiences interacting with parents and caregivers in that placement or any others they had completed. Visibly frustrated with the question, Sarah, a sophomore mathematics education major, responded, "I don't know how to find parents." As Ben reflected on that statement, he realized, with a start, that he didn't know how to find them for her, either—at least not in the context of an introductory field experience.

We and our colleagues think about how to design, support, and improve candidates' placements a good deal in SOE, which is known for its historical commitment to field-intensive educator preparation. Most of our programs have longstanding partnerships with local school districts and community agencies, and faculty work hard to codesign meaningful experiences that support growth for our candidates and offer value for our partners. Many of our undergraduates in teacher education tell us the opportunity to engage in fieldwork in their first year on campus serves as a key factor in their decision to matriculate. As many scholars have documented, however, it is difficult, labor-intensive work to launch and sustain field placements that offer consistently high-quality opportunities to learn, and such efforts are often fragile.[1]

Ben's foundations course presented these complexities in microcosm. Between twenty and thirty teacher candidates took the course each semester, with each needing to log a minimum of twenty-five hours in schools as partial fulfillment of our state's pre–student teaching field requirement. That one course placed candidates in half a dozen local school districts, each with different bell schedules, grade-level configurations, curriculum priorities, and instructional approaches. Despite regular communications with cooperating teachers and assignments designed to link course content with the placement, there was considerable variance in what candidates could observe and do. Ben learned quickly that he could neither predict nor guarantee any number of factors, including (1) who would actually engage with students, parents, or other teachers beyond the host, (2) what the circumstances of that engagement would be, (3) whether that engagement would link to concepts from his course, and (4) if there would be any data to guide reflection after engagement. Sarah's striking words suggested that Ben wasn't the only one aware of these challenges; at least some candidates seemed to be aware of the lack of consistent learning opportunities as well, judging from contrasting accounts of their experiences they shared in class.

A possible solution pathway opened up a few months after the exchange with Sarah when Ben met Steven Harris and learned about his work directing clinical simulations at SUNY Upstate Medical University, an institution in the State University of New York system that is Syracuse University's neighbor. Ben began thinking about how to tap Steve's standing roster of community theater actors who served as standardized patients for the simulations that Upstate, like nearly every other American medical school, runs daily to develop and assess the diagnostic skills of prospective doctors, nurses, and other health-care personnel.[2] Building from the conversation with Steve, Ben soon proposed an elective on parent and caregiver communications for SOE undergraduates. If he couldn't guarantee teacher candidates that they could find and engage with parents in traditional field practica, then he would design live simulations that would approximate those experiences. When Ben taught that elective on course overload the following year, Sarah signed up. She and her classmates participated in multiple simulated encounters on topics such as supporting students in crisis, responding to peer-to-peer bullying, and addressing parental challenges to required curricular materials. Not long after the course concluded, Ben made the first of many overtures to colleagues teaching subject-specific courses in the programs he served as a generalist teacher educator, and an ongoing line of inquiry into collaboratively designed simulations was born.

Flash forward nearly fifteen years, and clinical simulations are a fixture across multiple SOE certification areas. They have attracted funding from both public and private sources, including the Arthur Vining Davis Foundations, the Institute of Education Sciences, the National Science Foundation, and the Spencer Foundation. Ben's introductory course now features six different simulations that supplement in-person fieldwork, allowing candidates to explore a range of complex professional interactions predictably, including but not limited to parent communication. Educational leadership, an advanced study program that leads to certification as an administrator for experienced teachers, integrates simulations in eight of its nine required courses, helping to prepare future school leaders to dialogue with parents about equity issues, facilitate a resistant colleague's entry into a learning community, and provide responsive instructional supervision, among other areas of focus. To date, twenty-six colleagues who prepare educators for work in schools have collaborated with Ben to design, implement, and/or analyze data from at least one simulation, representing more than a third of SOE's full-time faculty members.[3]

This volume is an outgrowth of those collaborations. We editors initiated our simulation-related partnership when Ben invited Kelly to codesign some discipline-specific scenarios for use in the English methods course accompanying the first of two student teaching placements in secondary education. Not long after that experience, Kelly was appointed as SOE's associate dean for research, and she helped Ben to organize a study group for faculty interested in learning more about simulations in educator preparation. The idea for an edited collection of multiple perspectives on simulations at Syracuse emerged from monthly meetings of that group over three years. All of the chapters that follow include at least one author who was a member.

The purpose of this book, then, is to argue, with examples from across our collective, that simulations enhance the preparation of educators. In our view, simulations allow faculty to support their respective cohorts of teacher, school counselor, or school leader candidates in ways that closely approximate authentic problems of practice but, crucially, reduce the complexity of the instructional context in manageable ways for novices; ensure all candidates have comparable opportunities to practice; and reduce the risk for K–12 students, families, and colleagues who interact with those novices before they master key skills and habits of mind. In addition, simulations help SOE faculty bridge traditional silos to examine vexing issues about communication, cultural responsiveness, equity, and community that are relevant to the preparation of educators across the disciplines. In the sections that follow, we unpack several of the components of our argument, starting first with how we define and enact simulations and then turning to a discussion of how we came to see them as what Lee Shulman calls a signature pedagogy for SOE and the field of education more broadly.[4] We outline what we see as potential benefits of the volume for readers who come to it with different needs and interests before we conclude with an overview of subsequent chapters.

WHAT IS A CLINICAL SIMULATION?

Simulations have been used across a range of pedagogical contexts, including but not limited to education, for many years. They vary along a number of dimensions, including how long they last, the degree to which they allow multiple pathways for learners, and the number of simultaneous participants they involve. In some instances, learners engage in simulation with known classmates—a design feature that reduces implementation complications but can also threaten perceived authenticity when peers break character. In other instances, learners engage with interlocutors not previously known to them, a feature that tends to increase verisimilitude but usually requires recruitment, training, and sometimes even compensation for interaction partners. A recent wave of attention has explored the affordances of digital technologies in facilitating simulations, with some initiatives involving instructor-facilitated online communication and others utilizing digital avatars with which candidates have no other contact. What nearly all simulations have in common, however, is their designers' interest in leveraging planned but unscripted interactions to help learners identify, use, and reflect on knowledge and skills relevant to success in a particular domain.[5]

At Syracuse—and in this book—we define a *clinical simulation* as a live, recorded interaction between an educator candidate and a trained actor portraying a standardized individual in an attempt to approximate a challenging situation in schools. We use the descriptor *clinical* when we speak and write about our approach to simulations to acknowledge our conceptual debt to medical education, where the use of that modifier is pervasive. We also use that language to emphasize the applied and instructional nature of the simulated encounters, which are distinct, in our view, from typical instructional approaches in most campus-based education courses as well as from typical field placements in schools.

We use the term *educator candidate* (EC) to refer to a future teacher, school leader, or school counselor enrolled in a preparation program, as these are the populations with which we have used nearly sixty different simulations so far at Syracuse. Depending on the programs offered by your institution, you may also opt to employ simulations with other preprofessionals in education or other helping professions where success hinges on interpersonal communication, including school psychologists, social workers, occupational therapists, and athletic coaches.

In our model, the other person in a simulated interaction besides the candidate is a *standardized individual* (SI), a phrase drawn from medical educator Howard Barrows's original use of what he called *standardized patients* within clinical simulations. Standardized patients are actors who are carefully trained to present distinct symptoms and communicate questions and concerns to future medical professionals in a standard, consistent manner such that multiple medical professionals-in-training engage with the same set of patient circumstances, concerns, and medical data.[6] Face-to-face with the standardized patient in an exam room, each physician is challenged to move beyond a traditional, distant analysis of the "case" and instead conduct a diagnostic assessment, communicate with the patient, and construct a plan of action or treatment regimen.

Adapted to the needs of educator preparation, standardized individuals are actors playing the role of a school stakeholder such as a parent, a student, or a colleague. In our context, multiple actors enact the same schools-based scenario, which we usually refer to by the first and last names of the SI, for a group of candidates in a program or a course. Whether we have as few as three or as many as ten actors playing the same SI for a given simulation depends on the size of the candidate cohort. Most SIs have considerable acting experience; some are theater majors at local colleges, while others participate in local and regional productions. On occasion, most often in our educational leadership program, a simulation requires specialized knowledge to maintain plausibility. In these situations, we recruit and hire individuals with expertise in the profession (such as a retired building principal to portray a veteran teacher resisting recommended collaborations with other colleagues). Whether we specify particular identity categories such as race and gender in hiring SIs depends on the content of the simulation. Some scenarios are designed to explore the impact of such constructs directly, leading us to ensure that all candidates interact with actors who portray them consistently. In scenarios where a construct such as gender is not foregrounded, we typically select a pool of actors with varied identifications, allowing candidates to consider the impact of that difference in their whole-cohort debriefing but not holding it constant across individual simulated experiences.

As part of their training, SIs receive a three- to five-page, single-spaced interaction protocol that provides extensive character-building information as well as specific verbal triggers—the exact background, statements, questions, and nonverbal mannerisms that each SI must present and embody. SIs meet for one to two hours as a group with Ben and/or a relevant program faculty member to review this document in advance of the simulated encounters. At this time, the actors ask clarification questions, flesh out aspects of character motivation, and sometimes make suggestions for improvement that are subsequently integrated into the protocol.

We should note that our use of the term *standardized* to refer to the role actors play is intended to emphasize our desire for multiple candidates—both within and across cohorts—to engage with the same important content in a given simulation scenario. In no way do we intend to suggest, to ECs or to readers of this book, that we see all K–12 students, parents, or colleagues (or even all actors) as the same. Indeed, it is worth emphasizing that the interactional nature of our model means that individual candidates have varied simulation experiences shaped by their own choices, creating comparable but distinct learning pathways that can subsequently be unpacked with peers and instructors.

In fact, because a key objective of all simulations is for candidates to develop their ability to think on their feet during real-time professional exchanges, their instructions are much less detailed than those for the actors. ECs typically receive a one- to two-page, single-spaced protocol about a week before the scheduled simulation that provides background about the school and classroom context as well as a limited rationale for the pending interaction. A few simulations include supplemental documents, although most do not.[7] The protocol is intended to help candidates understand why they are about to engage with a particular SI but not to prescribe their actions, decisions, or communications. Instead, we encourage candidates to engage in the simulation using any prior training, experience, and professional judgment that seems relevant to them.

When we began implementing simulations, nearly all of the taped interactions took place in small conference rooms within Upstate Medical University's Clinical Skills Center, which is equipped and staffed to support medical simulations.[8] Basic subcontract and purchased-service agreements allowed us to utilize spaces wired with permanent cameras and microphones and to access actor rosters for SIs. As our simulation initiatives grew, we began to use other spaces, including traditional classrooms and faculty offices, for interactions we documented with portable devices such as iPads. Using multiple spaces and different recording technologies gives us flexibility in implementing the variety of simulations you'll read about in this book as well as reduces some of our implementation costs. The variety of our current approaches suggests that you need not be located near a medical school to pursue simulations, although reaching out to colleagues at such an institution may uncover useful resources and expertise if such a school is in proximity.

We allocate an eighteen-minute window for each candidate to engage in the simulated encounter—enough time, we have found, for the learning experience to take shape. Each simulation that we facilitate is digitally recorded and immediately available to the candidate. ECs then have seven to ten days to deconstruct their respective simulation videos, supported by debriefing guides that focus them on specific triggers presented in a given simulation or specific practices they may have used or referenced during the interaction.

With but few exceptions, all educator candidates in a given cohort engage in the same simulated encounter on the same day, uniformity that promotes shared analysis. In subsequent class sessions, ECs typically select and share segments of their videos with their classmates, prompting both individual and shared consideration of the simulated situation. These debriefing sessions provide candidates with time and space to reflect on their practice, grounding their reflections in clear data and seeking input from their peers to help them judge the effectiveness of their decision-making in the simulated encounter. Figure 1.1 offers a distillation of the process that candidates typically experience when participating in a simulation.

FIGURE 1.1 Overview of the simulation process

Candidates receive the candidate interaction protocol for review from their instructor.
One Week Later:
Candidates complete a brief preinteraction survey. Candidates engage in a videotaped interaction with a standardized individual. Candidates participate in an instructor-led debriefing session with other candidates who interacted with the same SI.
One Day Later:
Candidates receive access to digital video of their interaction with the SI. Candidates receive instructions about how to reflect on their experience in writing, with timestamps to reference particular moments in the video.
Seven to Ten Days Later:
Candidates share and discuss video clips they have selected for review by the class or cohort. Candidates submit final written reflections on the experience.

EMBRACING CLINICAL SIMULATIONS AS A SIGNATURE PEDAGOGY

In SOE, we trace our application of the term *signature pedagogy* to describe simulations to the transcript of a speech by Lee Shulman, past president of the Carnegie Foundation for the Advancement of Teaching, that many of us read and discussed during a study-group retreat in the summer of 2016.[9] In that speech, Shulman explored how four professions—medicine, engineering, law, and the clergy—utilized distinct pedagogies to prepare their respective practitioners. In each preparatory environment, faculty implemented a pedagogical approach pervasively and routinely. Over time, the very routine and extensive use of these pedagogies resulted in signature status within each profession. For example, Shulman cited the clinical rounds of medicine, where small teams of medical residents attend to and carefully study various patients each day, discussing diagnoses, regimens of treatment, and communications with patient and family. Shulman also described Socratic seminars in the field of law, where a presiding faculty member guides a group of law students through the careful review of a legal case and a rigorous dissection of their peers' arguments for or against the facts of that case.

Shulman argued that these signature pedagogies help novices move beyond the cognitive apprenticeship of thinking like a medical or legal professional to practicing like one. In this view, new practitioners must acquire a distinct knowledge base, but this knowledge is rote and inert if they are not also taught how to shift that knowledge into action. One must also learn how to *be* the professional; that is, to gradually develop the ethos, character, and identity of the medical, legal, theological, or engineering practitioner. Shulman's emphasis on teaching preprofessionals the "knowing, doing, and being" of the given profession led him to articulate a set of design features. He proposed that signature pedagogies across the professions are designed to be "habitual, routine, visible, accountable, interdependent, collaborative, emotional, unpredictable, and affect-laden."[10] Linking these key features together, Shulman outlined his thesis—that signature pedagogies in education are pedagogies of uncertainty, engagement, and formation (tenets that Ben explores in more depth in chapter 2). As we discussed the article content in light of our program-specific efforts, it was clear to us that live simulations as we were enacting them represented all three of these constructs.

That others were seeing simulations as a potential signature of preparation at Syracuse was also becoming increasingly clear. Discussions with current students and alumni across several programs revealed that many viewed their simulation participation as a vividly memorable and important rite of passage in becoming a professional. Our admissions personnel began to incorporate discussion of simulations into our student recruitment efforts, where it sparked considerable interest among prospective applicants and their families. Several faculty coalitions working on curricular revisions for specific programs or groups of programs made sure to embed simulations into their proposals.

Even as simulations were taking hold across SOE, they were not—and still are not—the only approach our faculty uses. Many of us employ and research other initiatives designed to serve as a bridge between campus-based coursework and fully contextualized practice in K–12 schools, including teacher educator–guided rehearsals by candidates in subject-specific methods courses; critically oriented, project-based field placements that allow faculty, candidates, and certified teachers to serve K–12 students in shared space; and lesson study.[11] We see all of these approaches as theoretically compatible with each other—as all grounded in common assumptions about the need to "turn away from an intense focus on the knowledge needed" for teaching, leading, and counseling and toward the situated use of that knowledge that Pam Grossman and others characterize as "practice-based" preparation.[12] We expect that a range of learning opportunities, including extended student-teaching apprenticeships in schools, will continue to be available to our candidates. But simulations have generated the most unifying traction across SOE as a whole, reaching more candidates and involving more faculty than any other practice-based initiative to date, suggesting that it is not a stretch to apply the signature pedagogy description in this case.

And we are not the only scholars to make strong claims for simulations' potential in education. As we have deepened our local commitment to this work, we have also interacted, both directly and indirectly, with many others using simulations in their own contexts. Some of these connections are linked to Ben's research collaborations beyond Syracuse—for instance, to subcontracts from an Arthur Vining Davis grant to colleagues interested in integrating aspects of our model into simulation work at Vanderbilt University and the University of North Carolina. Researchers from institutions as varied as the Massachusetts Institute of Technology, the University of Pittsburgh, and the Technical University of Munich visited our campus to observe simulated encounters. When they did, we learned more about the innovative aspects of their own simulation initiatives. And we read widely in the published simulation literature, to inform both particular research projects and our participation in the simulation study group.

We have been more apt to see simulations as a signature pedagogy as we have expanded our sense of how they might be used. As described above, our initial designs focused on simulations with parents and caregivers, with subsequent efforts exploring other kinds of discipline-specific interpersonal communication that are challenging for novices to navigate in schools. Cross-program discussions in the study group helped us realize it would be productive to focus our attention even more specifically on how such interactions implicate our longstanding, SOE-wide interests in *inclusive schooling*—which we define as schooling designed to support engagement and achievement for heterogeneous groups of learners, including but not limited to students with disabilities—in educative spaces where individual differences are seen as assets and not deficits.[13] This exploration has taken—and continues to take—two forms: (1) reexamination of existing protocol documents and accompanying interaction data with an inclusive lens and (2) design of new simulations that foreground these concerns more explicitly and with more critical and intersectional nuance. Most recently, racially biased police brutality in the United States, disparities related to COVID-19, and consciousness-raising student activism on our own campus have led us to set a new common focus around integrating antiracist principles more systematically in our simulation work. We will be helped in that regard by joint reading and discussion of a new book by Elizabeth A. Self and Barbara S. Stengel, early collaborators of Ben's from Vanderbilt, who have adapted a number of our procedures to this particular purpose.[14]

We cannot be certain that simulations will become as central to educator preparation as Socratic questioning is to law school. But we hope the many examples of how they're used at Syracuse will convince you of how generative they might be in offering your candidates opportunities to engage in authentic activity, develop aspects of professional identity and strategy, and recognize that their experiences are grounded within and hold implications for the larger classroom and school culture.

HOW THIS BOOK MIGHT HELP YOU

While planning, writing, and editing this book, we have found it helpful to envision you, our audience, as potential members of our simulation study group—colleagues like us who are committed to improving practice through experimentation, inquiry, and reflection. Such a stance reminds us to be invitational and candid in tone, as our best group discussions have typically been those in which participants felt welcomed to the table and free to speak directly without judgment. This stance also reminds us to anticipate and to welcome differences in knowledge and experience related to simulations and other practice-based approaches to educator preparation. That our group has productively included both our newest and our most veteran colleagues across five SOE departments suggests that simulations are an approach with a lot of "flex" to them—a pattern that informs our hunch that readers with varying background knowledge about simulations will find useful insights in the text, even if they're not the same insights.

What you gain from the book will likely depend on your positioning and your goals for reading it. If you are an individual teacher, leader, or counselor educator interested in integrating simulations into a particular course or sequence of courses you teach, we hope that the book will demonstrate the potential benefits of doing so and spark ideas about the aspects of your course content that might be generative to simulate.

If you are faculty or staff involved in the redesign or expansion of a teacher, leader, or counselor education program, shared reading and discussion of the volume may help you consider new angles on practice-based approaches that can unify the program. We hope the descriptions of collaboration threaded across the volume will also illustrate the value of undertaking simulations as a team.

If you are a graduate student in teacher education, leadership, or counseling, you might be reading this book as part of a course or seminar. We hope that it presents compelling ideas about how you and others may shape preparation of professionals in those fields in the future. Numerous graduate students have contributed to the efforts described in these pages, with several pursuing excellent dissertations about simulations that are themselves worth reading.[15]

And, finally, while we expect that our core audience is likely to be those who work primarily in postsecondary institutions, we see a role for simulations in K–12 contexts as well. Ben Dotger and chapter 7 contributors Joseph Shedd, Leela J. George and Diane Canino-Rispoli have worked with central-office and building leaders from districts in both New York and North Carolina to design and implement simulations that speak to in-service professionals' pressing concerns and continuous learning needs. If you work in schools rather than higher education, this book may spark ideas about how to support adult learning that will help you avoid the passive pitfalls associated with persistent professional development models such as the one-day workshops led by external experts.

In our view, one of the strengths of this volume is that it presents the simulation experience from multiple perspectives. You will see across the chapters how faculty working in different programs adapted our common processes to disciplinary and developmental agendas, which we believe will illustrate both the principled core that drives our design work as well as the implementation flexibility it offers. A constraint associated with this strength, however, is that space limitations prevent chapter authors from providing fine-grained details about such topics as funding simulations or training actors. If you desire additional information about what we call the "how to" explanations, we refer you to several of Ben's texts already in print.[16] If your interest in simulations is ignited, we also encourage you to follow the trail of the notes in individual chapters, as many of the authors have published findings from simulation-focused work in discipline-specific, peer-reviewed journals.

HOW THIS BOOK IS ORGANIZED

We've sequenced this book intentionally into three sections where the lens zooms out, then in, and then out again. Section I, Background and Conceptual Underpinnings, includes this chapter you've just read and chapter 2. The latter lays out the conceptual foundations that make Syracuse-based simulation work coherent while allowing for disciplinary and programmatic variation. It applies Shulman's lenses of engagement, uncertainty, and identity formation to various efforts in SOE and offers multiple examples of how these lenses are enacted by our faculty.[17]

Section II, Program-Specific Uses of Simulations, includes five chapters focused on how simulations can address interaction-based problems of practice anchored in varied disciplinary contexts. Each chapter draws on empirical data from one study or multiple studies conducted by the author or author team. Each shares at least one insight or takeaway related to the use of simulations that is discipline-specific and at least one other insight related to an issue of interest to faculty preparing educators in other disciplines.

The first three chapters in section II focus on different dimensions of single-encounter simulations for candidates seeking initial teacher certification. Chapter 3, by Duane T. Graysay and Joanna O. Masingila, focuses on the role of postsimulation group debriefing in developing candidates' knowledge for mathematics teaching. Chapter 4, by Michael L. Norris, Luis Columna, and Benjamin Dotger, explores how simulations provide practice for candidates in assessing the skills of students with disabilities and considering appropriate modifications to support their participation in physical education. Sharon Dotger and Benjamin Dotger share design tenets in chapter 5 for simulations requiring elementary education candidates to explore explanations of scientific phenomena, a practice at the center of the influential Next Generation Science Standards.

The last two chapters in section II expand the focus beyond classroom teaching to include other school professionals. These chapters also consider what happens when education faculty design multipart simulations enacted at two or more time intervals, rather than a single sitting. In chapter 6, Sharon L. Bruner and Melissa M. Luke demonstrate how nested simulations—candidates' multiple encounters with newly unfolding aspects of the same scenario—permit robust and integrated attention to four key domains in counseling. Chapter 7, by Joseph Shedd, Leela J. George and Diane Canino-Rispoli, describes how carefully sequenced, and in some cases linked, simulations across the educational leadership program prepare candidates for what these authors call "difficult conversations," including feedback and evaluation conferences with underperforming colleagues.

Section III, Cross-Program Perspectives on Clinical Simulations, includes two chapters that return to a wider-angled lens, drawing on data and offering insights that transcend any single SOE program. Chapter 8, by Christine Ashby and Megan E. Cartier, reviews candidate data from five different simulations with a common focus on disability and difference—an analysis that reveals several productive directions for multidisciplinary faculty collaboration around simulations. In chapter 9, Kelly Chandler-Olcott examines the intentions, processes, and outcomes of SOE's simulations study group to inform recommendations for how you might undertake collaborative design, implementation, and inquiry into simulations in your own contexts.

We hope that this volume inspires you to launch that work soon if you are new to it or deepens your commitment if you have already begun.

CHAPTER 2

The Conceptual Underpinnings of Clinical Simulations

BENJAMIN DOTGER

Elizabeth, a social studies education major, stands to the right of a giant video screen at the front of the classroom. She shifts nervously from side to side, adjusting her gaze back and forth between the giant screen and the audience of twenty-eight other teacher candidates. As the instructor, I am huddled behind the computer station to the side, silent and as inconspicuous as possible.

Although visibly nervous, Elizabeth captures the entire classroom, saying, "The clip I'm going to show is where I screwed up. I'll show it, and then—well, then I guess I want to hear from you." Elizabeth nods at me, and I push the button to play the simulation video clip she has cued up. Elizabeth, her peers, and I all watch the large screen carefully. In that short clip, Elizabeth is sitting across the table from a visibly worried father. With his hands clasped, the dad says to Elizabeth, "I don't know what to do. I'm not sure what's wrong with my kid!" Elizabeth responds with a very flat, matter-of-fact tone, saying, "Mr. Bolden, I don't know either."

Back in the classroom, Elizabeth nods at me to pause the video and turns to her peers, saying, "I picked this clip because I wasn't sure if I should say to a parent, 'I don't know,' and then there's this long silence between us that was just awkward. So?" As Elizabeth begins to facilitate her peers' questions and comments, I know this is an important moment. Elizabeth is in a vulnerable position. She's uncertain about what she said in the simulation.

And she's uncertain about what her peers—who also sat face-to-face with the same worried dad in their own simulations—are going to ask about her video clip.

Using the whole-group debriefing anecdote—and many other moments in the clinical simulation process—this chapter outlines the conceptual frameworks that guide simulations in the School of Education (SOE) at Syracuse University. As previewed in chapter 1, I center this chapter on Lee Shulman's three tenets of a signature pedagogy, beginning with the tenet of *engagement* to explicate how simulations immerse educator candidates (ECs) in authentic practice within and across disciplines. I then examine the inherent *uncertainty* that is baked into the exploratory actions and decisions of the novice educator. Finally, I conclude with Shulman's *formation* tenet and the promise of simulations to shape professional ethos and identity. As you read about how Shulman's framework guides our simulations, remember Elizabeth—engaging from the front of the classroom, showing a video of her recent actions in simulation, and toggling between the uncertainty of what she said and did in the simulated encounter and what she'll say and do while analyzing it with her peers. Facilitating whole-group discussion of her simulation video, like several distinct experiences within the simulation process, supports Elizabeth to build and blend the voice, presence, and skill of a professional educator.

USING SIMULATIONS TO ENGAGE IN AUTHENTIC PRACTICE

Building from Shulman's concept of signature pedagogies, our design and implementation of simulations at Syracuse hinge on EC engagement.[1] Very intentionally, our simulations situate candidates in the immediate and visceral demands of professional practice. We prioritize this active engagement as the baseline expectation so we can then leverage this learning experience into opportunities for individual ECs and peer cohorts to further engage in accountable, collaborative, and video data-informed analysis.

My initial simulation designs served as a response mechanism to mathematics education major Sarah and her peers' lack of opportunity to engage with parents and caregivers. Since then, the input and guidance of colleagues at Syracuse and across the US have expanded the design of simulations much further. Together, my colleagues and I now use simulations to ensure candidates in teacher education, school leadership, and school counseling can engage in a range of learning experiences that we cannot otherwise guarantee through traditional coursework and field placements. To illustrate this range, consider two very different learning experiences:

helping a student solve a mathematical equation and engaging with an individual with suicidal ideation.

In our secondary mathematics education program, my colleagues strive to equip their teacher candidates with the content knowledge and pedagogical skills necessary for teaching middle and high school mathematics. The field experiences for mathematics teacher candidates are deliberately varied to provide them opportunities to practice teaching different content (such as geometry, algebra, and trigonometry) as well as garner experience with learners in different grade levels. The variance in learning contexts offers the cohort a range of instructional opportunities to draw on but introduces challenges when it comes to discussing shared experiences coherently.

Responding to the need for focused experiences with and faculty-mediated review of specific instructional practices, my colleagues and I wrote, received, and utilized a National Science Foundation DR-K12 grant to design a series of secondary mathematics and science simulations. One of the resulting designs, the Jennifer Boyton simulation, situated mathematics teacher candidates in a face-to-face interaction with a standardized individual (SI) who was struggling to construct an equation that represented the relationship between two quantities. The context of this simulation was an after-school help session, akin to opportunities in secondary schools where students can drop in for extra help from a designated teacher from that department. In cooperation with SUNY Upstate Medical University's Clinical Skills Center, we recruited actors who were at least eighteen years old but who looked youthful enough to approximate a fifteen- or sixteen-year-old struggling in math. This small cohort of actors became our standardized students for the Boyton simulation, and we trained them to consistently portray Jennifer, a student who struggles with constructing an equation to represent a relationship given verbally. Through this simulation, we provided all of our mathematics teacher candidates with a common learning experience to experience individually and deconstruct collaboratively.

As a second example, consider the moment when a novice school counselor engages with an adolescent who is exhibiting signs of suicidal ideation. This is a clear moment for professional action, with striking potential consequences. My counselor education colleagues and I designed the Jasper Johnson simulation to center on the crucial moment of professionally interrogating whether an adolescent client has suicidal thoughts. In this simulation, candidates engage with a standardized student who recently transferred to the school and is showing signs of disengagement from family, full social media withdrawal from out-of-state friends, and longer-term changes in interaction patterns, dietary habits, and irritability. As in the algebra simulation, a small pool of actors was recruited to portray this standardized student. Training included emphasis on how each actor presents the signs of suicidal ideation but doesn't use the actual word *suicide*. By design, we positioned counselor candidates to interrogate whether the SI had considered suicide and how detailed their plans were.

The Jennifer Boyton and Jasper Johnson simulations are both informed by the historical design tenets undergirding medical education simulations that have been articulated by Howard Barrows and Stephen Abrahamson. The tenets serve as conceptual guideposts for our transfer of the simulation concept from medical to educator preparation.[2]

My colleagues and I anchored the Boyton simulation with the prevalence tenet, recognizing that all secondary mathematics teachers would likely encounter this common mathematics instructional situation and should have opportunities, through simulation, to engage and practice guiding a student to represent quantitative relationships across communication modes. In direct contrast, we grounded the Johnson simulation with the instructional importance and clinical impact tenets, recognizing that this situation is less common, holds significant implications if mishandled, and is a situation for which school counselors must prepare and practice thoughtfully, even though their traditional practica may not present opportunities for in-the-field engagement. By design, this simulation provides counselor candidates with the opportunity to practice documentation, direct questioning, and generation of follow-up actions to support a student in distress. In these two simulation examples and in the many others we utilize, the driving emphasis is to ensure opportunities for our ECs to engage and practice in very distinct professional situations—some that will be frequent in future practice, some less common, and some with distinct implications for a person or broader community.[3]

As we have designed clinical simulations for our ECs, the process has highlighted the concept of engaging authentically to ensure "in situ" learning. To illustrate, imagine ECs studying fully inclusive school environments. Ethically, this is a critical concept. Practically, this is an expansive concept, which a guiding faculty member could approach from many angles. Traditional study of fully inclusive classrooms might include subjects like special education and disability rights law, classroom and school structures that typically exclude students, different coteaching models meant to support and include students with disabilities in the general education classroom, and the educator's role in forming and implementing individualized education plans for students. To teach these subjects, a faculty member might utilize detailed book chapters, case studies, short films, and classroom observations as instructional approaches.

These instructional approaches do provide an EC with information and conceptual grounding on fully inclusive environments, and SOE faculty use all of them. Yet ECs can look past the PowerPoint slides, attend distantly to disability law, review, judge, and then forget the written case and discount the details present in classroom observation. As a result of these instructional approaches, the candidate may remain invisible, uninvested, unaccountable, and inactive.

In SOE, our simulation efforts center on ECs engaging in professional situations and examining the resulting video data. As faculty guide ECs to unpack their simulation data, we focus on outcomes for that specific situation, as well as broader implications for the school and community in which the situation is grounded. Our work links directly to how John Brown, Allan Collins, and Paul Duguid frame learning as situated cognition.[4] These authors highlight authentic activity as a means toward enculturation within a given community. They argue that learning is situational and scaffolded, where one learns by experiencing and taking action and, in doing so, begins to understand the broader culture in which those experiences and actions contribute and are grounded. That is, "activity, concept, and culture are interdependent. No one can be totally understood without the other two."[5] As faculty, we wrestle with how, when, and in what depth to teach our ECs professional concepts, tools, strategies, and activities. We struggle even more to help our ECs assimilate to the broader culture in which these tools and strategies are enacted. Brown, Collins, and Duguid distinguish between traditional school activity—the distant, rote assignments, readings, and calculations—from authentic activity, defined as "the ordinary practices of the culture."[6] Engaging in authentic activity brings the learner closer to the purpose of the culture—in our case, the purpose of the school culture—and the messy, complicated, meaning-making one derives from daily practice within schools.[7]

As simulation designers, we strive for authentic representations of K–12 education. Our focus is simulating specific situations where individual ECs can enact their knowledge and skills while also gaining experience with the landscape of K–12 systems and service. We emphasize both EC actions and decisions in simulation as well as the ways the EC makes meaning within and about the culture of K–12 schools. As we focus on the individual EC within the larger K–12 school culture, we have an expectation of growth and development for both. Through simulations, we expect ECs' experiences and their review of actions and decisions to lead toward more deliberate and principled future practice. In parallel, we seek growth and development in the broader K–12 school culture, with novice teachers as potential catalysts for change toward more democratic, fully inclusive learning environments. As ECs engage in simulations, they experience discrete snapshots of K–12 school culture. As they gain experience and exposure to K–12 school culture, ECs do so in a structured postsimulation environment that allows them to review current school inequities and work toward change. Our goal is not for candidates to simply experience and acquiesce to the "ordinary practices of the culture" but rather for them to experience, challenge, and enact equitable, just orientations toward changing K–12 schools.[8] As we center on helping ECs engage with the practices and culture, we also center on constructively critiquing how the K–12 culture can advance in principled steps.

To further illustrate how we balance ECs learning in the simulated situation alongside ECs experiencing opportunities for positive K–12 systems change, consider how they engage in a music education simulation. When my colleagues and I began to design the encounter, we knew that music teacher candidates would have had multiple past opportunities to audition themselves, to navigate audition scores and ratings, and to demonstrate their talents on stage. We knew they would have had much more limited opportunity to engage with parents about audition expectations, rating systems, and the reasons some teenagers are (and are not) selected for a given high school musical. In response, we designed the Marissa Collins simulation to situate music teacher candidates in conversation with a parent who questioned why her daughter wasn't successful in auditioning for the spring musical. By design, we were trying to blend the authentic activity of speaking with a concerned parent—which these teacher candidates had not experienced at all—with the rich musical performance culture with which these music teacher candidates closely identified.[9]

We knew such an interaction was rare in traditional field placements, and we also knew that navigating this situation would require music teacher candidates to synthesize different knowledge and skills, as they outlined performance expectations, listened carefully, described rubrics and resulting scores, and suggested options for future participation. In navigating this simulation with a concerned standardized parent, the music teacher candidate might utilize clarifying or follow-up questions, could use positive reinforcers to indicate what the unsuccessful student did well in the audition, or might choose to take notes on Ms. Collins's concerns, while maintaining an open disposition during this interaction. That is, in this music education simulation and others, we intended for ECs to engage in rich, complex interactions that closely represent authentic K–12 school practices. We also hoped to widen the lens on those practices to open up space for consideration of issues related to equity and access, such as who gets access to extracurricular opportunities, how to encourage greater participation for all, and what it means to be successful in K–12 schools.

Our design and facilitation of simulations are fundamentally grounded in Shulman's tenet of engagement, situating ECs in practice. As Elizabeth experienced in leading her peers through whole-group analysis of her simulation video segments, engagement within authentic situations provides multiple entry points for data-informed reflection and meaning-making. As ECs engage—in simulated encounters, small-group debriefings, individual video analysis, and whole-group debriefings—they experience Shulman's second tenet of a signature pedagogy: uncertainty with professional unknowns.

USING SIMULATIONS TO EXPERIENCE AND NAVIGATE UNCERTAINTY

Shulman suggests that signature pedagogies foster uncertainty in the preprofessional, where a path forward isn't predictable or clearly mapped out and where the demands of practice exponentially increase.[10] This uncertainty comes from two sources—not quite knowing what to do as the novice professional, yet still having to take action and be held accountable for that action in an environment visible to others.

When I started simulations at Syracuse, Molly was a mathematics teacher candidate who volunteered to participate. Emerging from her first simulation, Molly walked with me toward the small-group debriefing room at Upstate Medical University's Clinical Skills Center. As we walked, I asked her, "How'd it go?" Molly stopped abruptly, looked directly at me, and replied, "Honestly, I'm sweating! That was tough!" I smiled, knowing she would have much more to say to me and her peers when we started our debrief.

The short walk from simulation to small-group debriefing room is one that I've taken more than 2,400 times with ECs. My pace is quick, but the brief walks with ECs are often filled with bursts of off-the-cuff processing, expressions of emotion, hurried recounts of acute moments, and genuine "What should I have done?" questions. In postsimulation hallway chats and debriefing sessions, ECs consistently reflect on the uncharted territory they just tried to navigate in the simulation; the unexpected variables that emerged in simulation; their uncertainty of if, how, and when to engage with these variables; and their basic physiological responses of mild panic and perspiration.

Molly's frank response about perspiring during her first simulation aligns with many other candidates who acknowledge their own physiological responses of "adrenaline rush[es]," "heart[s] pounding," "trouble catching my breath," and nervous reflections of "I'm just not sure how well I did."[11] Candidates aren't sure what to say or when to say it, if taking notes is rude or professional, if asking a parent about home is off limits, or if leaving the door open during challenging interactions is recommended. In essence, simulations command ECs' focus and energy by presenting many unknowns that feel risky and uncertain.

When candidates engage in their first couple of simulations, they often report feeling overwhelmed by all that they have to process in the moment. What they are speaking to reflects Piaget's theory of equilibration.[12] The uncertainty and disequilibrium emerge as one works to build schema quickly and make sense of a new experience or environment in real time.

Encouragingly, though, the unknowns and uncertainty lessen across multiple simulations. This, too, represents Piaget's theory in action, as ECs utilize their new schema for creating a plan of action or for knowing when and how to ask clarifying questions. Many accommodate and begin preparing their own advanced organizers for the simulations. They often increase the notes they bring to an encounter and fine-tune how they document what was said and done, both during the actual simulation and afterward as they watch their respective videos. As they engage in and build from experiences in simulations, they report less frequent and less acute physiological responses. When engaging in longer series of simulations, a noticeable shift starts to occur in ECs—from an initial focus on themselves toward the simulated challenge at hand. For example, when teacher candidates engage in their fifth and sixth simulations as part of my Study of Teaching course, I typically hear matter-of-fact presimulation verbalizations of, "OK, let me get in there [the simulation room] and handle this." What I'm hearing is both an acknowledgment that unknowns and uncertainty await in the forthcoming simulation but also a recognition and even an emerging trust in self that they can and will do their best to engage, speak, and make decisions as the professional. Across multiple simulations, experience is teaching them to engage with professional uncertainties.

In addition to the general uncertainty of engaging with professional unknowns, my colleagues and I intentionally design simulations to introduce specific uncertainties. We do so because there are some professional situations that we need novice professionals to navigate well and that have significant consequences if mishandled.

For example, consider the verbally aggressive standardized student who recently expressed wanting to physically fight a peer and then later indicates to the school leader candidate in simulation, "Don't worry. I'll take care of them." When the school leader candidate hears that scowling, sulking student say, "I'll take care of them," her blood pressure should rise. Not knowing the teenager's intent—whether to issue an empty threat, start a fistfight, or use a weapon—means the candidate must navigate well this uncertain situation. The consequences are simply too great if the school leader does not determine the meaning behind "take care of them."

As a second example, consider the future biology or health teacher candidate who encounters in simulation an angry parent with strong objections to the school district-approved unit on reproductive education. In a demanding manner, the standardized parent insists the teacher candidate take three courses of action: "provide an alternative for my kid," "get this filth out of the public schools so no kid experiences this," and "reassure me that my kid has a teacher with some morals!" There are risks to candidates in this simulation about challenged curricula, and there are significant consequences if mishandled in licensed practice. Consider the consequences if the teacher candidate acquiesces to the parent entirely and no longer allows any student in class to learn reproductive biology or health. Consider the broader community context—how quickly anticurricula movements can build and how poorly that novice teacher could be positioned.

Across these two scenarios—the student who will "take care of" his bullies and the loud parent demanding the removal of approved curricula—we see clear examples of risk, uncertainty, and sharp consequences. Each situation presents multiple variables and perspectives that have to be considered. Each situation requires in-the-moment synthesis of school structures, professional responsibilities, and school policy. Each situation is ripe with opportunities for employing an impatient disposition, mollifying some and disadvantaging others, or making statements and decisions that are indefensible.

Fortunately, these tough situations exemplify one of the key constructs of simulations: they are bounded, limited engagements where one can practice with professional uncertainties in a forgiving environment. Because each of the above situations is simulated in a clinical environment, ECs can engage, make decisions, utilize a tone of voice or disposition, and designate follow-up steps, all without lasting consequences and with the time and video data to unpack what they said and did in simulation. For example, when the school leader candidate engages with the standardized student who says, "I'll take care of them," she may choose a hard-line course of action, including admonishment and punishment. In the same simulation, another candidate may choose actions that more deliberately seek to understand what the student said, why he said it, and what the student is being teased about on the bus. The risks and uncertainties to either course of action remain the same: the student in question could cause others physical harm. Unlike fully contextualized work in schools, though, this communication with an upset student is not interrupted with intercom all-calls, colleagues knocking on the door, or the responsibilities of after-school bus lot monitoring. The simulation structure holds constant all other variables and professional considerations that would otherwise demand and divert the administrator's time and focus. That particular situation—and the school leader candidate's actions and decisions—are the sole focus.

Clinical simulations are not certain. In fact, we use simulations in educator preparation to introduce and leverage uncertainty. Introducing uncertainty initiates a process of learning how to act and be the future school professional. The simulation process approximates the layering of unknowns on a small scale for ECs so they may experience what licensed educators experience through daily school practice. To further illustrate the introduction and leveraging of uncertainty and unknowns, consider the Ashley Wilson simulation, which requires candidates in multiple educator preparation programs to sit down face-to-face with a mother who has requested a meeting "to discuss a concern for her son, John." As Ms. Wilson explains to the EC, she is worried about her son's safety at school. She outlines several specific concerns, describing shifts in John's disposition toward school, a gaping tear in his favorite coat that he reports got "caught on a doorknob," and a visible, dark, fingerprinted bruise on both sides of his neck. Ms. Wilson explains that she gently confronted John at home, asking him what is going on. In response, John broke down crying, sharing that he was being beaten up at school because some upperclassmen "think I'm gay." After recounting to the EC what her son had reported, Ms. Wilson directly states, "I'm here to discuss how we're going to stop this assault on campus. Where should we start?"

In this simulation, Ashley Wilson introduces multiple professional uncertainties, including student well-being, physical safety, bullying, LGBTQ identity, school team response plans, mandatory reporting and documentation, and school-to-home communications. To begin, the EC learns of a situation where a kid is being physically assaulted, calling for an immediate response on the part of the candidate to acknowledge the serious nature of this situation, address John's safety concerns, and do so with a clear plan of action that includes the appropriate school personnel. Just below the surface of the interaction with Ms. Wilson, the EC also faces the demands of professional ethics. While the parent doesn't explicitly point this out in her dialogue, this simulation suggests mandatory reporting and documentation procedures be enacted. By design, the EC begins to feel that ethical pull, where the situation suggests more than a simple, quick response and instead requires clear documentation, reporting, and a systematic response. Additionally, John is being assaulted on campus because some upperclassmen "think" he is gay. When the actor playing Ashley Wilson shares this in simulation, ECs must consider this aspect of identity as they determine how to move forward.

While the Ashley Wilson simulation presents layered educational uncertainties the EC must navigate, the structure of the simulation environment compounds these uncertainties. The EC is situated in a simulation room, where multiangle cameras and microphones are recording everything. Ms. Wilson shares with affect and sincerity her son's situation and her concerns for him. At no point will this parent call a time-out so that the EC can think about what she has said before responding. At no point will she ask a question or express a concern and then pause so the EC can hustle off to write a reflection paper about this situation. As Shulman notes, professionals often have to take action, even when there is uncertainty about a situation or complete knowledge isn't readily at hand. The structure of the simulation environment introduces professional uncertainty. Even when the EC is likely uncertain as to how or on what fronts to take action, the demands of the simulation environment require engagement. In short, Ashley Wilson is sharing important information, asking for help, and expecting thoughtful responses.

As Shulman describes the tenet of uncertainty that undergirds signature pedagogies, he notes the growth and maturity of the preprofessionals as they "transform debilitating fear into tolerable anxiety."[13] Through simulations, my colleagues and I simulate professional situations that are uncertain and sometimes risky but that our ECs will nonetheless need to navigate well in licensed practice. Our goal is to give them a chance to practice within the uncertainty, experience the feeling of not quite knowing which path(s) to choose, make decisions, and then deconstruct the video data. Ultimately, we engage our educator candidates in the uncertainties of practice in an effort to form and shape their professional identities.

USING SIMULATIONS TO FORM EDUCATOR IDENTITY

Shulman's final tenet of signature pedagogies attends to the formation of the professional identity and the ways engagement and uncertainty lead to the broader development of the professional ethos.[14] I associate the formation tenet with Sasha Barab and Jonathan Plucker's title—"Smart People or Smart Contexts? Cognition, Ability, and Talent Development in an Age of Situated Approaches to Knowing and Learning."[15] Their title strikes at exactly what we're working toward in SOE: designing situated learning experiences that foster and develop novice professionals.

Through our work with simulations, my colleagues and I are beginning to understand the illuminating nature of this pedagogy. We have made great strides by designing nearly sixty distinct simulations that illuminate what ECs know and can do in the moment. The resulting data are rich, and even small samples of simulation data are telling analytic experiences. Specifically, simulation data sets hold formative promise in demystifying ECs' dispositional development. We define an educator's *disposition* as "trends in judgment and action within ill-structured contexts."[16] The following example of a simulation focused on disability and inclusion exemplifies how simulations can both illuminate ECs' professional dispositions and challenge faculty to look carefully at what ECs know and can do.

In 2009, my colleague Christy Ashby and I designed the Elizabeth Meyers simulation, structured as a getting-acquainted conference between elementary teacher candidates and a standardized paraprofessional. By design, the standardized individual in this simulation is a middle-aged female who does not hold a teaching license but has worked with elementary-age students for fourteen years. That is, the paraprofessional who is established in that particular school and in her ways of working with students with disabilities is juxtaposed against the novice status of the candidate.

We designed this simulation to illuminate how teacher candidates interact with a standardized paraprofessional who is trained to indicate—only once—that she typically removes any students with special education designations from the general education classroom and works with them in the corner of the school library. The ECs who first engaged in this simulation were in their final student teaching placement for a dual degree in inclusive elementary and special education. This program prepares candidates to support the full inclusion of students with disabilities in the general education classroom. We knew our teacher candidates had taken multiple courses on disability, inclusive teaching practices, and supportive school and community structures. In designing the simulation, we wanted to know how these teacher candidates would engage with a new colleague, the standardized paraprofessional, who suggests the exact opposite of what they had been taught to enact across the program.

This simulation yielded very telling data about what ECs had learned in prior coursework and how ECs' dispositions shape the enactment of that knowledge in practice. Only a third of our teacher candidates engaged with the paraprofessional as they'd been taught—by challenging the paraprofessional's references to pulling students out of the classroom with counternarratives and strategies for teaching all students in the general education classroom. Approximately a third of the candidates simply and quickly acquiesced to the one-time suggestion of the paraprofessional, surrendering instructional responsibilities for students with disabilities to a person not licensed to teach. The remaining third responded to the paraprofessional by citing conditional approaches to full inclusion, using phrases like, "Let's see how the first week goes" and "We can start off in the classroom." In almost every one of those simulations, what started off as conditional inclusion soon slipped into a discussion of which disciplinary content (e.g., "maybe for science and math") the students with disabilities would learn about in the corner of the library instead of the general education classroom.[17]

Some of the most illuminating data emerged not in the simulated encounter but in the small-group debriefings we facilitated with these candidates immediately after their simulations concluded. In two different debriefing groups, Susannah and Nancy made comments that spoke directly to how their novice educator identities and dispositions emerged in simulation. When prompted to reflect on the simulation process itself, Susannah compared the simulation experience to other programmatic efforts, noting, "Sometimes I feel like we write what someone else wants us to write. Like, I could tell you the best inclusive answers that are out there, but that's not necessarily my opinion, you know. In this [simulation], you have to be a little bit more, 'What do I expect in my own classroom?'" In a separate small-group debrief, Nancy's words reinforced Susannah's position: "I felt like because it [the simulation] wasn't graded, I could really say what I thought as opposed to what a professor would like to hear, and I felt that was a big difference."

While this simulation was particularly illuminating for faculty associated with this specific educator preparation program, we see additional examples in other programs of simulations surfacing and demystifying candidates' dispositions. For example, in a spring 2019 session of my Study of Teaching course, one social studies teacher candidate noted in her end-of-semester simulation meta-analysis that she saw evidence across six data sets of her tendency to simply brush past and ignore opportunities to ask follow-up clarifying questions of other adults. This candidate verbalized a trend in action, where in multiple simulations her impatience led her to push forward with her own points of conversation, instead of pausing to inquire deeply about and better understand the standardized individuals' perspectives and positions. In that same cohort, another candidate reflected on his nearly opposite disposition in engaging with parents and caregivers, reflecting his continuing anxiety about speaking and engaging. His repeated written and verbal reflections across a six-simulation semester summarized his reserved and timid disposition, whatever the nature of the simulated situation. Both of these candidates benefited from the simulation-generated opportunity to reflect on the affordances and constraints offered by their interactional preferences in professional contexts.

Across the chapters in this book, you will read other examples of EC identity development and ways our simulation processes illuminate candidate ethos and disposition. As we continue to explore the formative nature of simulations, we recognize the need to design additional simulations that expose and fight injustices and inequities at both the system and individual levels, within and across our programs. While we maintain our core commitments to inclusive schooling, we fail any basic code of ethics if we do not use the illuminating nature of simulations to surface and combat racism and discrimination. Later in this book, colleagues discuss both promising and challenging trends in ECs' responses to disability and difference across multiple preparation programs. There, you'll see the antiracist imperative rightfully called for, recognizing that priorities for inclusion and difference go only so far without explicit attention to dispositions that challenge racist discrimination.

THE HIDDEN TENET: COMMUNITY

While Shulman outlines engagement, uncertainty, and formation as the three tenets of a signature pedagogy, I suggest he points to a hidden fourth tenet: community. Signature pedagogies become "signature" not because of their distinct outcomes but because of their pervasive use across communities of teachers and learners who wrestle with, interrogate, and expand their use. As communities work together to build a pedagogy, this collective effort denotes its status as a signature.[18]

At first, ECs feel very alone in the simulation room. Cameras are on, the room is quiet, and the SI's knock on the door reminds the EC that they are the only one in the room to engage. Feelings of isolation also come from the immediate demands of practice; simulations illuminate what individual candidates know and can do in the moment. They reveal the professional terrain which ECs must navigate, even though the paths to take in their decisions, actions, and communications are not always clear. As ECs engage with the uncertainties of the profession, simulation data point to and inform EC dispositions.

The action-taking rests with the individual EC, but the meaning-making engages the peer community. The moment ECs exit their individual simulation rooms and enter the small-group debrief, the community blossoms. There, ECs have their peers to rely on and draw from as they make initial sense of what just happened in simulation. Later, as candidates reflect further in whole-group debriefings, simulation data highlight specific practices and K–12 school contexts, reinforcing the responsibility of the EC in individual practice and in connected service to the broader school community.

Consider again Elizabeth, the social studies education major from the vignette that opens this chapter, and her classroom facilitation of discussion about an excerpt from her simulation video. In front of her peers, Elizabeth displayed video data that highlighted the experiential process of transitioning knowledge into practice. Elizabeth learned through practice in simulation that teachers must learn how to say "I don't know" and that teachers connect with parents and caregivers through empathy and support. These are two (of many) critical practices that effective educators master over time. Engaging in situ fostered uncertainty in Elizabeth, such that she was focused in the simulation moments and very attuned again, later, in small- and whole-group debriefings. The engaging simulation and the professional uncertainties it fostered supported Elizabeth in formatively building portions of her emerging identity as a teacher.

The hidden tenet is there, too. What Elizabeth said and did in simulation was in response to that particular SI's concerns and included how she might draw on the school community's resources to address those concerns. Soon, Elizabeth pored through her simulation video, examining both her actions and decisions in the simulation and the ways her responses aligned with or challenged the broader K–12 school structures. A few days later in the whole-group debriefing, Elizabeth facilitated her simulation video analysis in front of her entire EC peer community. While Elizabeth focused on her own data and ways those data tied to school structures, her peer community was there for Elizabeth. As she displayed, responded to, and interrogated her own practice, Elizabeth's peers shook their heads affirmatively. They had been in the same simulated situation that Elizabeth was reflecting on. They understood her struggles and successes, and as a community, these candidates were making meaning together.

As you explore the voices and ideas in this book, I hope you also consider the conceptual shoulders on which they rest. The groundbreaking work of Harold Barrows spurred not only the medical education community in the 1960s but provided a foundation for problem-based learning initiatives in other communities well into the future. Lee Shulman's powerful scholarship and his tireless leadership at the Carnegie Foundation for the Advancement for Teaching complement Barrows's work, extending exploration of pedagogy across knowledge domains and professional disciplines. The many scholars exploring situated cognition—such as John Brown, Allan Collins, and Paul Duguid—recognize the power of that framework to explain individual experience in the moment and shared learning within the broader community, both grounded in sociohistorical perspectives. In SOE, we build from these scholars and others. There is much to explore through the emerging signature pedagogy of clinical simulations. In doing so, we continue to see intersections with both historical and contemporary lines of scholarship.

SECTION II
PROGRAM-SPECIFIC USES OF SIMULATIONS

CHAPTER 3

Simulations in Secondary Mathematics Teacher Education

The Role of Debriefings in Providing Opportunities to Develop Knowledge for Teaching

DUANE T. GRAYSAY AND JOANNA O. MASINGILA

Seven educator candidates in secondary mathematics are meeting with a mathematics teacher educator to debrief their experiences in a clinical simulation.[1] *Before the debriefing, each candidate engaged in a simulated interaction with Jennifer Boyton, a standardized individual (SI) representing a high school student who is learning to write equations to represent quantitative situations from two word problems.*[2] *The first problem was,* "Write an equation using the variables *M* and *W* to represent the following statement: 'There are three times as many women as men working at a school.' Use *M* for the number of men and *W* for the number of women." *In response, Jennifer presented the equation* 3W = M. *Each candidate subsequently engaged in dialogue with Jennifer and tried to help her revise her response to arrive at the correct equation* M = 3W. *The second problem was,* "A laboratory used some fence posts in an experiment comparing two types of paint. Six fewer than twice as many fence posts were painted with paint *A* as were painted with paint *B*. Write an equation to represent the relationship between *A* and *B*." *Jennifer responded to this problem by telling candidates, "I don't even know where to start. Where do I begin?" Each candidate then attempted to help Jennifer think about creating an equation to represent this situation.*

Now, in the debriefing, the cohort of candidates uses the shared points of reference created by the standardization of Jennifer's behavior to discuss their responses and experiences in the simulation. All but one note that the approaches they used to help Jennifer understand the need to change her equation for the first word problem did not work as well in assisting Jennifer to make sense of the second word problem. Jane describes drawing images of people to help Jennifer revise her equation for the first problem, which she refers to as a diagram, but says that the diagram approach did not work well for the second problem. Jane laments, "I wish I wouldn't have . . . tried to draw a diagram [for the second problem]." Carla and Rick sympathize, each noting similar issues with drawings for the second problem. Reflecting on what they would do differently if another student came to them with the same questions, the candidates in the group agree that they might use drawings to support the student in the first word problem. However, they express lingering uncertainty regarding how to help the student understand why $A = 2B - 6$ *is a correct equation for the second problem but* $B = 2A - 6$ *is not.*

In recent years, clinical simulations in various forms have emerged as a developing pedagogy in mathematics teacher education. As illustrated in the preceding vignette, simulations can provide opportunities for each educator candidate (EC) in a group to engage in the individual, in-the-moment work of deciding how to respond to student thinking. Postsimulation debriefings allow the group to have a shared conversation about the different choices that teachers might make in response to the same situation and the consequences of those choices. The vignette illustrates how simulations can offer interactive contexts in which candidates encounter and explore common difficulties that students exhibit when learning mathematics.

In this chapter, our goal is to examine the opportunities simulations provide for candidates to develop useful pedagogical knowledge and pedagogical content knowledge that will support them in making sense of student thinking and responding in ways that support students' progress. We begin by outlining the problem that undergirds our interest in simulations. We subsequently describe a framing for our analysis of data from our implementation of simulation debriefings in secondary mathematics education and for our reflections, as teacher educators, on our opportunities to learn from developing and facilitating simulations. We then present our findings related to the opportunities evidenced by ECs' reflections on their experiences, followed by our reflections on what we have learned as mathematics teacher educators.

THE PROBLEM: PASSIVE, PROCEDURE-FOCUSED INSTRUCTION

For decades, mathematics educators have advocated for change in the dominant instructional paradigm in mathematics in the United States. The findings of James W. Stigler and James Hiebert reporting results from an examination of mathematics instruction in the United States, Germany, and Japan are characteristic of the concerns that have motivated that advocacy.[3] Stigler and Hiebert hypothesize that US students during the period under review were learning a more fragmented and superficial mathematics than their international counterparts. They position this finding as a consequence, in part, of a model of teaching, then prevalent in the United States, that positions students as passive recipients of mathematical knowledge within instruction that is highly procedure-focused—presenting terminology to students, demonstrating procedures for students, and then having students practice those procedures. Further, Stigler and Hiebert note that US instruction utilized mathematics problems that involved less reasoning and were less advanced in content than the problems found in classrooms in Germany or Japan.

For decades, mathematics education researchers have reported valuable insights about instructional practices that are most likely to support significant student learning. The National Council of Teachers of Mathematics (NCTM) summarized the findings of that body of literature in terms of eight high-leverage mathematics teaching practices.[4] Those practices include, for example, engaging students in tasks that promote reasoning and problem solving, engaging students in mathematical discourse, and using purposeful questioning to assess students' thinking and to support progress toward mathematical goals. Through their certification examinations, states have begun to require mathematics candidates to provide evidence of their abilities to engage in similar practices. Namely, candidates must demonstrate readiness to engage students in developing conceptual understanding, procedural fluency, reasoning, and problem solving while using formative and summative assessments to attend to student thinking and then to use that thinking to shape instruction and support student learning.[5] Nevertheless, efforts to shift mathematics teachers' practices from the passive, procedure-focused model toward more active models with a richer image of mathematical competence seem to have had limited impact, even when those efforts have led to changes in teachers' beliefs and self-perceptions of their readiness to use more ambitious practices.[6]

HOW DO SIMULATIONS ADDRESS THIS PROBLEM?

The dominance of the passive, procedure-focused instructional model makes it likely that candidates begin their professional preparation with images of themselves as teachers explaining to students, demonstrating procedures, and monitoring as students practice those procedures.[7] To learn to engage in the kinds of teaching practices described by the NCTM, candidates need to witness and enact such practices.[8] However, field placements occur in classrooms where teachers face multiple pressures, such as state-mandated high-stakes assessments or district-level initiatives. An understandable response to those pressures is for teachers to narrow their curriculum, evaluation, and pedagogical practices to focus on topics and tasks aligned to the high-stakes assessment.[9] These pressures can also lead teachers to shy away from cognitively demanding tasks or high-leverage teaching practices and fall back on memorization and drill instruction, particularly with students in disadvantaged schools where the pressure to improve scores is high.[10] An unfortunate consequence is that cooperating teachers may not feel comfortable supporting candidates who experiment with instructional practices in the context of tasks that demand reasoning and problem solving.

In recent years, researchers and scholars in teacher education have used simulations to provide contexts in which candidates can experience approximations of essential situations that teachers encounter in the relational work of teaching. For example, some simulations model common issues surrounding secondary students' interpretation and creation of graphs, while others simulate elementary students' ways of carrying out multidigit addition or elementary students' understandings of fraction.[11] Some have also simulated conversations with students to support and examine candidates' emerging abilities to elicit, interpret, and respond to student thinking.[12] An advantage of such simulations is that they liberate candidates from the looming threat of students' performance on high-stakes assessment and from the ancillary effects of pressures faced by cooperating teachers. The control that simulations offer to mathematics teacher educators could create conditions that allow candidates to experiment with, for example, eliciting student thinking and responding to that thinking.[13] These opportunities frame much of the existing rationale for developing simulations as instructional tools for teacher education.

In line with these efforts, we have each designed and implemented content-focused clinical simulations intended to support candidates in developing knowledge and skills for secondary mathematics teaching. Some key features of our programs are summarized in figure 3.1.

FIGURE 3.1 Program overview for mathematics education

Educator candidate (EC) population:
Undergraduates dually matriculated in mathematics and mathematics education; graduate students matriculated in a master's program in mathematics education

Program length:
Four years for undergraduates; fifteen months (summer, fall, spring, summer) for graduate students

Simulation timing:
Varies

Because simulations are a relatively new part of mathematics teacher education, we recognize the importance of empirically assessing the opportunities for growth that are created by candidates' participation in such simulations. In this chapter, we present analyses of transcripts from two debriefing sessions to illustrate some of what we are learning about a critical question:

- What opportunities do simulations offer for candidates to learn about mathematics, students, and teaching by engaging in content-focused clinical simulations in mathematics teacher education?

We also explore our reflections, based on our experiences, regarding the following question:

- How might mathematics teacher educators benefit from designing and orchestrating content-focused clinical simulations in mathematics teacher education?

CONCEPTUAL FRAMING

Mathematical Knowledge for Teaching and for Teaching Teachers

A construct that is useful for developing, using, and analyzing simulations with candidates is *mathematical knowledge for teaching* (MKT). Research on teachers' knowledge has flourished following Lee Shulman's presidential address at the 1985 American Educational Research Association's annual meeting, where he introduced the idea of pedagogical content knowledge.[14] This knowledge, which Shulman called the "missing paradigm" in research on teaching, linked knowledge of teaching pedagogy with knowledge of the specific content that was taught.

As a result of Shulman's speech and the research that followed, Deborah L. Ball and colleagues introduced MKT, which describes the mathematical knowledge required for teaching mathematics.[15] This framework expands Shulman's categories of subject-matter knowledge and pedagogical content knowledge by identifying three domains of knowledge within each category. Of particular relevance to this chapter are the domains that Ball and colleagues identified within the category of pedagogical content knowledge. These domains are *knowledge of content and students* (KCS), which includes (but is not limited to) knowing how students might approach tasks or what challenges they might encounter as they engage with those tasks; *knowledge of content and teaching* (KCT), which includes (but is not limited to) knowledge about how to represent or explain mathematical ideas, how to respond to students, and how to support student activity; and *knowledge of content and curriculum* (KCC), which represents the teacher's knowledge of school mathematics curriculum content.[16] Supporting candidates' MKT in these domains is important because of the central role these domains of knowledge play in the work of teaching.

Similar to the MKT framework, we also consider the notion of *mathematical knowledge for teaching teachers* (MKTT)—defined as the mathematical knowledge needed by mathematics teacher educators to help candidates develop MKT, both through creating the tasks involved in the simulations and facilitating candidates' reflecting on and analyzing their experiences within the simulations. Deborah A. Zopf defines MKTT as "the mathematical knowledge used by mathematics teacher educators in the work of teaching mathematics to teachers" (xi) and claims that "the major purpose of the work of [mathematics] teacher education is beginning with people who already know some mathematics and developing that knowledge into mathematical knowledge for teaching" (165) using practices applicable to the discipline of mathematics.[17] The Conference Board of Mathematical Sciences holds that "prospective teachers need mathematics courses that develop a deep understanding of the mathematics they will teach."[18] Similarly, mathematics teacher educators also need experiences that enable them to develop deep understandings of the mathematics that they teach to candidates and that support those candidates in understanding mathematical ideas deeply. To do their work successfully, mathematics teacher educators need to use their mathematical knowledge and knowledge about their candidates to design and implement mathematical experiences and critical discussions regarding these tasks with a goal of developing candidates' MKT. We hypothesize that designing mathematical simulations can support mathematics teacher educators' development in these areas.

Simulations in Mathematics Teacher Education

We begin by offering a broad definition of simulations in mathematics teacher education, followed by a brief examination of some relevant research findings on the uses of simulations in mathematics teacher education.

What Constitutes a Simulation in Mathematics Teacher Education? As a starting point, we extend the defining features of clinical simulations to define a *mathematics education simulation* in a way meant to unify the diverse ways that teacher educators and researchers have designed interactive approximations of practice. We propose, for this chapter, to define mathematics education simulation as an approximation of an interaction around a mathematical task by an education candidate serving as a teacher in a simulation event and a trained actor playing the role of a standardized student, with a mathematics teacher educator serving as facilitator.

A variety of approximations of practice in mathematics education have these characteristics, to varying degrees. The most obvious variation is in how students are represented within the simulation. For example, Carrie W. Lee reports using virtual avatars, controlled by a simulation specialist, to embody SIs and to engage elementary candidates in rehearsing a mathematics instructional activity.[19] In contrast, Benjamin Dotger and colleagues describe clinical mathematics simulations in which researchers carefully trained actors to embody SIs representing secondary students. The researchers designed the SIs to present secondary mathematics candidates with a common problem related to the interpretation and construction of graphs.[20] Further, others have reported using the LessonSketch platform as the medium for engaging elementary candidates in teaching simulations.[21] In spite of these variations, we include each of these types of interactive experiences under the broad umbrella of mathematics education simulations.

What Do We Know About the Affordances of Simulations? Dotger and colleagues analyzed candidates' interactions with an SI secondary student around problems of interpreting and creating graphs in algebra and candidates' comments during postsimulation debriefing sessions.[22] They found that the simulations offered candidates opportunities to recognize, act on, and critique their actions relating to their instructional responsibilities toward the

SI. Dotger et al. further note opportunities for candidates to select strategies to address student misconceptions and to critique the kinds of questions they used to elicit and respond to student thinking within the simulation. Additionally, simulations offer candidates opportunities to receive in-the-moment feedback and use that feedback to shape their decisions. Corey Webel and colleagues, for example, note that simulations through the LessonSketch platform offered opportunities for elementary candidates to experience the results of their choices within the simulation. This feedback provided candidates opportunities to reconsider their interpretations of student thinking and think critically about their decisions within the simulation.[23] Similarly, Lee notes that simulations using virtual avatars created opportunities to highlight the ways that open-ended questioning elicits different responses from students than literal questions as well as opportunities to highlight the ways that candidates' responses to students position those students as competent or not.[24] However, there has been limited research reporting the impact of simulations on prospective secondary mathematics teachers' emerging mathematical knowledge for teaching.

DESIGN AND IMPLEMENTATION OF SECONDARY MATHEMATICS SIMULATIONS

In this chapter, we report on data collected from debriefing episodes from implementations of three different clinical simulation protocols: the Word Problem simulation, the Numerical Approach to Generalizing simulation, and the Figural Approach to Generalizing simulation. These simulations approximate individual conversations between a teacher and a single student. While most people in everyday life imagine teaching to be primarily an interaction between a single teacher and a moderately large group of students, individual conversations with students about their mathematical thinking or understanding are a regular feature of student-centered teaching. In the subsequent two sections, we describe these simulations and provide an abbreviated summary of the interaction protocols for each simulation.

The Word Problem Simulation

Through a National Science Foundation Discovery Research K–12 (DR-K12) exploratory grant (award #1118772), Benjamin Dotger, Sharon Dotger, Joanna Masingila, and colleagues designed seven secondary mathematics and science clinical simulations. Three of these were mathematics simulations intended to engage candidates with students struggling with problems or situations that the students found mathematically challenging. For the purposes of this chapter, we focus on one of these simulations, the Word Problem simulation. Findings related to other simulations from that project are reported elsewhere.[25]

The Word Problem simulation is designed to simulate a conversation with a standardized individual (SI), Jennifer Boyton, who has worked on two challenging word problems and represents the relationship between two variables incorrectly. The problems and Jennifer's initial equations are presented in the vignette at the beginning of this chapter. The purpose of this simulation is to provide candidates with the opportunity to work with a student who is making "a literal, direct mapping of the words of English into the symbols of algebra" or "a static-comparison" interpretation where the student uses the equal sign to express a comparison rather than an equivalence.[26] The candidate has the opportunity to recognize that the SI has represented the word problem situation incorrectly. If the candidates recognize this, they can engage the SI in checking the validity of the algebraic representation and developing a correct representation.

The Approaches to Generalizing Simulations In separate work, Duane Graysay led the design of clinical simulation protocols to model approaches, as documented in empirical research, that students might take in response to linear generalizing tasks.[27] These protocols engage candidates with an SI who is attempting to generalize from a set of geometric figures to predict the number of squares needed to construct additional figures, using the Tiling Squares Problem (adapted from Joanne Rossi Becker and Ferdinand Rivera) shown in figure 3.2.[28]

The simulations are designed such that two SIs model a different approach to the task. The interaction protocols differ in the ways that they simulate each student's navigation between figural and numerical representations, their approaches to counting elements of a figural representation, and the challenges that students have in translating their verbalizations of pattern into symbolic expressions.[29]

In the Numerical Approach to Generalizing simulation, Nellie McNally, the SI, describes to the candidate a pattern, based on numerical values, that she has recorded in a list but struggles to represent that pattern in a way that leads to an explicit formula. In the Figural Approach to Generalizing simulation, the SI, Susie Greenberg, recognizes that each figure is constructed by adding four additional squares to each arm of the preceding figure but struggles to write an appropriate symbolic expression for the pattern. The protocols are designed to present to candidates two students

FIGURE 3.2 The Tiling Squares Problem *(Adapted from Joanne Rossi Becker and Ferdinand Rivera)*

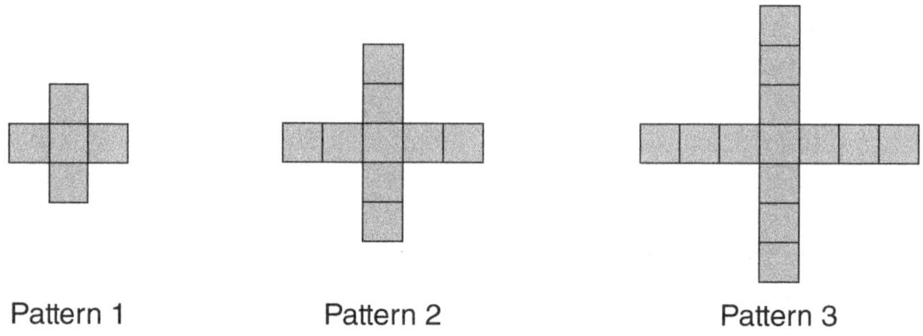

1. How many blacktiles are needed to make Pattern 4? Pattern 5?
2. How many blacktiles are needed to make Pattern 20?
3. How many blacktiles are needed to make Pattern *n*?

who recognize similar patterns of increase but from different underlying representational registers and in ways that lead to different (albeit equivalent) symbolic expressions of a pattern. The goal of these simulations is to provide candidates opportunities to engage in the practices of eliciting, interpreting, and responding to student thinking.

In this chapter, we report findings derived from a debriefing session conducted with participants from the Word Problem simulation designed by Dotger et al. and from a debriefing session with participants from the simulations designed by Graysay.[30] Both protocols are described in table 3.1.

METHODS

Our primary data source for this analysis consisted of transcripts of the debriefing sessions to examine the opportunities for secondary mathematics candidates' learning. The first debriefing session, led by Joanna, was with seven candidates (Carla, Farrah, Jane, Linda, Nia, Patrick, and Rick) who had engaged in the Word Problem simulation with Jennifer Boyton.[31] Before engaging with the SI and task, candidates had been given some general information about Jennifer Boyton as a student. They received a copy of the two word problems. They were told that the problems had been assigned as homework and that Jennifer would be coming to discuss the homework assignment before the school day began.

TABLE 3.1 Overview of mathematics simulation protocols

Simulation	Word Problem	Figural Approach to Generalizing	Numerical Approach to Generalizing
Candidates	Prospective teachers in either the undergraduate or graduate mathematics teacher education program		
Standardized individual (SI)	Jennifer Boyton	Susie Greenberg	Nelly McNally
Context	Individual after-school help session	Individual after-school help session	Individual after-school help session
Summary of instructions for the standardized individual	• For the first problem, admit uncertainty about your answer, and ask if it is correct. • Explain the thinking behind your answer, and ask why it is wrong. • After the teacher discusses the problem with you, ask how you can check your equations to see if they're correct. • For the second problem, state that you are unsure where to start. • Respond to the teacher as best you can. If you don't understand what they are telling you or asking you, say so.	• Start by showing the teacher the table that you have already created. • Focus only on the numbers you have written, and say that you see them going up by four each time. • State that you think the formula should be "$n + 4$." • If the teacher tries to show you a different way to approach the problem, insist on doing it "your way." • Resist any attempt from the teacher to explain a solution to you. • If the teacher prompts you to reexamine your work, you should notice that the formula doesn't work for any values other than $n = 1$. Suggest that maybe the formula should be "$4n$" since the value goes up by 4. • As the teacher encourages you, without telling you the answer, note that $4n$ doesn't work either. • As long as the teacher continues to encourage you, without telling you the answer, note that $4n$ works if you add 1 to it—"$4n + 1$."	• Explain that you see five squares in every figure. Start a two-column table and write 1 and 5 in the first row. • Note that figure 2 has the same five squares with one more added to each arm. Add a row to your table containing 2 and 9. • Describe figure 3 as the "same five squares" with "two sets of four squares" added. Add a row containing 3 and 14 to the table. • Describe figure 4 as "five squares with three sets of four added." • Describe figure 20 as "five squares plus nineteen sets of four." • State that you aren't sure about how to write the formula. • Resist any attempt by the teacher to explain the pattern or formula to you. • After some encouragement from the teacher, propose "$5 + n * 4$" as the formula. • If the teacher asks you to investigate your formula, note that when $n = 1$, the formula gives the value for figure 2, and for $n = 2$, it gives the value for $n = 3$. Correct the formula to $5 + (n - 1) * 4$.

The second debriefing session, led by Duane, was with three candidates (Alice, Callie, and Diane) after their engagement with the actors playing Nellie McNally and Susie Greenberg. Before the simulated encounters, Alice, Callie, and Diane received copies of the Tiling Squares Problem. They solved the task, shared their ways of solving the task, and considered as many different ways of solving the task as possible. Duane also provided them with a brief overview of research-based constructs for anticipating and describing how students might approach a linear generalizing task. Both the Word Problem debriefing and the Numerical and Figural Approaches to Generalizing debriefing were started by the teacher educator asking an open-ended question (such as "What are your reflections on your experience working with this student?").

To analyze the data, we partitioned the transcript into conversation threads by identifying commonalities in the subjects of candidates' statements within each debriefing session, such as "Sharing approaches to teaching in the simulation" or "Attending to student thinking or understanding." We then coded statements according to which domain of subject-matter knowledge or of pedagogical content knowledge was most directly related to each statement. In the case of a statement that did not relate to the simulation's mathematical content, we tagged it as "no code." For example, we used the knowledge of content and teaching (KCT) code for any statement in which a candidate referred to their actions relative to a concept, procedure, or representation during the simulation event; the knowledge of content and students (KCS) code for statements that referred to the standardized student's way of thinking, understanding, or behaving relative to the mathematics of the task; and the knowledge of content and curriculum code for any statement that described how the mathematical task related to curriculum for school mathematics. Finally, we used frequency counts of codes within each thread to identify themes within the conversations and concerning the potential for growth in candidates' mathematical knowledge for teaching.

FINDINGS

In the Word Problem debriefing session, we identified two primary conversation threads related to pedagogical content knowledge: "Sharing approaches to teaching in the simulation event" and "Attending to student thinking or understanding." In the Numerical and Figural Approaches to Generalizing debriefing, we found one primary conversation thread related to pedagogical content knowledge: "Attending to student thinking." The threads that focused on teaching and student thinking provided candidates opportunities to develop their KCT and KCS.

Opportunities for Prospective Teachers to Develop Knowledge of Content and Teaching

The primary conversation thread in the debriefing of the Word Problem simulation involved candidates sharing and comparing their approaches to responding to the SI's errors in symbolic representation of relationships among quantities in the two word problems that formed the simulation context. As illustrated in the opening vignette, candidates shared the strategies they used to help Jennifer recognize her error and arrive at a correct representation of the scenario for the first word problem. As they shared, they also compared their approaches to those of others, either stating that they had used a similar strategy or else presenting a new approach to teaching. Within this conversation thread, we coded nineteen candidate statements. Four statements were not related to mathematical knowledge for teaching. We identified twelve statements as KCT, two statements as KCS, and a single statement relating to KCC, leading us to characterize this thread primarily as affording opportunities for the development of KCT. Examining the contents of candidates' statements, we identified this opportunity's focus as the development of knowledge of the affordances and limitations of representations within teaching.

Opportunities for Candidates to Consider the Affordances of Multiple Representations An essential aspect of KCT is knowledge of a repertoire of representations that can be employed to communicate mathematical ideas to students.[32] Prospective teachers' statements in this conversation thread suggest that the Word Problem simulation provided them with opportunities to consider and to respond to different ways of representing ideas to students. In general, candidates' statements tended to focus on the representations they had used to respond to Jennifer as they attempted to support her in creating an equation to represent the relationships among quantities in each word problem. In this conversation thread, candidates shared multiple mathematical representations they used in their conversation with Jennifer, including tables, diagrams or pictures, specific cases, graphs, and lists of algebraic representations of quantities and variables.

For example, as described in the opening vignette, some of the candidates discussed their attempts to use drawings to help Jennifer Boyton make progress on the problems. Linda, however, introduced the possibility of using tables of values to try to help Jennifer:

> I made a table [of values], and then she thought that was really useful to see . . . that hers was wrong 'cause it wasn't matching up, but then I tried to make it for the second [problem], and I used one and ended up getting negative numbers, so . . . and I was like "All right, well, let's just . . . that's okay . . . let's just . . . ."

As the conversation continued, Patrick introduced the possibility of using a graph to draw attention to slope and ratio:

> You have $W = 3M$, so if we were to graph this thing, you know, it simply means that the slope of the graph is three, which is three over one—for every man there would be three women. So I mean, that was a way of showing the student that the slope is constant: it's a linear relationship. For every one man, you will always have three women.

By sharing and comparing the kinds of representations they used during the simulation, candidates created opportunities to contrast their own use of representations with those of the peers in their cohort, including discussing which representations seemed effective in supporting Jennifer's work in each problem. Such opportunities are valuable for expanding the set of representations that a candidate might see as viable resources in their future work with students, which is an important opportunity to develop KCT.

Opportunities for Candidates to Discuss the Limitations of Representations In addition to having a repertoire of representations that mathematics teachers can use in teaching, KCT also includes understanding "the instructional advantages and disadvantages of representations used to teach a specific idea."[33] The candidates' statements in the debriefing suggest that the Word Problem simulation created opportunities for them to think about this critical aspect of KCT.

As candidates shared their approaches to working with Jennifer, several of them mentioned that the strategy or representation they used effectively to address Jennifer's misunderstanding in the first word problem did not work as effectively for the second word problem. For example, Linda explained that she had used a tabular representation to illustrate relationships for the first word problem, that Jennifer "thought that was really useful to see . . . that hers was wrong 'cause it wasn't matching up," but that when she tried it for the second word problem, she "ended up getting negative numbers," which was problematic given the nature of the quantities described in the problem.

Similarly, Jane reported that she "drew little people diagrams" for the first word problem and asked Jennifer, "How many men are there to women, and then how would you express that in an equation?" The representation seemed useful. Yet for the second word problem, although Jane initially tried using another diagram ("I was, like, 'We'll try another one!'"), she found it harder to do so than she had during the first problem: "Then I was, like, 'No, no, no, forget about that. Let's think about it.'"

These quotations and others similar to them are evidence that the simulation experience and the subsequent debriefing created opportunities for candidates to reflect on and share the limitations of some representations for illustrating relationships among quantities in a given situation. Discussion of the limitations of representations created an important opportunity for the candidates to frame their emerging repertoire of representations by an understanding that the representations that one might use in a given situation also depend on the characteristics of the mathematical task. The ability to draw on a range of representations, with an understanding of the relative possibilities and limitations of those representations, is an important part of KCT.

Opportunities for Prospective Teachers to Develop Knowledge of Content and Students

The second primary conversation thread from the Word Problem debriefing and the primary thread from the Approaches to Generalizing debriefing involved candidates describing their activity in ways that focused on eliciting evidence of student thinking. In the Word Problem debriefing, Rick initiated this thread. He stated that he was still struggling with strategies for helping the student understand "a good way to determine which variable to put where—like, Why wasn't it $B = 2A - 6$? Why was it $A = 2B - 6$?" We identified fifteen statements from the Word Problem debriefing that were part of this conversation thread. Of these, we coded nine as relating to KCS, four related to KCT, and the remaining as not about mathematical knowledge. As a result, we characterize the opportunities offered by this thread primarily as opportunities to develop KCS.

These threads in the debriefings contributed to opportunities to develop KCS in two ways. First, candidates made explicit statements connecting their actions within the simulation to an intention related to Jennifer's thinking in the simulation. Second, in response to the teacher educator's question asking what they had learned from their experience in the simulation, candidates described their thinking about the more general role that anticipating and attending to student thinking plays in teaching.

Opportunities for Candidates to Actively Attend to and Respond to a Student's Thinking An important component of KCS is knowledge of "what students are likely to think and what they will find confusing about mathematical tasks and content."[34] This is essential for teaching that actively attends and responds to student thinking. Prospective teachers' statements in this conversation thread provided evidence of their opportunities to describe how they attended and responded to Jennifer's thinking within the simulation experience. For example, in response to Rick's initial statement, other candidates agreed that they had also been thinking about how best to support Jennifer in her thinking. The candidates described how this goal shaped the questions they asked and their actions within the simulation. Jane responded first, connecting one of her questions to an intention to determine whether the order in which the variables appeared in the text of the problem was the primary influence rather than relationships between the quantities that the variables represent:

> [I asked,] "Why are you putting *A* here and *B* there?" And she explained it, and I still wasn't sure if it was because of the syntax or because of the dependency of the variables. So I [asked her to] explain it to me one more time, and she was, like, "Well, . . ." And she explained it, and [I said], "Okay, I'm making sure it's not because that's the order you were given, so that's how you're plugging it in." So I was kind of proud that I checked for understanding.

Patrick recounted asking Jennifer to write both *A* as a function of *B* and *B* as a function of *A* and connected the question to an intention to determine "if she understands what three more means, plus three means, and one half means in the context of the problem." By asking Jennifer to rewrite her equation to solve for *B* as an expression of *A* and to interpret the new equation, Patrick sought to determine whether Jennifer "could interpret [that] the other equation [*B* as a function of *A*] was quite different from the other one [*A* as a function of *B*], even though they represent the same relationship."

In their responses, Jane and Patrick indicated that during their interactions with Jennifer they were each focused on her thinking and understanding. Each described their questions as intending to determine whether Jennifer's written equation represented an understanding of relationships between the quantities in the problem. In the process, they created opportunities for themselves and their fellow candidates to consider the understandings and the thinking that occur as students construct equations to represent relationships among quantities.

Opportunities for Candidates to Consider General Roles of Anticipating and Attending to Students' Thinking One way that teachers draw on KCS is during the planning process as they anticipate common understandings and partial understandings that might shape how students interact with tasks. As the Word Problem debriefing continued, the candidates gave evidence that the simulation provided an opportunity to develop an awareness of this general role for KCS. When Joanna asked candidates what they thought they had learned from their experience, they responded in ways that shifted focus away from recounting their actions in the simulation and toward general principles related to anticipating and attending to student understanding as resources for teaching. Patrick described the importance of trying "to think of as many ways as possible that students might interpret the question," which Nia echoed, stating that "as a new teacher I think it's all about preparation, . . . how you think about the problems and what you think the students might ask and how you think you might explain it." Statements such as these, when raised during debriefing, provide evidence that the simulation experience created opportunities for candidates to consider the general role that anticipating student thinking plays in effective teaching.

Opportunities for Candidates to Develop KCS by Comparing and Contrasting Student Thinking Knowledge of content and students plays an important role in supporting teachers to anticipate student thinking. It is useful to anticipate different approaches students might take different to the same task.[35] In the Approaches to Generalizing debriefing, candidates gave evidence that their interactions with the Generalizing simulations and their conversation in the debriefing session helped them to consider multiple potential approaches to the same problem. The contrast seemed to focus on how well each candidate thought they understood the SI's approach. For Callie, understanding Susie's approach was difficult:

> I guess Nellie was a lot easier than the other . . . Susie's . . . a tricky one. . . . I honestly . . . had trouble following what she was doing until the end, then I kind of got it but not even completely. So I struggled with it. I didn't really know what she was talking about.

Diane agreed with Callie, but Alice disagreed:

> I'm kind of different. I thought Susie was easier. But it's also because . . . [in preparing for the simulation] I literally went through the same thought process that Susie went through. So I completely followed what she was doing. So that helped me a lot. And Nellie's—I don't know. . . . There was one point in that part where I got lost because the way that I was thinking about it was using the [image], and that confused her. So I had to try in the moment to think of something really, really fast, and try to not use the [image] as much to try to get her to get it. So that one was a little harder for me.

In their descriptions of their own reactions to each SI's way of approaching the task, Alice, Callie, and Diane recognized approaches to the task that were different from their own ways of thinking. This is important for developing knowledge of the many ways that students might think about and approach mathematics. However, although we use simulations in part to address the well-known gap between development of knowledge about teaching and development of the capacity to use that knowledge in action, it is important to acknowledge that the relationship between knowledge and action is not simplistic. The capacity to act does not directly follow from the capacity to recognize and understand a student's way of thinking. Diane, commenting on her understanding of each SI's approach, made this subtlety clear:

> Having looked at it before, I could understand where [the SIs] were coming from. . . . I understood the different approaches, but I just didn't know how to . . . use that knowledge to help them better than I did.

Part of the importance of KCS for secondary mathematics teachers is understanding the range of responses and approaches that students might use in a task. Such understanding is necessary, though not always sufficient, for a teacher to be prepared to recognize and respond to student work. The conversation thread observed among Alice, Callie, and Diane gives evidence that the simulation experience provided opportunities for each candidate to attend to student thinking and to recognize similarities and differences among the approaches that the candidates used in the presimulation activity and the approaches taken by each SI. In doing so, candidates had the opportunity to broaden their understandings of different ways that individuals might think about and respond to a common mathematical task.

DISCUSSION

The broad problem of practice that anchors this chapter is overcoming passive, procedure-focused instruction by creating opportunities for candidates to engage in core practices of teaching in contexts that free them from concerns about content coverage, standardized testing, and other pressures. Mathematics teacher educators need to ensure that candidates can engage with student thinking in ways that build their repertoire of strategies for teaching and the knowledge base needed to anticipate and to interpret student thinking.

Our findings suggest that simulations have the potential to create opportunities for candidates to develop stronger mathematical knowledge for teaching, including in the domains of knowledge of content and teaching and knowledge of content and students. Standardization of the student misconceptions and approaches created conditions in which candidates could, in the debriefing session, compare and contrast their experiences with a common frame of reference. By sharing and comparing strategies and observations, candidates contributed to conversations that had the potential to raise new possible representations, acknowledge important limitations of representations, and recognize and normalize diverse student approaches to tasks, all in ways that are richer than any single candidate might have recognized in their individual reflections.

Reflections on Opportunities for Mathematics Teacher Educators to Develop MKTT

Constructing and facilitating content-focused simulations require a significant investment of time and attention by teacher educators. A natural question to ask is whether the potential gains of that work are worth the investment of resources on the part of mathematics teacher educators.

In part, based on the opportunities for candidate learning, we argue that the investment has an important payoff that cannot be reliably replicated through field experiences or coursework without opportunities to engage in teaching. We also think it is important to consider how we, as teacher educators, may benefit from the activity of constructing and facilitating such simulations.

Orit Zaslavsky and Roza Leikin suggest that mathematics teacher educators develop knowledge in two ways: "*through learning*, as facilitated by a [mathematics teacher educator], or *through teaching*, when they facilitate [mathematics teachers'] learning."[36] Our reflections focused on developing our knowledge gained through teaching—specifically, through (1) developing the mathematical tasks and simulation protocols for the simulations and (2) using questions to facilitate the candidates' reflection on their experiences working with a student in the simulation.

Opportunities for Mathematics Teacher Educators to Develop Knowledge Through Task Creation As discussed previously, we each designed simulations to engage candidates in approximations of teaching practice. A critical component of practice-based teacher learning is a well-designed and well-facilitated task.[37] By task, we mean not only a well-designed mathematical task for the standardized student, but a well-designed task for the educator candidate. As Edward A. Silver et al. explain, well-designed tasks "can provide opportunities for teachers to rethink and reorganize the mathematics that they encounter in their practice, thereby allowing them to render their mathematical knowledge more useful and usable."[38] These are the types of tasks that we sought to create for use in the simulations.

To create well-designed tasks, we drew on the mathematics education research literature for types of mathematical problems with which students struggle and for ways that students approach different types of tasks. Additionally, the research team involved in the NSF-funded study interviewed experienced secondary mathematics teachers to obtain their perceptions of challenging concepts for students to learn. They worked to design tasks that would engage the candidates in supporting students (represented by an SI) with challenging mathematical problems and provide opportunities for ECs to learn from their attempts. By drawing on the knowledge of the experienced mathematics teachers and the knowledge of the mathematics education research community, we each had opportunities to discuss with colleagues and think carefully about challenging mathematics concepts and ways candidates might engage in supporting students who are struggling with these concepts, and this deepened our MKTT.

Opportunities for Mathematics Teacher Educators to Develop Knowledge Through Facilitating Candidate Reflections To grow as mathematics teacher educators, we recognize that we need to use our mathematical knowledge and knowledge about our candidates to design and implement mathematics experiences and critical reflections on those tasks to support candidates in developing MKT. This requires mathematics teacher educators to have high-level metacognitive and mentoring skills.[39] The essential goals we have for engaging candidates in simulations, having them view their videos of the simulation interaction, and then having a group reflective debrief are to provide the candidates opportunities to practice supporting learners and developing their pedagogical skills and to make the work that teachers do explicit. We want our candidates to think deeply about what mathematical challenges students encounter in the tasks and what they can do to support students in developing better understandings of these mathematical relationships.

Thus, we thought carefully about how we would structure the reflective debriefing sessions for the cohorts after candidates viewed the videos of their interaction with the SI. We planned a series of questions, knowing other questions would arise in the moment to build on comments made by the candidates. We started by asking the candidates to discuss their reflections on their experiences working with the student on the mathematical tasks. Our next questions asked the candidates to discuss why problems like these are challenging for students, followed by a query about what they did that they thought helped support the student's learning. We also asked what they might have done that they believe was not helpful and what they would do differently. We then asked what they would do in subsequent lessons to support students in better understanding these mathematical ideas and what they have learned about planning, instructional strategies, and assessment.

Designing and then facilitating the reflective debriefing sessions supported our learning through teaching. In considering what questions to ask during these sessions, we thought carefully about what instructional moves the candidates might make and where they might struggle in trying to support the students' learning. In the same way that we tried to support our candidates in decompressing their compressed mathematical knowledge to be able to teach students mathematics, we also worked to decompress our compressed MKT to think carefully about what MKT our candidates might utilize or learn by participating in these simulations and thus to choose questions to help scaffold our candidates' learning.[40]

REFLECTIONS ON THE CHALLENGES OF DESIGNING MATHEMATICS-FOCUSED SIMULATIONS

As we conclude this chapter, we anticipate that some readers might be thinking about the potential of content-focused simulations and the challenges of designing and implementing them. One of the challenges inherent in such simulations is the development of SI interaction protocols that will effectively guide an actor to speak and behave in ways that model some form of student understanding or student thinking. Such protocols need to be thorough enough that they do not require mathematical confidence on the part of the actor and detailed enough that the actor's own mathematical understandings do not become part of how he or she embodies the SI. At the same time, the protocols need to be flexible enough to allow actors to improvise around the protocol so that they engage dynamically with candidates during the clinical simulation. This is a serious challenge for designers. Similarly, protocols must provide the actor with a realistic and appropriate method for resisting efforts by the candidate to push the SI into ways of thinking or understanding that are beyond what the protocols have prepared them to do. Perhaps simple statements such as "I really want to think about it my own way" are sufficient. In some situations, the SI may need to be designed to make an excuse to leave the simulation if the actor feels pushed by the candidate beyond the boundaries of the protocol.

We also acknowledge that there are issues of identity and representation that the interaction protocols for these simulations do not address directly but that are important as we and others in the field continue the work of designing and implementing simulations in mathematics teacher education. Attending to how the identities—or perceived identities—of SIs may affect how candidates interact with them during a simulation will be an important area for future research and inquiry.

We believe, as do our colleagues in mathematics teacher education, in the importance of the work of preparing mathematics teachers. We recognize the significant challenges associated with preparing a teacher workforce with the knowledge base and skills to teach in ways that may represent empirically validated practices but that also may deviate significantly from the teaching practices they observed and experienced as students of mathematics. We have found that simulations, while not a perfect vehicle for candidate learning, have significant potential to support those teachers in developing a broader range of perceived possibilities with respect to representation use and with respect to anticipating student thinking. We encourage others to continue to experiment with such simulations, while attending critically to both the learning benefits and the investment costs of developing and facilitating such tools.

CHAPTER 4

"How Can She Participate?" Examining Inclusion in Physical Education Through Simulation

MICHAEL L. NORRIS, LUIS COLUMNA, AND BENJAMIN DOTGER

All three of us are crowded together, shoulder to shoulder, in the small control room of SUNY Upstate's Clinical Skills Center. In front of us is a large screen, showing both camera angles of a simulation room. In that room is Geno, a physical education candidate, sitting very straight in his chair, waiting on the standardized parent, Brad Winston. We see the door open, and Mr. Winston enters the simulation room. He shakes hands with Geno and sits in the chair nearest to him. Before Mr. Winston has even settled in his chair, Geno nervously asks Mr. Winston how he can help.

With a worried, scrunched-up face, Mr. Winston begins to explain that his daughter, Erin, will soon be a fourth grader in Geno's class and that she is excited about physical education. He shares that Erin was injured at home several years ago, losing complete vision in one eye and partial vision in the other. His shoulders fall, suggesting that he still feels terrible about the accident. Just a few seconds later, though, he seems to shrug off the weight and starts describing Erin's progress after the accident. He beams with pride about all that she has done in recent years, even with the challenges of limited vision. Mr. Winston pauses. When he starts speaking again, he asks simply, "How can she participate?"

Mr. Wilson has said quite a bit in just the first minute of this simulation. Geno might respond in a number of different ways. Will he tell Mr. Winston that "everything will be fine"? Will he convey his enthusiasm for having Erin in the class or his own anxiety about how to address her needs? Can he describe exactly how Erin will participate in class? A few seconds lapse. Geno has to say something. It is not easy for the three of us to watch.

This vignette illustrates physical education (PE) candidates' engagement in the Brad Winston clinical simulation, an experience designed to support and complement their broader program of study. In its design, this simulation brings together the disciplinary expertise of Michael Norris and Luis Columna, faculty in physical education, with the simulation expertise of Benjamin Dotger, a generalist in teacher education. Like other codesigned simulations in Syracuse University's School of Education (SOE), the Winston simulation challenges education candidates (ECs) to engage in a situation, call on their requisite skills, and make decisions toward an outcome in a structured environment. As this vignette shows, such simulations challenge candidates to balance many different variables as they work to support children with disabilities in physical education settings through deliberate, inclusive practices.

In this chapter, we briefly review literature related to K–12 students with visual disabilities in physical education settings. Then we describe how the Winston simulation was designed, with a focus on how the education candidate could articulate supports to a standardized individual (SI), the parent of a student with a visual disability. We examine the resulting data from the Winston simulation. Finally, we look to their implications within PE and across the broader spectrum of educator preparation.

BACKGROUND AND CONTEXT

In the United States, the number of children with disabilities engaging in physical education alongside their peers without disabilities is on the rise.[1] In 2019, the American Community Survey showed 547,083 children (under eighteen years of age) with visual impairments.[2] To support students' development of social and play skills so they can obtain the benefits of physical activity, educators need to provide and support inclusive settings for students with visual impairments.[3] Including students with visual disabilities in PE settings means enhancing the preparation of PE teachers to recognize potential challenges, including lack of opportunities (within and outside of school) that students with disabilities encounter and parents' fear of injury.[4] Most PE educator preparation programs support only one introductory-level adapted physical education (APE) course, thereby offering less development of ECs' attitudes and intentions to include children with disabilities into their educational programming.[5]

As teachers work to recognize students' strengths and help them engage challenges, they must do so while also communicating with students' parents and caregivers about those strengths and challenges. As physical education teachers learn about their students, their attitudes and intentions toward students with disabilities can be influenced by the severity of the disability.[6] Still, when PE candidates are provided opportunities to interact with students' disabilities in inclusive settings, they develop more positive attitudes.[7] ECs with more experience teaching students with disabilities tend to self-assess themselves as feeling more competent and more aware of factors under their control that affect their ability to teach students with disabilities in general physical education than those with less experience.[8] In addition, ECs must also be attuned to and prepared to navigate the perceptions of parents of student with disabilities, where parental worries include the extent to which their children will be provided PE adaptations, along with fear of injury and concern about the stigma of low expectations.[9]

We believe inclusive physical education is a deliberate approach to health and physical activity, where educators attend to student difference, modify learning experiences accordingly, and uphold expectations for participation by all. As we recognize student differences and structure fully inclusive physical education environments, we do so by modifying objectives and activities with an emphasis on equity. That is, we expect our physical education candidates to support their K–12 students with resources and adaptations that meet the needs of the individual learner within heterogeneous learning communities.[10] SOE's historical foundation in inclusive education, coupled with our beliefs about the importance of physical activity for all, led us to consider how these fundamental positions would manifest in the preparation of physical education teachers. Specifically, we wanted our ECs to engage in a simulation that centered on a student with a visual disability, interrogated how she would be included, and surfaced the input and concerns of a parent.

THE BRAD WINSTON SIMULATION DESIGN AND METHODOLOGY

We recognize that parents and caregivers of students with disabilities often have increased responsibilities in helping mediate learning opportunities for their children. Despite this pattern, family members' contributions and potential insights can often be overlooked by school personnel.[11] The Brad Winston simulation was designed in recognition of these contributions and intended to help ECs link home and family contexts to the physical education classroom. It was also designed in recognition of teacher educators' struggles to ensure that all teacher candidates will get to work closely with parents and caregivers to support students with disabilities during their student teaching placements.

Recognizing the importance of and variance in ECs' opportunities to work with students with disabilities and their parents/caregivers through field practica, we sought to design a simulation that honored families' contributions in physical education contexts. In previous chapters of this book, we outline Harold S. Barrows's four design tenets for medical simulations and ways we have used them to guide our design of simulations in educator preparation.[12] Two of Barrows's tenets—clinical impact and social impact—serve as the conceptual foundation for the Winston simulation design. Barrows notes the opportunity to design simulations that approximate less common learning opportunities, such as working with parents of students with disabilities, and that have potentially great impact on the individual (clinical impact) or community (social impact). As a result, we situated physical education candidates in a one-to-one interaction with Mr. Winston related to his daughter, Erin, with specific attention to making and communicating decisions about modifications of physical education activities. In centering this simulation on Erin and her visual disability, we anticipated that ECs who enacted knowledgeable, inclusive responses could positively impact both Erin and her peer community.

The Winston simulation was guided by two interaction protocols—one for the novice PE teacher and a second for the actor playing Brad Winston. The EC protocol situated each candidate as a newly hired novice teacher in an elementary school enrolling grades K–5. The scenario indicated that in preparation for the start of the academic year, the school guidance counselor alerted the teacher that a parent, Mr. Winston, has requested a meeting to discuss his daughter Erin and her transition into the teacher's PE class. The EC protocol was intentionally sparse, providing just enough information to help the ECs understand the situation in which they would engage in simulation but offering no information that would direct or otherwise script their actions or decisions.

In contrast to the EC protocol, the SI protocol provided much more background context on Erin, her visual impairment, and Mr. Winston's concerns. It outlined Erin's accident, at age four, that resulted in a significant loss of vision. Additionally, the SI protocol described Erin's many accomplishments since the accident, her excitement about the new swimming pool and rock climbing wall in the school, and her parent's worries about how she would engage in physical education activities. Figure 4.1

provides an overview of the protocol, including the verbal triggers that each standardized Mr. Winston used in simulation with ECs.

Participants, Data Collection, and Analysis

SIs were recruited by SUNY Upstate Medical University staff and trained in accordance to procedures outlined earlier in this book. Opportunity to participate in the Brad Winston simulation was extended to all ECs currently enrolled in the physical education program, with a final sample consisting of candidates across the four-year program sequence. (See figure 4.2 for an overview of key features of the program.)

FIGURE 4.1 Brad Winston simulation overview

Educator Candidates (ECs):
Undergraduates in physical education (PE)

Standardized Individual (SI):
Brad Winston, the father of Erin, a child with a visual impairment

Context:
Parent-initiated conference with the teacher

Summary of Instructions for the Standardized Individual:

- Provide background on Erin's accident and significant vision loss, and note her engagement in activities and assignments in previous grades.
- Ask how Erin can participate.
- Ask how the teacher supports students with visual disabilities in PE settings.
- Outline Erin's struggles with small, moving objects, and ask how the teacher can support.
- Ask the teacher if there are PE activities that Erin might not participate in, due to concerns about safety.
- Ask the teacher if there are additional PE activities that parents can practice with her at home to build confidence and skill.

FIGURE 4.2 Program overview for physical education

Educator Candidate (EC) Population:
Undergraduate students matriculated in a K–12 physical education program

Program Length:
Four years

Simulation Timing:
Varies

All ECs had either completed or were enrolled in a course on adapted physical education. In addition, some ECs had voluntarily participated in a community-based program, Fit Families, directed by Luis Columna, for children with disabilities and their families.[13] All ten ECs (five identifying as female, five as male) consented to allow the author team to analyze transcripts from the simulated interactions and from small-group debriefings. For this particular simulation, no whole-group debriefing occurred. ECs' pseudonyms, year, gender, race, and cultural community background are identified in table 4.1.

On the designated date for the simulated encounter, educator candidates arrived at Upstate's Clinical Skills Center and attended a brief orientation to simulation logistics and postsimulation debriefing procedures. ECs then entered their assigned simulation rooms to meet and converse with Brad Winston. Video data were collected in the simulation rooms via the established multiangle cameras and audio recording devices, yielding mp4 (QuickTime) videos for researcher transcription. NVivo 11 software was used for analysis. Analysis by the first and second authors included data categorization through identifying codes and meaningful labels.[14] Additional analysis of the transcribed data set was conducted independently by the third author. Initially, these analyses led to preliminary codes of philosophy of inclusion, preassessment, modifications, individual activity, language/word choice, communication plan, and peer engagement. Additional discussion between the first and second authors and subsequent post-hoc analysis

TABLE 4.1 Educator candidate demographics

Participant	Year	Gender	Race/Ethnicity
Monte	First year	M	White
Calvin	Sophomore	M	White
Tina	First year	F	Hispanic
Ronda	Junior	F	White
Lisa	Sophomore	F	White
Bre	Junior	F	White
Geno	Sophomore	M	Hispanic
Lena	Sophomore	F	Hispanic
Will	Junior	M	White
Mark	Junior	M	African American

by the third author led to a distillation of the codes into the two themes—assessment of skills and inclusion through modification—that organize our findings.

FINDINGS

Data from the candidates' simulations centered on two primary themes: candidates' intended assessment of Erin's skills and their plans for including Erin through modifications to physical education activities. Embedded within these themes are examples of ECs' positive descriptions of students with disabilities. As we conclude discussion of our findings, though, we provide examples of ECs' description and positioning of students with disabilities that represent potential areas for improvement for both candidates and the program.

Assessment of Skills

As PE candidates learned more about Erin and her visual impairment from their conversation with Mr. Winston, much data indicate their desire to assess Erin's strengths as well as the areas in which she can gain and grow in skills. Seven ECs explicitly referenced an assessment of her skills, indicating that they would like to see Erin perform a variety of physical activities in class. Bre stated, "I would say . . . we would just start off with basic drills, and then we would assess her strengths and weaknesses." Will echoed Bre, saying, "We can provide anything that she really needs. If she needs extra time, maybe if assessments or something she struggles with, maybe we could keep her after class and do an assessment that way." Ronda's response connects the in-class assessment to future communications with Mr. Winston, explaining,

> That is something that I would like to do [assessment]. I could let you know how she does with certain activities. If we could do an evaluation sometime with you and I and she, that would be great. I don't know if you would have time for that. Then we could figure out what she could do at home to help and being more involved in in the class.

Other ECs introduced the assessment of Erin's skills but did so through an informal evaluation of the entire peer group, including Erin, as Lena exemplifies:

> We use the TGMD 2 [Test of Gross Motors Development 2] and with this form [assessment] evaluate her skills and how she's jumping

> and [doing other skills] as well as how she cooperates with other children. Moving forward, we see where she's at [her development] and modify activities based on her skills.

As they communicated about a future skills assessment for Erin, the ECs also gathered additional information through questions of Mr. Winston. For example, both Lisa and Ronda asked follow-up questions regarding Erin's degree of sight in each eye, while Lena clarified whether "peripheral vision" was stronger or presented a challenge. Only one EC (Ronda) asked about any past individualized education plans that might have been in place to support Erin. These clarifying questions, coupled with the references to skills assessments, represent a cluster of data centered on Erin, her current abilities, and the ECs' intentions to help Erin progress forward.

As ECs gathered additional information and context, they began offering developmental perspectives. With reassurance for Mr. Winston, Geno noted, "It's just about seeing progression. It doesn't have to be a vast impact; it's just to see [Erin] improve [her] motor skills." Similarly, Lena noted her intention to "start slow and see where skills are." As Lena continued, she referenced basketball and visual acuity: "The peripheral vision is very—like, very—needed in that sport, so I feel, like, slowly she can adapt to the situation. So we'll definitely take it easy with her." Referencing a different sport, Bre spoke to "step-wise progressions" in soccer, helping Erin first learn in close-proximity groups and then engage on the soccer field at a greater distance from her peers.

The first theme centers on ECs' need to assess Erin's skills and abilities, buttressed by expressions of progressive growth in the future. These lines of dialogue around skill assessment led to broader conversations about Erin's inclusion in the PE classrooms through modifications.

Inclusion Through Modification

All ECs noted the need for an early skills assessment, and all but one of them described the assessments from a positive, inclusive perspective, noting that they would do everything they could to help Erin feel included in PE class. Ronda offered a somewhat conditional response to Erin's full inclusion, noting, "It's definitely a goal of mine . . . to have full inclusion when—when it's needed and when the student can do it. I'd be willing to accommodate any of her needs." With more definitive support, Lisa communicated Erin's inclusion in a confident manner: "she will fit in . . . she will be perfectly fine, and she won't be, like, left out." Monte blandly referenced the "challenge" of visual impairments but then offered clear reassurance, "I can't really think of any reason why she wouldn't be able to participate in everything." Geno verbalized how some physical education environments can lead to exclusion in contrast to his own plans for Erin. He connected the inclusive philosophy he espoused to his identity—within a different kind of PE teacher collective:

> A lot of teachers within a health and physical education setting . . . most of the time they ostracize or push students with disabilities off to the side. What is most important is . . . we [health and physical education teachers] need to work with everyone in class and keep them engaged.

Ronda blended a broad commitment to inclusion with reference to specific modifications for Erin, saying, "My goal is that she learns exactly the same thing that any of the other students do and even if it's in her own way." Ronda's peers were not as succinct, but like her, they also transitioned from reassurances of full inclusion to more concrete dialogue about activity modifications to ensure Erin's safety.

As outlined in the SI protocol, Mr. Winston asked all of the ECs how they envisioned Erin's involvement in traditional PE activities (such as basketball and jumping), shared with them Erin's interest in climbing wall activities, and expressed concern about Erin's safety in PE. As anticipated, ECs offered general reassurances of safety and care in all PE activities. Still, this verbal trigger cued ECs to bring forward examples of modifications. Monte outlined how he would offer Erin verbal cues on the climbing wall. Calvin noted, "There's a ton of adaptations" he could make and then quickly offered examples related to color-coded basketball goals. He also suggested that he might put a tether between Erin and himself to help teach concepts related to proximity and movement. As he spoke, he shared a sample physical education lesson plan he'd brought with him into the conversation with Mr. Winston. Calvin wasn't cued by faculty to bring in this document. Taking this initiative, though, he literally pointed to modifications he'd made in another physical education lesson, providing additional detail and further support to his responses to Mr. Winston.

As each conversation with an EC unfolded, the actor playing Brad Winston expressed more specific concerns about how Erin would interact safely with flying objects, as directed by the SI interaction protocol. In some encounters, this statement by the SI transitioned the conversation from the ECs' more general references to safety to more specific descriptions of modified equipment and activity. In quick succession, Ronda described one visual modification and two auditory supports she would provide in class:

> [During] individual sports, I can make those adaptations by differentiating various colors for activities and having a peer partner for support during activities like throwing and catching a beep baseball. . . . [Then] her partner could support her when she must run to first base, or I could have someone standing there clapping, so that way she knows the location/direction of the base as she's running.

Will offered a different modification, describing how he would adjust basketball movement in consideration of Erin's limited peripheral vision: "We want a three-man weave where you're passing to the side. Maybe we target that so it's more face on, so you don't have to worry about her getting hit in the side of the head with the ball."

A number of ECs—including Calvin, Geno, and Lisa—offered ideas about modifying equipment for the whole class, not just Erin. In an attempt to reduce potential stigma associated with use of such equipment by one student alone, Lisa noted, "The equipment can definitely [be] used by [all students] for class as well, and instead of getting enough for her, I can use them for the whole class. Everyone will use it." In excerpts like these, we see examples of ECs invoking inclusive approaches in the physical education environment. At different points in their conversation with Mr. Winston, ECs linked the expression of an inclusive philosophy—meaning a stated commitment to equitable access to resources and appropriately modified opportunities—with discussion of PE practices that would yield a better understanding of Erin's skills and more opportunities to be involved with her peers.

The Brad Winston simulation revealed ECs' emphasis on skills assessment and inclusive modifications for Erin. Aligned with both themes, though, are additional data that point to one clear area for growth—how ECs describe students with disabilities. For example, it was notable that Lisa tried to convey assurances by stating twice, in near repetition, that she'd "keep a close eye on her." Just a few moments later, still working to reassure Mr. Winston, Lisa indicated, "I work really well with these types of students." Lisa's words were pointed, showing little sensitivity to students with visual impairments, whom she positioned as "other" with her language choices. Her words represent ableism, communicating discriminatory undertones about students with disabilities. Speaking to his inclusive philosophy and his support of Erin, Mark stated, "[excluding her] would just be not only unfair to her but unfair to any student that had some issue that wouldn't be able to participate." Like Lisa, Mark's poor word choice (i.e., 'some issue') hinted at some ableist undertones.

Two other ECs cited potential discomfort, for Erin or her peers, as one factor influencing Erin's participation in class. Lena outlined potential plans for student groups, seemingly in an effort to preserve Erin's feelings: "We probably categorize her in different situations. We like to put her with children that are in the same level as her so she doesn't feel as, like, socially awkward." Tina was less focused on Erin's feelings than Lena was, instead emphasizing the feelings of Erin's hypothetical peers: "Some of the games we do, she might not be able to participate in those. Just like I said with her disability, other students might not, like, feel comfortable." These perspectives trouble us a bit, as candidates enacting a more fully realized inclusive philosophy would be less concerned about preserving students' comfort level in such contexts and more concerned with creating a learning community where such differences would be expected and normalized.

Overall, the physical education candidates' interactions with Mr. Winston reveal data to celebrate. In real time, ECs demonstrated a synthesis of knowledge and skill from prior learning experiences and utilized a student-centered perspective that acknowledged Erin as an individual and a member of the peer community. Still, there is more work to be done, focused on how ECs talk about students with disabilities. This area for growth implicates both the physical education program and broader teacher education efforts as we center on how language connotes perspective toward disability.

DISCUSSION AND IMPLICATIONS

We ground our discussion in Mr. Winston's question, "How can she participate?" His question is directional, not conditional. Mr. Winston is not asking *if* Erin can participate in gym class. He assumes participation and is, instead, seeking clarity from the ECs on what her participation might involve. Mr. Winston's question has broad implications, encompassing Erin's opportunities to engage with peers, build confidence, learn new skills, and maintain health. While his question emerged in the context of Erin utilizing the gymnasium's climbing wall, ECs' responses were much bigger than whether Erin would participate in a singular activity. Candidates' responses to Mr. Winston's questions and concerns were deeply connected to much broader issues of access, modified supports, and community acceptance.

As we noted earlier, EC protocols do not script or direct candidates in their simulation responses. Instead, candidates must synthesize in the moment what they have learned through coursework and field experiences, employ professional judgment, and communicate actions and decisions. We highlight simulations as moments of synthesis to call attention to the data presented above, focusing closely at the interwoven nature of personal assessment, inclusive philosophy, and appropriate modifications.

Responding to Mr. Winston, ECs emphasized the importance of assessing Erin's skills to determine strengths and areas of challenge. This strand of data is very encouraging. It represents an approach to physical education that centers on development and growth, focused on Erin's strengths, challenges, and a plan forward. Many of the transcripts indicate this dialogue on skills assessments occurred early in the simulations, representing not only a developmental philosophy toward physical education but also a conceptual and communication emphasis that is person-centered.

Like other contributors to this book, we consider how these simulation data reflect prior learning experiences. Tracing EC actions and decision in simulation back to prior learning experiences is a complex task that we have begun but not fully completed yet. Still, we think about how ECs' emphases on skills assessments likely connected back, for most individuals, to their prior experiences in the required motor behavior class. This course focuses on several assessment tools, including the TGMD-2 that Lena mentioned in her simulation, and provides ECs opportunities to practice assessment techniques using video samples of children at varying stages of development.

References to skills assessments show ECs were focused on Erin and her participation in physical education. This emphasis alone does not fully address Mr. Winston's fundamental question of *how* Erin can participate. Encouragingly, ECs exemplified Erin's inclusion in the physical education environment by citing specific modifications to support participation. Like ECs' references to initial skills assessments, when we see simulation data that point to inclusive environments and activity modifications, we start to think about where our candidates learned these approaches to physical education and how the Winston simulation illuminated their knowledge and skill.

In our physical education program, ECs learn to design appropriate learning tasks that allow for skill development in an instructional environment that works toward mastery. The goal is helping K–12 students become physically literate, such that they develop the confidence, skills, and desire to be physically active throughout life.[15] Our goal of physical literacy does not extend only to those that society considers "able-bodied." This goal applies to all, respects differences in learners, and employs appropriate modifications.

In addition to our broad goal of physical literacy, the Brad Winston data highlight at least two learning opportunities: the required adapted physical education course and the optional Fit Families program. The ECs who took the course in their sequenced program of study learned to scaffold forward from initial skills assessments, modifying and adapting physical activity in a manner consistent with learning objectives and student strengths. On a voluntary basis, some ECs had also engaged in the Fit Families program, supporting younger students with disabilities and their parents/caregivers in making and engaging in adapted physical education activities.[16]

Mr. Winston's question—"How can she participate?"—is deceptive. At first pass, the answer is obvious and quickly given: "Yes, she can participate." To respond to the SI's question with more than simple affirmation, though, ECs must bring together knowledge and skill from past learning experiences—those represented here in our discussion and those offered within our broader SOE. This is the challenge that simulations present to all educator candidates, within and across all disciplines—synthesizing what one knows into what one can do for students. As we continue designing simulations for physical education and other educator preparation programs, we envision a series of simulations that are mapped to program decision points. Placing simulations at intentional points across a program of study and ensuring the timely analysis of the resulting data provide education faculty with multiple, formative assessment points in the program. Instead of simply waiting until the conclusion of the teacher candidate's final student semester placement, the thoughtful integration of simulations allows faculty to look closely at how ECs are engaging as new professionals and connect their engagement back to specific points of preparation.

As we examine the Brad Winston data, we naturally consider the implications of those data on K–12 students like Erin and on ways ECs might structure inclusive, student-centered health and physical education environments in the future. Still, our program goals of physical literacy and lifelong wellness are not bound by the gymnasium doors. With this position, we see the Winston data in a more expansive light. Looking beyond the gymnasium, we consider how ECs' inclusive, start-where-the-learner-is-and-modify-accordingly approach holds promise for the broader K–12 school.

To exemplify, consider the universal spaces in a K–12 school—the hallways, bus lots, cafeteria tables, stadiums, auditoriums. Each space has its routines and traditions, and all professionals hold responsibility to those spaces and the students in them. As these same ECs engage within their future schools, we wonder if the same inclusive, learner-centered perspective will be similarly employed in the physical spaces shared by all. To illuminate this potential transfer of knowledge and skill beyond the gym, we envision additional iterations of the Winston simulation, where physical education candidates might jointly work with other candidates in music or theater preparation programs and again with Mr. Winston. We wonder how our physical education candidates might apply what they know about skill assessment and inclusive modifications when the conversation grows more complex and shifts from Erin's participation in the gym to Erin's dance on stage. We also question how ECs might speak to Erin's opportunities in other spaces—such as the stage or marching band—where modifications for her visual disability might also meld with scaffolded opportunities for peer leadership. Ultimately, we look forward to continuing this work with our colleagues, recognizing our shared commitment to inclusion and welcoming opportunities to explore how PE candidates transition what they know into what they can do through simulations.

CHAPTER 5

Designing Simulations for Building Scientific Explanations with Elementary Teacher Candidates

SHARON DOTGER AND BENJAMIN DOTGER

The two of us are meeting in Sharon's office after many months of codeveloping a set of science-focused clinical simulations. Funded by the National Science Foundation, the project is intended to help elementary teacher candidates learn to prompt others to offer their own explanations of scientific phenomena. Although we are spouses who both work in teacher education, we do not often have the opportunity to work closely with one another. This project has required a great deal of collaborative research and revision, and we are excited to see the transcript data from the first simulated encounter between educator candidates (ECs) and the actors playing standardized individuals (SIs) with whom those candidates interacted.

The first simulation we consider has a focus on shoreline erosion. The scenario positions ECs as fourth-grade teachers coplanning with a standardized special educator for an upcoming field trip to the beach. We choose the transcript at the top of the stack and are initially excited by its length because a five-page, single-spaced transcript typically indicates a lot of talk happened. Yet as we read, we realize that the text is full of ideas from the EC and considerably fewer from the SI serving as conversation partner. We expected the simulation to reveal indicators of the candidate's content knowledge, and it does. We had hoped those indicators would come, at least partially, from the questions the candidates asked their SI partners to draw out their ideas. But across this first transcript, the SI partner responds to the candidate nineteen times with short utterances such as "mm-hmm," "right," and "yeah." At no point does the candidate ask a question to probe those utterances and elicit more elaborated thinking. The absence of such questions concerns us because it hints at how the candidate might proceed when interacting with children as well.

As we make our way through other transcripts in the stack, we see similar patterns in candidate talk. Do these patterns suggest gaps or deficiencies in ECs' preparation to date that need to be addressed, or are they consequences of the way we designed the simulation? We begin an animated discussion of how we might reduce the potential impact of the latter concern, with each of us taking copious notes. We know that designing simulations that prompt candidates to discuss a topic without telling them what to say is difficult. We have additional protocols to create, and we set out to try again.

This chapter describes the process for designing clinical simulations that focus on education candidates (ECs) in the inclusive elementary and special education program building explanations of science phenomena. We—a science educator (Sharon) and a generalist teacher educator (Ben)—conceptualized simulations to explore how our teacher education program was preparing future teachers of the elementary grades to support their students in building scientific explanations.[1] Our simulation design was informed by several sources: prior science simulation work for secondary science and mathematics content, the performance expectations of the Next Generation Science Standards (NGSS), *A Framework for K–12 Science Education: Practices, Crosscutting Concepts, and Core Ideas* (2012), and our commitment to using phenomena as a driver for science teaching.[2] We describe how each of these sources influenced the design of the simulations, contextualizing the design principles with two examples—one focused on water erosion at Niagara Falls and another focused on shoreline erosion. We use these examples to illustrate general outcomes of the simulations and discuss design considerations for future iterations of the simulations and the teacher education program.

THE STATUS OF ELEMENTARY SCIENCE IN US SCHOOLS

Relative to other content areas, science is not regularly taught in elementary classrooms. In a recent national survey of 919 elementary teachers, only 21 percent of teachers reported teaching science all or most days of the week.[3]

Thirty-nine percent reported teaching science some weeks but not every week of the school year. The study revealed an average of twenty minutes per day for elementary science, significantly less than the time spent in mathematics and English language arts classes. It also revealed that science content was not emphasized in respondents' elementary teacher education preparation programs. Only a third had at least three collegiate courses in the sciences—one each in earth, life, and physical science. Another third had two of the three, but the final third only had one course. Significantly for this simulation design, only 17 percent of surveyed elementary teachers felt very well prepared to develop students' abilities to do science, including developing models, explanations, and scientific arguments. A third of elementary teachers also thought that they should explain a scientific idea to students before having students consider evidence for that idea—a perception that runs directly counter to our goals in our teacher education program and those of the NGSS and supporting research.

Within our elementary teacher education program at Syracuse University (see figure 5.1 for an overview), candidates take two collegiate courses in the sciences. Although the content of these courses is not standardized, most candidates' learning experiences lean heavily toward the physical sciences. The courses, which are taught in another college and not the School of Education, tend to deploy traditional lectures, digital problem sets for homework, and multiple-choice quizzes and tests. Although these pedagogical strategies do not necessarily preclude students' engagement in the scientific practices for learning content, they often do. Therefore, most students' experience with the practices is now limited to a single science methods course.

The status of elementary science in schools also means that candidates have very limited opportunities to teach science during their field placements.

FIGURE 5.1 Program overview for inclusive elementary and special education

Educator candidate (EC) population:
Undergraduate students matriculated in a dual-certification inclusive elementary and special education program for grades 1 through 6

Program length:
Four years

Simulation timing:
Varies

Our teacher education program emphasizes interaction between candidates and classrooms each semester, but science is explicitly included in only one of six field experiences prior to student teaching. Candidates may have some opportunities to teach science during student teaching, but the performance assessment required for state certification that they must complete during student teaching addresses only mathematics and literacy, reducing the likelihood that science will be taught consistently. Given these systematic limitations, we determined that designing simulations that address science teaching could expand our students' opportunities to learn.

DESIGNING FROM THE STANDARDS

One of our positions is that when standards are well written, they form a baseline expectation of ideas that should be made fully accessible to all students. In this regard, we view meeting the standards as an equity requirement or as a means of empowering students' civil rights.[4] That said, we also understand that the standards are not always neutral and need to be consistently reevaluated through a social justice lens.[5] In the elementary context, the standards set a threshold for student learning that has yet to be met in US classrooms. The NGSS and the *Framework for K–12 Science Education* articulate for the first time a set of eight scientific practices that students need to participate in to learn. Constructing explanations is one of them. The eight practices are not intended to exist in isolation; instead, they overlap with and contribute to one another.[6] In contrast to traditional assumptions associated with what some scholars call the "mythological" scientific method, these practices should not be treated in a stepwise order.[7]

Unlike other standards documents, the NGSS integrated what would have been traditionally described as "content"—known now as disciplinary core ideas (DCIs)—with the practices and the crosscutting concepts. The language adjustment to DCIs signifies the importance of science teaching focused on science ideas that are applicable to a broad range of natural phenomena. It also nods to the goal of reducing the breadth and increasing the depth of ideas studied in school science. The DCIs are organized within biology, physical sciences, earth science, and engineering. Seven crosscutting concepts represent important science ideas, like cause and effect, that are applicable across the four disciplines and can be useful for linking the disciplines to one another. Thus, every standard, formally labeled a "performance expectation," weaves together a DCI, a scientific practice, and a crosscutting concept.

When we began designing these simulations, the *Framework* was published and laid out the foundation of the new standards. Our initial aims were to emphasize explanation building, a practice we selected because we were aware of the research in science education for supporting explanation building with students, and we had early ideas about scientific phenomena that could be useful for prompting candidates in the simulation context. There was enough research available in science education about explanations for us to move forward, even as we waited for the NGSS to be finalized.

DEFINING EXPLANATION AS A SCIENTIFIC PRACTICE FOR K–12 SCIENCE TEACHING

The *Framework for K–12 Science Education* defines scientific explanations as "accounts that link scientific theory with specific observations or phenomena—for example, they explain observed relationships between variables and describe the mechanisms that support cause and effect inferences about them."[8] This definition is supported by other descriptors of explanations in the science education literature. Fundamentally, scientific explanations must include causal accounts of how a phenomenon—the existence of which is not in doubt—occurs in nature.[9] These causal accounts move explanations beyond descriptions of what is experienced. Instead, the explanations require a mechanism that often relies on abstraction. For example, here in Syracuse, application of salt onto roads and sidewalks occurs regularly in the winter. Students could describe that snow and ice melts around and beneath the salt crystals. To generate an explanation, however, they would have to emphasize that the salt lowers the freezing point of water. They could explain that the sodium and chloride ions—which are too small to be seen—impede the formation of ice as temperatures lower below the freezing point of pure water. This explanation relies on kinetic molecular theory and application of the idea that temperature is a measure of the energy of particles. Invoking the particulate nature of matter and kinetic molecular theory provides an explanation of what causes ice melting that is beyond a description that salt melts ice.

Science educators point out that explanation building, like all scientific practices, overlaps and has relationships with other practices, like argumentation and modeling. A key difference between explanations and arguments is that students engage in argumentation when they are evaluating two or more explanations considering the evidence available.[10] Over time, argumentation results in the advancement of an explanation that is best supported by the evidence. Models can show patterns in observations or can describe aspects of systems or phenomena or explain how or why an event occurs.[11] Modeling is closely related to explanation building. Models focus on critical features of a system and are useful for predicting how the system might respond to changing conditions. Models can apply explanations to a specific case.

SEARCHING THE STANDARDS AND DETERMINING CRITERIA FOR DESIGN

To begin designing the elementary science simulations, we focused on some pragmatic factors specific to our teacher education program. Candidates enroll in six credits of science content and three credits of science methods. The science methods class is held in the semester immediately preceding student teaching. ECs are coenrolled in mathematics methods and English language arts methods, along with a technology course, a field placement, and a seminar. Since the mathematics and language arts methods courses focus on teaching elementary students in the intermediate grades, which is the upper limit of candidates' certification, placements typically occur in those grades, too. Our initial goal, then, was to select performance expectations from the grade levels where our candidates would have science teaching practice.

For these reasons, our initial search of the NGSS standards focused on grades 3, 4, and 5. Using Next Generation Science Standards (nextgenscience.org), the website that houses the NGSS and links to the *Framework for K–12 Science Education*, we searched for performance expectations that included the practice of constructing explanations. This resulted in eight performance expectations for consideration. In the standards, constructing explanations in science is sometimes paired with designing a solution in engineering. Performance expectations that emphasized designing a solution were eliminated from consideration since we expected to design simulations that could be completed in a short period of time and the engineering standards expected students to generate and compare solutions—work that should take more than the fifteen to eighteen minutes that our experience suggested is the outer limit for a productive simulated encounter. By removing from consideration performance expectations that mentioned designing a solution, our initial pool of eight performance expectations was reduced to four.

Our initial analysis of these four possibilities revealed challenges for simulation design. Some of these performance expectations addressed content that was not addressed in prior coursework for the ECs. Although we wanted to prioritize explanation building, we wanted to design simulations that might facilitate candidates' drawing on their prior knowledge from content that at least some candidates in each cohort had practice with. In essence, we did not seek to assess content knowledge and explanations simultaneously. Unfortunately, by focusing only on DCIs that explicitly named explanation building in our initial search, we narrowed the field so much that there was no overlap with candidates' prior content learning opportunities.

As a result, we revisited all of the performance expectations for grades 3, 4, and 5, which was an initial list of forty-one. We eliminated those that were directly associated with designing solutions, reducing the possible list to thirty-five. We then resumed our quest to narrow the focus for designing again.

To illustrate what we prioritized in that next round of standards review, consider performance expectation 3-LS1-1: "Develop models to describe that organisms have unique and diverse life cycles but all have in common birth, growth, reproduction, and death." This standard clearly expects a descriptive, as opposed to an explanatory, model. While this is appropriate given that the standard is for third graders, whose opportunity to learn more about unseen mechanisms explaining how these life cycles work had not yet materialized in school, this modeling expectation did not overlap with the explanatory goals of the project. Further, we struggled to conceptualize a range of life-cycle examples from various organisms with which the ECs could rapidly familiarize themselves before engaging in conversation with a standardized individual. Given that we had many other standards to choose from, we eliminated 3-LS1-1 from consideration.

We evaluated the remaining standards based on a loosely defined concept, captured with the question, "Is this standard 'sim-able'"? This question was our shorthand way of asking if the topic we were considering could be reasonably approximated given the constraints of the simulation model. As we saw it, there were multiple factors to evaluate. We wanted to choose topics we could make accessible through affordable hands-on materials, photographs, or other media to the EC and the standardized individual (SI) with whom they would interact in the simulation room. Relatedly, we needed concepts and materials that could be reasonably explored and discussed within fifteen minutes. We also wanted topics that at least some candidates would have had an opportunity to learn in prior semesters in the program. Since we wanted the simulations to explore candidates' capacity to help students construct explanations more than we wanted to evaluate their science content knowledge, we selected the performance expectations with ECs' prior learning opportunities in mind.

We knew that we wanted to recruit adults as SIs for these simulations. In previous simulations with a secondary focus, we either recruited adults to serve as standardized parents or young-looking college students to serve as standardized students.[12] With this project, however, we assumed that asking college students to portray elementary children would violate our emerging awareness that simulations are more successful for ECs when they are as realistic as possible. Asking college students to portray children risked a level of silliness we feared might convey a lack of sincerity in the situation. We wanted the ideas that were shared by the SI to seem reasonable and to be conveyed with a language and cadence that would make the encounter seem realistic to the EC.

Relatedly, we did not want to recruit children. We intended to construct the simulation such that the SI would say things we knew to be scientifically incorrect or naive to prompt the EC to respond with an opportunity to explain. We were influenced by the decades of science misconception research that clearly indicated the difficulties of changing students' ideas and therefore feared that actively teaching children to convey these misconceptions would be difficult to "unteach." Therefore, we wanted to choose scenarios where we could envision a reason for two adults to discuss the content and generate explanations to improve the potential realism of the simulation.

Finally, since we wanted the simulation to focus more on explanation building and less on the evaluation of content knowledge, we considered the amount of information we would provide the EC prior to the initiation of the simulation. In other simulations, we want the EC to respond to the situation off the cuff because many encounters between teachers and other school stakeholders are spontaneous and not always amenable to an intentional plan. However, we were certain that we did not want the simulation to be limited by the EC's capacity to recall prior content learning on the fly during the interaction. Therefore, we provided the ECs with a candidate interaction protocol at least a week prior to the encounter, which permitted them an opportunity to review how the phenomenon in question worked. However, we did not provide information about explanations because we did not want to stipulate the EC's encounter too explicitly in advance.

THE SIMULATIONS

Table 5.1 overviews the six simulations we designed for elementary science. They are listed in the order in which we designed and tested them and accompanied by a short title. The simulations are linked to the performance

TABLE 5.1 An overview of six simulations designed for elementary science

Simulation	Title	Performance Expectation	Scientific Practice	Disciplinary Core Idea	Crosscutting Concept	Link to Explanations	Accessibility	Realistic Adult
1	Niagara Falls	4-ESS1-1	Constructing explanations	The history of planet earth	Patterns	Explanations were the focal practice in the performance expectation.	A local phenomenon, supported by photography	Docent at a visitors' center talking with an adult patron
2	Shoreline Erosion	4-ESS2-1	Planning and carrying out investigations	Earth materials and systems; biogeology	Cause and effect	There is a reciprocal relationship between designing investigations and explanation building.	Images before and after hurricanes make shoreline landfall	Colleagues planning a field trip
3	Collisions	4-PS3-1	Constructing explanations	Definitions of energy	Energy and matter	Explanations were the focal practice in the performance expectation.	Easy-to-use provided materials	Docent at a local museum talking with an adult chaperone
4	Shadows	5-ESS1-2	Analyzing and interpreting data	Earth and the solar system	Patterns	Analyzing and interpretation data informs modeling and explanations.	Map of school grounds	Teachers working on a design committee
5	Water Quality	5-PS1-1	Developing and using models	Structure and properties of matter	Scale, proportion, and quantity	Both models and explanations can address how and why a phenomenon occurs.	A local phenomenon	Summer camp counselor talking with a parent volunteer
6	Yellowstone	3-LS4-3	Engaging in argument from evidence	Biological adaptation	Cause and effect	Argumentation informs modeling and explanations.	Photographs of Grand Prismatic Spring	Summer resource educator with the National Park Service talking with an adult visitor

expectation from the NGSS that guided their design. The next three columns specify which of the scientific practices was emphasized in the performance expectation, the disciplinary core idea, and the crosscutting concept. The next column overviews how the simulation addressed explanations, especially if the focal practice was not an explanation. The accessibility column overviews how we brought the phenomenon into the simulation. The last column identifies how the simulation addressed our design criterion of having a realistic adult as interlocutor.

All of the six simulations included what we saw as a realistic adult as the standardized individual. However, after the simulations were written and the candidates engaged with them, we realized this feature of the simulation design fell into a pattern. Of the six examples, three relied on the EC talking with an employee at an informal science education center such as a museum, nature preserve, or national park. The other three relied on the EC talking with another educator: planning a field trip with colleagues, working on a committee, or discussing student thinking. Given this pattern and limited space, we have elected to detail one of each type of simulation to illuminate their designs and discuss broad outcomes from them for the ECs. Therefore, we focus on the simulations for Niagara Falls and Shoreline Erosion.

Niagara Falls

The first simulation we drafted was based on standard 4-ESS1-1, which we called the Niagara Falls simulation. As New York State residents, we had multiple opportunities to visit Niagara Falls ourselves, and we expected our students had at least heard of the falls and that some might have visited them on their own. Sharon's prior methods teaching had given her multiple opportunities to help teacher candidates plan science lessons about the falls, and so she was aware of some of the history of the falls and their management. For example, she knew that the flow of water over the American side of the falls had been diverted in the 1960s following an evaluation by the International Joint Commission and later by the US Army Corps of Engineers. She found twenty-one photographs online that were taken when the American falls were dry and showed students the size of the boulders at the bottom. She used these photographs previously with individual ECs when they were asked to teach about the falls in their field placements.

When we decided to draw from this phenomenon for a simulation, we started with the group of photographs. We limited the set of photos to five—two images with opposing side views of the falls and with people included for scale, two views from the bottom with people for scale, and one view from across the falls with the water flowing and with a boat for scale. The people and boats were important inclusions in the photographs because without them it would have been difficult for viewers to comprehend the size of the boulders, many of which were two to three times the height of an adult person. These photographs emphasized the boulders rather than the falls themselves and tended to lead others to ask how the boulders arrived at the base of the falls and why they were so large.

After the design of the simulation and completion of initial data gathering, we realized we failed to capitalize on an opportunity to raise our students' awareness of the land around Niagara Falls and its relationship with Indigenous Peoples. We later learned that the Niagara River and the falls sat at the intersection of at least three Indigenous Nations: Wenrohronon, Haudenosaunee, and Attiwonderonk.[13] Arrival of European colonizers began in the 1600s, and the land remains unceded by the Nations. We could have included this information in the Niagara Falls simulation, as well as in three other simulations to help our ECs consider how our land representations position the interests of the Nations within the United States.

As was the case with each of the simulations, we constructed an interaction protocol for educator candidates and a separate one for standardized individuals. For the ECs, we explained that they had been hired as a guide for patrons of the Niagara Falls visitor center. After setting the general guidelines for the job, we explained that the guides were usually asked many questions about the project and that they should be prepared to "make an effort to help [visitors] craft a scientific explanation of the erosion that has occurred." The protocol contained the photographs they would have available during the simulation, and there were large printouts of the photographs on the wall in the simulation room for them to refer to during the interaction. With this information, ECs could explore on their own any additional information they might need to understand the phenomenon and anticipate how their simulation would unfold.

In the training and protocol for the SIs, we explained that they were the caregiver of a family traveling the northeast United States on summer vacation and that their latest stop was Niagara Falls. We encouraged them to go to the visitor center and examine the photographs of rock faces on the walls. After looking at the pictures, we wanted them to "open" the simulation by saying, "Wow, the waterfall must be really powerful to push those giant rocks downstream!" Recall that in this simulation, the EC is playing the role of a docent in the visitor center while the SI portrays a visitor. We emphasized that SIs should answer questions asked of them by the EC—questions that the EC was supposed to be generating to elicit information about the SI's thinking. If the EC was not asking questions that would lead to a discussion of change over time, we coached SIs to ask the EC, "Have the falls always looked this way?"

When we evaluated the explanations provided or supported by the ECs, as captured in the simulation videotapes, we looked for them to address the fact that the large boulders at the base of Niagara Falls are a result of erosion of the rock face obscured from view by the falls themselves. Some of the layers of rock beneath the Niagara River are more susceptible to erosion by water. This differential erosion means that some layers erode back more quickly than others, leaving some layers to stick out and weaken since they are unsupported from lower layers. Eventually, this weakening leaves the rock face to break and fall to the bottom, to be pummeled by the water falling over the falls and eventually break into ever smaller pieces.

When the ECs engaged in this simulation, they asked the SI questions to elicit ideas from the SIs less than 10 percent of the time. Instead, they offered their own explanations 85 percent of the time. Most of the explanations the ECs offered were very close to their written explanations of the phenomenon, which they recorded on a computer shortly before the beginning of the simulation. Following the simulation, during our debrief meetings, we asked the ECs how they prepared for the encounter. They explained that they looked up erosion of Niagara Falls using an internet search and repeated what they remembered on their preencounter form, as well as during the simulation itself.

Shoreline Erosion

The second simulation was written shortly after Hurricane Sandy struck the northeastern US coastline in October 2012. Since our university draws most of its students from this region, we expected that a shoreline erosion concept would be relevant to teacher candidates. Additionally, many ECs who participated in this simulation had an opportunity to practice teaching peers or K–12 students lessons about water and erosion. During these experiences, they used stream tables, sand, soil, and water to replicate multiple conditions. We chose not to use these same materials in the simulation, however, because they are difficult to reset (thereby necessitating a new setup for every student), they make a substantial mess, and their outcomes can be variable. Instead, we decided to provide ECs with a series of before and after photographs of shoreline erosion, gathered from the United States Geological Survey website. These included images showing elevation changes, aerial photographs before and after hurricane landfall, and graphs showing the beach volume, shoreline change, and elevation change as a function of distance from the landfall point.

In the interaction protocol document provided to the EC before the encounter, we explained to the candidates that they would be planning a fourth-grade field trip with colleagues. The ECs were to assume they had prior experience with visiting the Barnegat Lighthouse on Long Beach Island, New Jersey, and would be expected to use the images described above to help a colleague explain how they could use the lighthouse visit to help students generate explanations in keeping with the standard. In the future, as with the Niagara Falls scenario, we will improve the interaction protocol with an acknowledgment that the Barnegat Lighthouse sits on land previously occupied by the Lenni-Lenape, the first tribal group to attempt a treaty with the newly formed US government after the signing of the Declaration of Independence.[14]

To prepare the standardized individuals, we explained that they would act as a special education teacher at an elementary school who is tasked with collaborating with the EC to plan a field trip. The SI was the person who asked how the field trip could link to the elementary science subjects they were studying. They were made aware that there would be images that the EC could elect to show them during the simulation. We hoped that the EC would ask questions about the images to elicit SIs' explanation of what happened at the shore.

When ECs were providing or eliciting explanations, we anticipated that they would indicate that the storm surge—resulting in a larger volume of fast-moving water—was capable of picking up, moving, and depositing sand away from the beaches and toward the inland areas. The evidence from the multiple images is useful in noting that the energy of the storm is highest near the eye and decreases with distance. Lower energy in the storm results in reduced movement of sand.

During the simulated encounter, the ECs asked the SIs more questions than they did in the Niagara Falls case. Additionally, the cohort of ECs made fifty-four separate comments about how they would plan for student learning for the Shoreline Erosion simulation, compared to no such references for the Niagara Falls scenario. Although we acknowledge that we had no expectation that ECs would discuss student learning in the simulation, we interpret this difference in focus as an outcome of the ECs being asked to talk with a colleague planning a field trip in which some form of student learning would be expected. When comparing the two simulations, we also found that the shoreline example elicited more content discussion about erosion, particularly on the impact of erosion on changing the landscape.

This difference surprised us, but we think that the short time frame over which the erosion occurred in the case of the hurricane may have made it seem more significant to the ECs than erosion at Niagara Falls, which has been slower and interrupted by human intervention.

DESIGN IMPLICATIONS

Simulations can be designed to address professional standards, even when those standards focus on what should be taught in classrooms. Our evidence suggests that the simulations were successful in getting our candidates talking about their thinking related to the phenomenon at the focus of the case. Our postencounter discussions revealed that our ECs relied on internet searches to inform their explanations. Additionally, some ECs recalled that they learned science content related to the phenomenon in prior courses, but they preferred to use an internet search rather than use their resources from their classes.

Our findings that few ECs were able to generate content-accurate explanations have implications for the design of the simulations and for our broader teacher education program. Regarding simulation design, we hoped that giving ECs information about the content of the scenario would allow them to review the content as needed to elicit an explanation. We now view this as a naive assumption. Essentially, the ECs did not have enough background knowledge to be aware of how much background knowledge they needed. They were able to use a few words related to the phenomenon but not to use them entirely correctly. Thus, we may need to embed the simulations more fully in the program—an issue to be explained further below.

Regarding simulation revision, the ECs' preference for focusing discussion on pedagogy could be useful for further revision. We could capitalize on this by modifying the simulations to focus on situations where they would talk about lesson design. The situation and the trigger statements for the SIs would need to focus on lesson design for explanations. This possibility would require that we remove the docent role from the SI and may mean we need to alter the scenario accordingly. For example, in the Yellowstone simulation, we could still use the Grand Prismatic Spring phenomenon but ask the EC to invite the SI to discuss a lesson that would lead students to generate an explanation of how this works. The spring is a useful case for the simulation, especially since a photograph provides sufficient opportunity to observe the various bacteria and gives enough information to be discussed in the simulation. If we edit this location away for other reasons, we still believe that choosing a phenomenon that can be discussed within the limits of the simulation experience will remain important.

In terms of program revision, one improvement would be to embed the simulations in multiple semesters, including potentially in the science methods course. The data make clear that ECs need more opportunities to build their own explanations of the phenomena and then more practice eliciting those explanations from others. We could revise the science methods and curriculum course to emphasize this, recognizing that improving explanations might happen at the expense of time on modeling or argumentation practice. Additionally, we could work with colleagues to provide more opportunities for our students to learn about science teaching by either adding a course or adding content to other courses. Another option would be to work more deliberately with local schools to continue to support our graduates in learning about content and pedagogy into their continuing professional education.

CONCLUDING THOUGHTS

Our experiences suggest that it is possible to design content-focused simulations for use with future elementary teachers. We realized that as teacher educators, we balance several factors in designing simulations within the overall context of our programs. As demonstrated by the selection of topics, we work to address students' prior knowledge, professional expectations for instruction as designated by the standards, contextual factors that place constraints on program structure, and challenges candidates are likely to face in their future classrooms. Regarding the standards and the NGSS, the simulation structure provides an opportunity for us to assess our students' readiness for teaching to inform program adjustments as edits to the standards are made over time.

In the elementary context, we remain humbled by the vast array of ideas our future teachers need to understand and the limited opportunities we have to prepare them for this array in a four-year teacher preparation program. These challenges suggest to us that one way to improve the knowledge, skills, and practices of future teachers is to improve their opportunities to learn science in K–12 settings. We presented the challenges to elementary science as a matter of a lack of opportunity for these future teachers to practice teaching science, but it also means that over their thirteen years in schools as students, the cumulative effect of minimal learning places too much pressure on resolving this knowledge gap during college.

Additionally, as we expanded our own knowledge as White teacher educators about land as a site of pedagogy and Indigenous ideas of sustainability, we realized that we failed to begin to address even fundamental land acknowledgments in these site-based simulations and will make those corrections in our future work.[15]

The candidates' knowledge of the disciplinary core ideas, crosscutting concepts, and the explanations revealed during the simulations remains under analysis. Yet we can confidently say that our candidates are not yet ready to elicit explanations from others. Instead, they generally approached these simulations as a mechanism to provide right answers as grounded in the protocol documents we provided and the internet inquiry they undertook as preparation for the simulation. This suggests to us that our program needs to improve our ECs' skill and capacity for supporting others in building explanations. Nevertheless, these simulations provided them with structured opportunities to practice communicating about topics that they would be expected to teach in their future classrooms and that more traditional field opportunities were not providing them consistently.

learning.[2] Peer-to-peer role-plays are complicated by preexisting relationships, varying abilities to engage a role, and potential performance anxiety.[3] Although these pedagogies represent forms of active engagement called for in adult learning theories, they also challenge counselor educators' ability to equitably assess learning across cohorts of ECs.[4] Similarly, just like colleagues in teacher and school leader education, counselor educators struggle with how counseling practicum and internship experiences offer ECs inconsistent and varied opportunities to practice the synthesis of knowledge and skill.

Despite the depth and breadth of literature demonstrating the effectiveness of simulations within education professions, particularly in teacher education, there is limited evidence of simulations within the training of school counselors.[5] This is curious for two reasons. First, school counselors work alongside teachers and school leaders within K–12 educational systems and must therefore learn to collaborate with other school professionals, access shared resources, and bear collective responsibilities within an education system more broadly.[6] The importance of school counselors' interprofessional work in schools indisputably parallels that of clinical mental health counselors in integrated care or medical contexts, but the elaboration and use of simulations for such training have remained underdeveloped. Second, school counselors are frequently licensed and/or certified as teachers at the state level, with the specialty of school counseling through pupil personnel services. Although the use of simulations began in the preparation of K–12 general education teachers, currently simulations are expanding across special education, music education, and physical education (described elsewhere in this book), as well as higher education.[7] There has, nonetheless, been limited extension of these simulations to include the work of counselors practicing with and alongside other educators in K–12 school contexts.[8]

Although simulations originated within medical education, their utility as a training pedagogy has since been demonstrated across allied medical professions (including nursing, speech language pathology, and health sciences), as well as across education professions (such as teaching and school leadership). Over the last decade, the use of simulations as part of training mental health professionals has emerged in the empirical literature across social work, marriage and family therapy, psychology, and counseling. Of note, within counselor education, the use of simulations is focused almost exclusively on interprofessional training of clinical mental health counselors within integrated behavioral health contexts.[9]

We recognize both the value and challenges of experiential learning pedagogies, including simulations used in allied professions and clinical mental health counseling. Further, we place value in providing for all counseling candidates some common, shared learning experiences—such as supporting a student in crisis—that we cannot guarantee through traditional school counseling field placements and that require subsequent follow-up with families and other school professionals. As a result, we recognized in the work of Benjamin Dotger an opportunity to engage further with the experiential pedagogy of simulations through designs that engage counseling candidates in an active and intentionally scaffolded learning progression. Nested simulations, rather than single encounters, seemed particularly appealing given the nature of counseling as a field.

NESTED SIMULATIONS DESIGN IN COUNSELOR EDUCATION

Counseling is an ongoing relational process that occurs over time, necessitating the counselor to engage in professional activities in sessions with the client and between sessions out of the client's view. For school counselors, this involves working with their student clients in a typical counseling session and also with students' families, teachers, and other personnel within the broader educational system. Nested simulation designs in counseling connect the person-to-person components of counseling sessions, with the work done outside sessions and the broader situational context. Embedded—or "nested"—within a series of related simulations is the core situation. As the series of simulations unfolds, ECs experience the elaboration or unfolding of situational context over time in a way that intentionally scaffolds multiple opportunities for ECs to engage in session with the standardized individual (SI) but also through out-of-session debriefings and professional documentation procedures.

To start the nested design process, we selected the Ashley Wilson simulation. As described in this chapter's opening narrative as well as in chapter 2 of this book, the Wilson scenario centers on a teenage boy, John, who is being bullied and physically harassed by peers who think he is gay. We selected the Wilson simulation because it is used across SOE's teacher and school leader programs, and we wanted our nested design to build from a simulation that had been used successfully with other ECs.

Then we looked to the broader objectives of our program and the professional frameworks that guide our program, including the Council for the Accreditation of Counseling and Related Educational Programs (CACREP) counseling standards and the Multicultural and Social Justice Counseling Competencies (MSJCC).[10] As outlined in figure 6.1, our counselor education

FIGURE 6.1 Program overview for school counseling

Educator candidate (EC) population:
Graduate students matriculated in a master's program in school counseling

Program length:
Twenty-four months (including summers)

Simulation timing:
Established with nested designs; varies depending on syllabus

program is a graduate-level program that prepares thoughtful, effective, responsive, empathetic counselors, focusing on student advocacy and cutting-edge practices. Prior to these efforts, we had not implemented any other simulations within or across program coursework.

Multiple intersections between the program's introductory course, the broader program of study, the CACREP standards, and the Multicultural and Social Justice (MSJ) competencies were identified to support the design of the nested simulations. For example, one objective of the program's introductory course is to focus on how counselors' roles and responsibilities align with student populations that have historically been underserved, including English new language learners, students with disabilities, and lesbian, gay, bisexual, transgender, intersex, and questioning (LGBTIQ+) students.[11] As a second example, the broader school counselor program expects ECs to practice "outside-the-counseling-session" consultation and collaboration with systemic resources, across a given school and community.

Building from the connections between the counseling program and national standards, we then turned to Melissa Luke and Kris Goodrich's scholarship in "LGBTIQ+ Responsive School Counseling Supervision" to identify the links between the narrative in the first Ashley Wilson simulation and our forthcoming designs for the second and third Wilson simulations. The first simulation surfaces the core situation: Ms. Wilson reports her son, John, is being bullied and physically assaulted. In this initial simulation, Ms. Wilson explicitly indicates she's meeting to talk about her son's assault on campus and not about whether some kids think John is gay. Building from the core situation and the intentionally directed conversation toward the physical assault, we then outlined the next two simulation designs.

In these subsequent designs, the core situation remained nested within the context of the other two simulations that followed. For example, the second simulation again is initiated by the SI, Ms. Wilson. In this follow-up conversation, she reports the bullying and harassment of her son have not stopped. She also reports, though, that she has "discovered" communications between her son and a peer that suggest that her son, John, may be gay. By design, the situation grows more complex as Ms. Wilson explains to the EC that she's struggling with how to talk to her son. Thus, in this second simulation, candidates must dually engage with physical harassment on campus that still hasn't ceased, as well as a mother who is struggling with her son's identity and "how to deal with a gay kid." We intentionally designed the third simulation to position the counselor candidate in an encounter with John. Under the guise of preparing for next year's course selections, the EC initiates a conversation with John. Stepping into the third simulation, the EC now has significant background knowledge of the bullying and harassment from two conversations with John's mother—one about the assault and another about her concerns for John and his sexual identity. The SI interaction protocol for this third simulation calls on actors to hint that "things aren't going well" and to be forthcoming with the EC if they interrogate John's insinuation of challenging times. Table 6.1 overviews these three simulations.

TABLE 6.1 Nested simulation protocols

Protocol	Candidates	Standardized Individual (SI) and Context	Summary of Instructions for Standardized Individuals (SIs) and Key Triggers
Ashley Wilson 1	School counseling	First parent-initiated conference between parent and school counselor after parent learns her son is being bullied at school	• Provide background on your experience as a single mother raising John. • Say that you appreciate that John is active in band-related activities at school. • Express anger about recent bullying incidents, and ask what the school counselor can do to stop the harassment. • Express concern that John will be embarrassed by your coming to school and/or that the visit could increase the bullying behavior. • Ask the school counselor to check in on John but to keep your visit a secret.

TABLE 6.1 *(Continued)*

Protocol	Candidates	Standardized Individual (SI) and Context	Summary of Instructions for Standardized Individuals (SIs) and Key Triggers
Ashley Wilson 2	School counseling	Second parent-initiated conference between parent and school counselor after bullying continues and parent has learned her son may identify as gay	• Share your worry about your son John because "the bullying hasn't stopped." • Mention that you observed bruises and torn clothing. • Communicate your anger (but not at the school counselor) that the bullying continues. • Only if asked, say you think you know why this is happening. The text messages you found between John and his male friend Bill have led you to think your son John might be gay. • Ask immediately, "How do I deal with a gay kid?" • Say, "I love him, but I don't know what to do with this! How do I talk to John about this? What do I say? This isn't how I pictured things." • Make it clear that you're not against John or the gay community but are a bit shocked by all that you've learned very recently. • Distinguish between your concerns for how to move forward with John and the need for the bullying to stop.
John Wilson	School counseling	Meeting with student being bullied after the second meeting with Ms. Wilson	• Answer the school counselor's questions vaguely, but hint that things are not going that well. • Be forthcoming if or when the school counselor asks you directly about harassment. • Focus on bullying and harassment, and if you're asked directly why this may be happening, blame yourself as "paying a price for something you said to a friend." • Describe a conversation with a male friend where you shared that you are not that interested in talking about girls and how they look or in kissing them, and you think your friend now suspects you're gay. • If the counselor asks if you are gay, respond by saying, "I don't know. I think maybe so. I may be gay." • Share that your intra- and interpersonal experiences are "different" from your male friends and that you aren't sure what this means for you and if or how you can approach this topic with your mother.

CONNECTIONS BETWEEN NESTED SIMULATIONS DESIGNS AND LEARNING ACROSS COUNSELING DOMAINS

The nested designs of the three Ashley Wilson simulations approximate the ongoing, iterative, and interactional processes that the school counselor might encounter when working with LGBTIQ+ students, their families, and personnel within a school counseling practice context. We embedded this nested simulation design in our program's introductory school counseling course because it highlights the different roles and responsibilities of school counselors in contemporary schools but also because this course focused on the personal, social, and academic needs of students identifying as LGBTIQ+.

Twelve counseling candidates were enrolled in this course and participated in the Wilson simulations in accordance with the implementation procedures outlined in the first chapter of this book. Following each candidates' individual simulation and immediate, small-group debriefing (standard procedures for all simulations in this book), the candidates also engaged in group learning activities in the classroom involving review and discussion of excerpts of their recorded sessions. This activity not only extended the simulations but also permitted the candidates opportunities to begin to develop reflective practice. Through the instructor-led application of the School Counseling Supervision Model in a group context, candidates were supported to take an active role in peer supervision, a standard professional expectation for practicing school counselors.[12]

In addition, the course syllabus included the expectation that candidates submit two different types of material based on their simulation roles—reflective and critical. After ECs engaged in the simulations, they responded in reflective subjectivity journals. They were given prompts to provide structure to the journal entries, but they were also encouraged to discuss and explore any additional material they chose. The five subjectivity journal entries were assessed based on the level of detail included in the reflections, as well as the openness with which ECs processed their personal reactions, biases, and beliefs. Finally, ECs were required to view a peer's clinical simulation video and provide one to two pages of written peer supervision—both observational and reflective in nature—for submission to the instructor as well as the classmate.

As a coauthor team, we approached these data with the goal of examining connections between the simulation and journal data corpus and the four counseling domains that undergird our program. Each author independently read simulation transcripts and coded the four domains that had been identified a priori. We compared the coded data and discussed to consensus the codes. Next, we followed a similar process when reviewing the journal data. We identified journal excerpts focused on the four domains. We then examined the transcripts and journal excerpts over time for development. As we examined the data, we elected not to assign gender-specific pseudonyms and instead refer to each as a counselor educator candidate (EC). Below, we share how the simulation data and subsequent journal and peer supervision activities align with the four counselor education domains: conceptual knowledge, intra- and interpersonal awareness, counseling skills, and social justice advocacy.

Conceptual Knowledge

Conceptual knowledge in counselor education reflects a broad range of concepts and skills related to understanding and engaging in the role of counselor. The Council for Accreditation of Counseling and Related Educational Programs (CACREP), the primary accrediting body for counselor education programs in the United States, identifies eight core areas of conceptual knowledge for counselors: professional orientation and ethics, social and cultural diversity, human growth and development, career development, counseling and helping relationships, group counseling, assessment, and research/program evaluation.[13] Each core area provides ECs with a foundational knowledge base from which to approach clients. Within the more specific context of school counseling, CACREP also requires that school counselors learn about the role of school counselors, the warning signs for adverse experiences, and K–12 school legal and ethical standards. In our counselor education program, we hope ECs can apply relevant knowledge from the eight CACREP core areas, learned through their coursework, to real-life situations.

In the initial simulation, ECs were situated in conversation with Ashley Wilson, a worried parent seeking assistance from the school counselor with the bullying and physical assault her son is experiencing on school grounds. Many ECs were initially unsure about how to respond. Some suggested the parent speak with her son, offering indirect approaches to that conversation: "I wouldn't suggest pushing the issue but perhaps just—like, just opening it up for discussion—like, 'I'm not exactly sure what's going on, but if you want to talk. . . .' Just make it a comfortable, open environment so that if and when he does feel like talking, he's comfortable to do so." Although this EC seemed to exhibit some understanding of the role of a school counselor, which doesn't necessarily include mediating between a parent and a child, the EC also seemed uncomfortable using broaching skills with the parent herself or as a model for the parent to adopt as she engages with her son later.

In another simulated encounter, the SI Ms. Wilson asked the counseling candidate, "Yeah, basically I just kind of wanted to know what is your policy for harassment in schools?" By design, the parent was expecting the counselor to address school policy related to resolving the bullying and assault. Although we recognize this is a simulation, as faculty we still expect the counseling candidate to demonstrate conceptual knowledge about school policy related to bullying and assault. In response, the EC asked, "Did he give you names of the students or just that it was three upperclassmen because we have a very, very, zero tolerance policy." The EC did demonstrate some beginning conceptual knowledge about school policy, but this response illustrates the importance of knowing and employing more precise language about reporting and acting on reports of bullying and assault in schools. As the conversation continued, the EC asked Ms. Wilson for additional information about the bullying and assault, reflecting an in-the-moment conceptual understanding that part of serving as a counselor means accurately reporting bullying behavior. On further reflection, an EC wrote in a journal entry, "In my clinical simulation, my client wanted to know specifically what the school's policy on bullying was, and I was not able to give her a specific answer." This knowledge gap, identified by the EC through the simulated experience, had the potential to complicate and challenge the tendency of ECs to rush into practicum without consideration of the knowledge they need to be successful in those field settings.

Across the small EC cohort, we saw several other examples of how the first simulation illuminated gaps in conceptual knowledge related to the roles and responsibilities of school counselors. For example, one EC suggested holding a school assembly on bullying as a part of a comprehensive school counseling program. This EC noted, "We can do anything, you know, that's going to help to get rid of bullying at this school because I want John to feel safe at this school." We see strength in this EC's suggestion of preventative services, but we also see a gap in knowledge when the EC suggested they could "do anything" to keep a student safe. There are ethical and practical boundaries for the school counselor that simply won't support having the counselor be with John every moment to ensure he is not bullied. In another simulation, a different EC demonstrated a lack of understanding about which school personnel are responsible for addressing student behavior. The EC shared with Ms. Wilson, "If we do have concrete information that bullying is occurring, then they would be punished—not by me, but by, uh, the people who punish." Additional conceptual knowledge about school structures, roles, and responsibilities could help this EC more fully inform Ms. Wilson and take the appropriate steps to link her and her noted concerns with the proper school administrator.

While this simulation demonstrated how some ECs struggled with understanding school structures, it also illuminated EC responses that bridge across the counseling domains. For example, in response to Ms. Wilson's question about school policy on bullying and harassment, one EC did not display a counseling orientation, instead stating, "With it being such a small school, do you think maybe he's feeling a little bit alienated as it is being a new student and not really knowing many people? How new are you to the district?" From our perspective as counselor educators, such a response suggests the need for us to discuss with the candidate what caused them to offer an alternative explanation for John's behavior before sharing school policy on bullying and harassment. Such a response—one that places additional inquiry and responsibility on the student being bullied—holds interpersonal or social justice implications. Thus, this example demonstrates how knowledge and skill related to the conceptual knowledge domain can cross over to other domains (such as intra/interpersonal and social justice advocacy) as well.

These data exemplify how simulations help us identify ECs' application of knowledge and skill, highlighting where further programmatic and candidate work is necessary to ground the conceptual knowledge domain within K–12 school contexts. Although these data illustrate the conceptual knowledge domain, we see within them and the simulation process itself emerging evidence of the second domain—intra- and interpersonal awareness.

Intra- and Interpersonal Awareness

The development of intra- and interpersonal awareness is a key aspect of counselor training. Counselors must learn to recognize their own internal biases and dispositions, as well as the impact of their own identities on interpersonal interactions in counseling practice. In addition, school counselors must learn about themselves as leaders and change agents, in alignment with CACREP standards and within the context of K–12 schools.

Through the simulation and journal data, we see evidence of intra- and interpersonal awareness. For example, one EC who engaged with Ms. Wilson asked, "Does that make you feel any better?" As a second example, an EC reflected in a later journal entry about a tendency to affirm others, saying, "I think I was wanting to be a people pleaser, and I thought compliments was

[sic] what makes someone feel better, but really giving honest observation can help more in the long run." The EC had engaged in prior coursework that directly addressed this interpersonal knowledge, but the simulation supported the transition of this course content into working knowledge for the EC to ingrain this knowledge in a new way.

In our roles as counselor educators, we sometimes see ECs' knowledge prioritized in the moment, thus obstructing interpersonal interactions. One EC demonstrated this, reflecting that in her simulation, "I am so concerned with saying the right thing in the right way that I end up getting totally lost in my head." Hearing this, Melissa was able to engage with the EC about strategies to navigate overthinking and to interrupt rumination. Later, in the second Wilson simulation, the EC reported practicing this skill. In related intrapersonal learning, several ECs reflected on how simulations and the subsequent small-group debriefings impacted their self-awareness. One EC said. "After my participation in the first clinical simulation, I left feeling as though I had let Ms. Wilson down." Another EC said, "The simulation experience was helpful in that I have been able to receive feedback and to learn about myself and my style through the process." This candidate voiced anxiety and uncertainty immediately after the simulation, but a later individual video review of the simulation data and whole-group discussion of the broader situation fostered in this EC a level of comfort and confidence. One of the core constructs of simulations—interacting with a standard individual—helped ECs to compare similar experiences. As those peer discussions progressed through processing in journals and class sessions, the broader process helped them to know more about themselves and the ways they engage with others.

Engaging in two nested simulations also helped ECs explore how their intra- and interpersonal awareness blends with their conceptual knowledge in real time. The simulation process highlighted ECs' hesitancy in broaching or engaging conversations about students' identity. Similarly, while ECs knew the roles and responsibilities of a counselor, the simulations highlighted a tendency toward information gathering rather than reflecting and the need to reassure without providing specific action steps. Blending conceptual knowledge with the demands of intra- and interpersonal awareness in demanding situations calls for specific counseling skill sets.

Counseling Skills

Counseling candidates must develop specific skills for engaging clients, parents, students, colleagues, and other stakeholders. For example, in preparing for professional contexts, ECs learn advocacy skills and processes for addressing barriers within their work settings. In preparation for counseling relationships, ECs learn about suicide models and skills for intervening with suicidal clients. In order to conduct and interpret assessments, ECs learn skills for effective assessment of risk for suicide or otherwise unsafe behaviors. Within the context of school counselor preparation, ECs must also learn skills that include evaluating home environments and home-school connections, strategies to promote equity, and skills to foster school counseling programs that decrease adverse school experiences, including bullying.

The two Wilson simulations illuminated a number of EC skills, including reflection, summarization, and information gathering. Additionally, more advanced skills (like broaching and challenging discrepancies) were employed by ECs. In one simulation, an EC utilized opening skills to orient Ms. Wilson to the space by sharing:

> You know you're free to speak about anything in this office. It's going to remain confidential with me. I do want to let you know, though, should I consider anything to be, you know, harmful to you or to anyone else, I would have to break confidentiality. And are you okay with me taking some notes during our conversation?

This EC also demonstrated this opening skill in conjunction with one of the eight core areas of conceptual knowledge, professional orientation and ethics—in this case, to highlight a duty to provide informed consent. Later in the simulation, the same EC practiced information gathering skills, asking, "Are you noticing a difference in his mood or his attitude—you know, when it's time to go to school or when he immediately comes home?" As faculty, we build on these early forays by encouraging ECs to continue practicing both skill sets—opening skills and information gathering skills—and to broaden the skill sets through open-ended questions and reflection-based skills.

There were very few examples of ECs engaging their emotional, content, or meaning reflection skills in the Wilson simulations. Emotional skills include the ECs' intrapersonal awareness and their ability to accurately perceive and respond to their client's positive and negative affect and to assess, integrate, and appropriately account for cultural and interpersonal dynamics between themselves and others. In this context, content skills refer to the EC's ability to think about school counseling theory, to differentiate varied school counseling roles and responsibilities, and to integrate school counseling law, ethics, policies, and procedures. Meaning reflection skills include the EC's ability to expand restated content to include a deeper understanding of the associated feelings, as well as their personal values and familial/ social significance.

In the simulated encounter, the SI was clearly discouraged and worried for her son, but most ECs focused on procedural responses, such as standing in a strategic place, reassuring Ms. Wilson, or employing more information-gathering skills. Although ECs didn't employ meaning reflection skills in simulation, journal data showed ECs using the simulation videos as a chance to reflect back on the missed opportunity for meaning reflection skills. In her journal, one EC noted, "I think that by summarizing and reflecting what they've said back, it will cause them to think about the emotions they are feeling in the present moment. This may also help them to work through these emotions, especially if they find them to be troublesome." In the whole-group class sessions that followed the simulations, similar journal entries provided opportunities for faculty and ECs to practice meaning reflections and discuss the impact of reflections on emotional processing. In a journal entry, an EC shared a feeling of pressure from having only a short amount of time with Ms. Wilson in simulation, noting the struggle to prioritize meaning reflection skills over what was perceived as a quicker solution.

Despite the time boundaries of the simulations, their nested design allowed us to consider more advanced skills in subsequent encounters. One EC demonstrated content reflection skills: "All right. So just to make sure I'm hearing you correctly: well, you're upset about the bullying, and you're upset about the fact that he might be gay." In the second simulation, a different EC connected with Ms. Wilson's emotions by saying, "I'm really glad you came in today. I can sense that you really do—I mean, you love your son, and it doesn't matter to you what choices he makes because, you know, I mean he's still your son." However, this EC then quickly shifted to giving advice: "I think the only thing you can do is support him. and you know, he is who he is, and as long as he knows that you love him and that you are happy for him—and you are proud of him still, [I] think that's the best thing you can do." Later in this simulation transcript, the EC then shifted the conversation significantly, suggesting potential discomfort in engaging in further conversation about John's sexuality with Ms. Wilson.

In counselor education programs, broaching is an important and frequently highlighted skill defined as "the counselor's ability to consider how sociopolitical factors such as race influence the client's counseling concerns."[14] Broaching should be proactive and counselor-initiated, acknowledge the complexity of identity, and generally occur within the first three meetings with a client. Broaching skills are relevant to the Wilson simulations in recognition of John's marginalized identity. The use of broaching skills represented a significant area of growth for some ECs, including Peter and Maria, whom we quoted in our opening anecdote. Both Peter and Maria had a hunch Ms. Wilson might be worried about her son's sexual identity but didn't directly broach those concerns. They and other ECs missed this opportunity for direct, counselor-led broaching of cultural factors important to Ms. Wilson. One EC demonstrated their effort with broaching cues ("Is there a . . . ? You brought up . . ."), asking Ms. Wilson, "I hear that you've . . . brought up the possibility that John might be gay a couple times. Is that something you'd like to explore?" While this EC's words were not straightforward, this was a clear attempt to broach this portion of Ms. Wilson's experience. The EC offered to talk more about this with Ms. Wilson, making it clear that their session was a space where Ms. Wilson could express her feelings and thoughts related to John's sexual identity.

Counseling skills are not utilized in a vacuum. They are deeply connected to the client's context. In these examples above and indeed within the broader design of the nested simulations, we see social justice contexts emerging. We now turn to explore this fourth domain of counseling.

Social Justice Advocacy

Counselor training focuses significantly on developing candidates' multicultural awareness, conceptual knowledge, counseling skills, and social justice advocacy. This includes preparing ECs to meet clients where they are in identity development, advocating for clients with marginalized identities in institutional and social contexts, and using their own positions to address barriers for students. Within school contexts, counselors learn to develop culturally responsive school counseling programs and address (and ideally, remove) cultural barriers in academic achievement for K–12 students. In our program, ECs are introduced early to knowledge and skills for social justice advocacy. In their initial course, ECs were introduced to social justice advocacy intervention, and the Wilson simulations provided us opportunity to examine if and how they were putting social justice advocacy knowledge and skill into practice.

In the second simulation with Ms. Wilson, there was a clear opportunity for social justice advocacy. Unlike the first simulation, where the SI only hinted about concerns related to her son's sexual identity, her verbalizations in the second simulation indicate this is a clear concern for her. In the first simulation, Ms. Wilson suggests that the bullying John is suffering may be connected to his presentation as "not a boy's boy." In the second simulation, Ms. Wilson disclosed clear information about John's emerging identity as a member of the LGBTIQ+ community. In response, some ECs placed the responsibility on John with phrases like, "Hopefully when he comes forward and lets us know what's really going on. . . ." Other ECs tried to reassure Ms. Wilson that everything would be okay: "Yeah, well. What you just said to me—like, I can see that you really care about him and you really support him, so just being honest with him is all you can do." In these two examples, the ECs were trying to affirm Ms. Wilson but fell short of advocating for John. Other ECs offered Ms. Wilson resources to support her communications with John. Later, one EC reflected on the importance of having information available for parents, noting, "The simulation helped understand the usefulness of a portfolio. I could have had literature and websites in my portfolio that I could have looked up and familiarized myself with the topic." The simulation presented a distinct moment when the EC felt the need to provide information and illuminated for the EC the connection between counseling practice and prior coursework portfolio assignments.

In the second simulation, the SIs portraying Ms. Wilson were trained to say, "I don't know how to be the parent of a gay kid. I don't know how to talk to him." Rather than using Ms. Wilson's words as an opportunity for social justice advocacy on John's behalf, an EC quickly shifted, saying, "Yeah, well, I, you know—I want to let you know on our end, I did make contact with some of the other administrative personnel that I work with here, so they are aware of, you know, the bullying that you had initially come in with some concern about." This EC's shift away from Ms. Wilson's comments about John's identity and back to the logistics of reporting the bullying incident demonstrated the EC's inability to recognize an advocacy opportunity. Ms. Wilson provided ECs with a clear opportunity to discuss how parenting a gay child is much the same as parenting any other child and to provide some information about what supports John might need from his mother.

As faculty, we see gaps in counseling domains that potentially influenced this EC's response. These gaps could be in intra- and interpersonal awareness, thereby influencing how the EC communicated with the SI. The gaps could be in conceptual knowledge, such that the EC didn't understand the implications of Ms. Wilson's behavior on John's exploration of sexual identity. Still, the gap could be in the skills domain, such that the EC was knowledgeable and interpersonally aware but simply lacked the skills to appropriately manage the conversation. Finally, this gap could represent intrapersonal awareness, such that the EC was personally uncomfortable with the topic of sexual identity and thus avoided further discussion. This singular moment demonstrates how simulations offer faculty insight into the links between educator preparation for social justice advocacy and opportunities for ECs to develop competency in advocacy.

In the Wilson simulations, some ECs attempted social justice advocacy. One EC enacted advocacy behaviors by educating Ms. Wilson on relevant laws, saying, "There's a law that they made for all students. . . . Here's a quick summary of it. . . . It's not acceptable to bully or harass or discriminate against students, and one of the things is, based on sexual orientation." This EC also shared information about Gay–Straight Alliance groups and encouraged Ms. Wilson to seek support for John and for herself. This is another example of EC growth through the nested simulation designs. This particular EC failed to acknowledge Ms. Wilson's concerns about sexual identity in the first simulation, but debriefing and self-reflection prompted the EC to address knowledge gaps. In the second simulation, the EC offered emotional support and concrete resources to support John and help Ms. Wilson talk openly with her child about his sexual identity. Reflecting on the second simulation, the EC had additional opportunities to refine his approaches. This set of subsequent experiences—comprised of action taking, deliberate reflection, and additional action taking—might not be replicated anywhere in the EC's practicum and internship experiences.

APPLICABILITY WITHIN AND ACROSS ALLIED PROFESSIONS

The design of the Ashley Wilson simulations provided counseling candidates multiple opportunities to engage with a core situation—a concerned mother reporting her son's physical assault and perceptions of his sexual identity. This situation was nested within all three simulation designs, threaded in a manner that allows candidates to approach the situation from a number of perspectives and use different knowledge and skills.

Our counselor education program is structured around four domains: conceptual knowledge, intra- and interpersonal awareness, counseling skills, and social justice advocacy. Data excerpts from the Wilson simulations, coupled with postsimulation journal reflections, suggest that the nested simulation designs offered candidates rich opportunities to apply knowledge and also demonstrate clinical and cultural competence in relationships with parents and caregivers. In contrast to most current simulation designs—where educator candidates engage in single, episodic situations that do not link to other simulations—the nested simulation design better captures the ongoing, iterative, and interactional processes associated with school counseling. To support the simulations, additional journal reflection assignments allowed ECs to give and receive formative peer feedback and meaningfully engage in self-reflection on which there was summative faculty feedback. There is much work to do, as further scholarship must consider the expanse of the four counseling domains, the different ways to interrogate the nested design, and the formative and summative opportunities within the postsimulation journal reflections. Specifically, counselor education scholars should consider how nested simulation design offer learning and research opportunities (1) with both individual and groups of stakeholders, (2) across in-person and virtual platforms, and (3) in the navigation of individual, systemic, and cultural worldviews, as has been done in social work training.[15]

Our scholarly and instructional expertise lies in counselor education. Still, counselor preparation frequently occurs within schools or colleges that include other allied professions, such as school psychologists, teachers, school administrators, or other health professions. Typically, the significant preparation requirements for each profession create silos such that counselor candidates do not regularly engage with candidates from other allied professions until they reach the practice-based portions of their programs, if at all. Across SOE's counselor, teacher, and school leader preparation programs, simulations have provided us with a shared approach to engage with our faculty colleagues and learn more about the specific preparatory work in their programs. In parallel, we believe that the interdisciplinary learning that faculty share through simulations could very much apply across multiple groups of educator candidates too. Similar to the nested Wilson simulation we outline in this chapter, we envision simulations between a teacher, parent, and school counselor where teacher candidates engage and learn alongside counselor candidates. As they simultaneously experience a shared simulation, ECs have opportunities to bring forward their respective knowledge and skills. For example, consider the dynamic between a teacher candidate and counselor candidate in their respective, culminating field placements. When working to support students in a K–12 school, both candidates may question how much student information they can or should share with the other. Simulating such an experience—where both teacher and counselor candidate are working to support a standardized student or parent/caregiver—can serve as one approach to teach the complexities of allied professional identities and responsibilities. We envision similar simulations between counseling candidates and school leader candidates, centered on how both might engage with (simulated) crisis situations that span across K–12 school contexts. Ultimately, we believe there is great opportunity in designing future simulations that nest or embed a core situation and provide multiple entry points for educator candidates across allied professions.

Initially, Ashley Wilson presents a challenging situation to counselor candidates: her son is being bullied by some peers who think he is gay. In a follow-up meeting, Ms. Wilson confirms her son's sexual identity and indicates she's struggling with what to say to her kid. As counselor candidates respond to Ms. Wilson across these simulations, their opportunities to apply knowledge and skill from the four counseling domains often present overlapping, interwoven demands. At the very moment a simulation begins, the resulting data are complex. Simulations require candidates to attend to the parent and situation in the moment, while activating and effectively transitioning what they know into what they can do. Complex simulations approximate the challenges that school counselors experience in K–12 school practice. As this work moves forward in counselor education, it is our hope that increasingly complex simulations, across our program of study, will enhance our candidates' performance as licensed counselors in schools.

CHAPTER 7

Using Simulations to Prepare School Leaders to Conduct Difficult Conversations

JOSEPH SHEDD, LEELA J. GEORGE, AND DIANE CANINO-RISPOLI

Jerry Michaelson has many years of teaching experience and isn't interested in what his principal thinks about his teaching. The actor who plays Michaelson in this clinical simulation of a performance feedback conference is trained to portray him as defensive, apathetic, and argumentative throughout the conference and not at all interested in addressing the evaluator's concerns or prepared to acknowledge the need to change. The educational leadership candidate who plays the building principal conducting the conference focuses on Michaelson's consistent use of teacher-centered lecture strategies, including notes that students are expected to copy from the board.

Based on classroom observations, the principal is convinced that Michaelson is burned out and uses teaching strategies that fail to engage or hold students' interest. Michaelson, however, argues that the strategies he is using have been successful for over twenty-five years, that most of his students perform acceptably on the state's standardized tests, and that he has no intention of changing how he teaches at this point in his career. The leadership candidate playing the evaluator must decide how to use the information they are given to get Michaelson to change his thinking and acknowledge the need to adjust his teaching.[1]

Approximately 160 leadership candidates have participated in the Jerry Michaelson simulation, which has been run once a year for eight years in either our Leadership for Adult Development course or our Administrative Internship seminar. Over this period, our candidates have fallen into a number of different traps, including the following: simply telling Michaelson that he must change without providing concrete evidence to justify their assertions; being so eager to put Michaelson at ease that their feedback and messages about what needs to change are sugarcoated and unclear; monopolizing the conversation without raising questions that promote self-reflection or press Michaelson to account for his approach to instruction; arguing with Michaelson over particular points without considering the overall message the evaluator wants to convey; allowing Michaelson to be noncommittal about concerns the evaluator has raised; and ending the conference without a clear plan for improvement or agreement on for the next steps each will take.

Although most of our candidates make one or another of these mistakes, they do not all make the same mistakes. Some recognize the need to communicate their concerns credibly and clearly but fail to appreciate that they must get Michaelson to accept their assessment of his need to change if they are to have any impact on his teaching at all. Others recognize that they must be open to Michaelson's perspectives, but they are so intent on putting him at ease that they fail to clarify any of their own concerns. It takes most candidates time to learn that if they are to have any chance of getting Michaelson to accept personal responsibility for changing his performance, they must be clear about their own perceptions and expectations and must listen carefully and respectfully to his perspectives. Balancing the two considerations is probably the most challenging part of the performance feedback process. In fact, this is a central dynamic in all our program's simulations and in many of those used in our sister preparation programs mentioned in this book.

Conducting difficult conversations with educational stakeholders is one of the core responsibilities of practicing school leaders. Yet few leadership preparation programs provide their educator candidates (ECs) with opportunities to develop and practice the skills required to conduct them. This chapter reviews how the educational leadership program in Syracuse University's School of Education (SOE) employs simulations in its preparation of school district leaders and principals. All our program's faculty members incorporate clinical simulations in their courses, but the authors of this chapter include two recently retired faculty (Joe and Diane) and the current program coordinator (Leela) who have made the most use of simulations over the longest period of time.[2] We provide a brief discussion of our general approach to using simulations in leadership preparation and then focus on the case of Jerry Michaelson and a handful of other simulations that aim to develop our educator candidates' skills in providing performance feedback to teachers.

We focus on two questions—one specific to the preparation of school leaders and the other a more general question about how all clinical simulations are designed. First, what kinds of skills do we want simulations to help our ECs develop when they conduct performance feedback discussions? Second, how can we design simulations that reflect the interactive nature of discussions in which one party is trying to get the other to change their behavior or thinking? We conclude with brief discussions of three issues that the Michaelson simulation illustrates but that apply to all our program's simulations and (potentially) to simulations in other fields: how we orchestrate debriefing discussions with our ECs after they have engaged in a simulation, how we integrate simulations across our entire preparation program, and whether and to what extent it might be possible to use simulations as summative assessments of individual ECs and/or our program as a whole. Figure 7.1 provides an overview of the educational leadership program.

USING SIMULATIONS IN THE PREPARATION OF SCHOOL LEADERS

The educational leadership program at Syracuse University has used a variety of clinical simulations as an integral part of school leadership preparation for over ten years.[3] These simulations deal with a wide range of issues, reflecting the complex roles of school leaders. They address closing the achievement gap, combating racism, evaluating instructional strategies, transforming

FIGURE 7.1 Program overview for educational leadership

Educator candidate (EC) population:
Teachers and other school professionals seeking preparation and certification as school district and school building leaders

Program length:
Thirty graduate credits; typically pursued part-time over three or four years

Simulation timing:
Currently used in eight of the program's nine required courses. Used twice in the course for adult development, twice in the seminar for administrative interns, and once each in the introductory course and courses in curriculum and instructional leadership, leadership for organizational development, leadership for inclusive schooling, and building leadership

student discipline, promoting inclusive schooling, building support for school programs and goals, promoting professional learning communities, and addressing the concerns of parents advocating for their children. Although the topics vary, each simulation requires leadership candidates to engage with standardized individuals (SIs)—trained actors playing parents, teachers, or other stakeholders—on contentious, often emotionally charged issues. A challenge that runs throughout all our simulations is how emerging leaders deal with conflict and navigate difficult conversations. Each simulation is designed to develop our ECs' abilities to communicate clearly, listen attentively, resolve specific issues, and critically reflect on their own performance. Table 7.1 details some of the courses in our program and the specific simulations used in each course.

TABLE 7.1 Selected examples of simulations used in leadership courses

Educational Administration Course and PSEL Standard	Standardized Individual	Sample Verbal Triggers
Leadership for Diverse Learners and Communities Standard 7: Professional Community for Teachers and Staff	A teacher who is resisting participation in a professional learning community	• I know my curriculum and do not need to collaborate with others in my department to know it better. • I consider it to be a waste of my time to listen to the concerns and problems of others. It is not my job to help them. As professionals, they should be able to figure this all out on their own.
Curriculum and Instructional Leadership for Equity and Excellence Standard 4: Curriculum, Instruction and Assessment	A teacher who is a "good person" and loved by all stakeholders in the community but whose instruction needs improvement	• I regularly attend workshops that are offered (even on my own time) and try to implement what I have learned. • Over the years, I have seen many ideas come and go, but I believe that helping students feel safe and happy is my primary goal.
Leadership for Developing Adult Capacity Standard 6: Professional Capacity of School Personnel	Jerry Michaelson, an ineffective and underperforming teacher	• After twenty-eight years of teaching experience, I have never been told that I am ineffective in any way, and I will not accept your assessment of my performance. • The way I look at it, it is my job to give them the information. It's their job to learn it. The way I do my job works, regardless of what some stupid test scores say.

TABLE 7.1 *(Continued)*

Educational Administration Course and PSEL Standard	Standardized Individual	Sample Verbal Triggers
Leadership for Organizational Development Standard 8: Family and Community Engagement	A parent adamantly opposed to their daughter being required to attend classes in sex education	• School isn't the place to address reproductive education. That's the parents' responsibility. • Discussing "safe sex" only encourages promiscuity. Abstinence is the only lesson students should learn.
Leadership for Inclusive Schooling Standard 3: Equity and Cultural Responsiveness	A teacher who is resistant to a principal's efforts to develop an inclusive model by promoting coteaching	• Special education students often are not able to perform the same tasks. They will feel bad if they are not able to be as successful as their peers. • Parents will be concerned that the education of their children in general education classrooms will be impacted by having the special education students in the class. They are already concerned about the emphasis that is placed on the state assessments and the learning standards and want to be sure their children are not short-changed.
Issues and Practices in Building Leadership Standard 3: Equity and Cultural Responsiveness Standard 6: Professional Capacity of School Personnel	A Black parent of a child with autism in a largely White school who is upset about a restraint of their son by the White male teaching assistant	• I am really concerned about what happened yesterday in the school cafeteria. Obviously, I'm pretty upset about this, and I have plenty to say about how Ms. Setmer and Mr. Jonas handled this. But I'm particularly interested in what you have to say. • Is it ever OK for an adult in your school to restrain a kid by wrestling him to the ground?

As is discussed in more detail in chapter 1 of this volume, actors who play SIs are trained on a specific simulation using a written interaction protocol that provides them a description of the character they are playing and information about how to react during the interaction with candidates. This training is designed to ensure that each SI presents the same persona, allowing our ECs to engage with the same situation, regardless of which SI they encounter, so that they can compare their experiences and approaches in the debriefing session that follows the interactions.

The actors we recruit to play SIs are retired teachers and/or administrators living in central New York. Although our leadership program initially used the same professional actors that our sister teacher preparation programs employed, our focus on issues that required detailed knowledge of K–12 classrooms has prompted us to use retired educators as actors for some simulations. Having SIs who have had the experience of dealing with teachers like Jerry Michaelson and who understand the issues that educational leaders face makes their portrayal of situations more realistic. These SIs also provide us with valuable advice when modifications to simulation scenarios and SI instructions are needed.

Our ECs receive an interaction protocol related to the standardized teacher or other individual they will deal with but usually are given very little direction as to how to proceed. The goals they set for their interactions with the SI are up to them, as are the approaches they will adopt to pursue those goals. (In fact, although most candidates quickly learn the importance of setting goals for themselves in these simulations, we never actually tell them that they must set them.) The actual exchange between the EC and the SI is video recorded, and the ECs watch their videos and complete self-reflection forms after engaging in the simulation. They then participate in a debriefing session with other ECs who have engaged in the same simulation, generally in a class session a week or two later.

As these general observations suggest, simulations are similar to case studies and role-playing exercises in some respects but are distinctly different in others. Like case studies and role plays, they provide all ECs with a common set of instructions and background information with which to begin exploring a situation. They require ECs to consider how they would grapple with authentic problems of practice that have no single right answers and then discuss with colleagues how they would deal with those problems. Unlike case studies and role plays, the simulations demand constant engagement with SIs who never step out of their roles and require learners to think on their feet and act in the face of imperfect information. The simulations are designed to develop ECs' interpersonal skills when conducting challenging, often emotionally charged conversations. The purpose is not just to develop their understanding of the issues posed in the simulations but to develop, practice, and continuously refine their skills in addressing these varied issues.

Like case study discussions, debriefings with others who have engaged in the same simulation help participants refine their understanding of the problem or issue and possible solutions, but they also allow them to identify the strengths and limitations of their own performance and understand why others held other perspectives and chose different strategies.

Simulations require ECs to examine the tensions and reconcile the differences between what has been called their espoused theories (what they know they ought to do) with their theories in use (what they actually do when required to act).[4] Simulations allow ECs to experience and decide how to act in situations they would otherwise just read and talk about.

USING SIMULATIONS TO PREPARE SCHOOL LEADERS TO PROVIDE TEACHERS WITH PERFORMANCE FEEDBACK

Most school leaders begin their administrative careers without ever having the opportunity to develop or practice skills at conducting difficult performance discussions with actual teachers. Many leadership preparation programs require leadership candidates to complete a practice evaluation during their administrative internship, but few school districts allow interns to observe and evaluate teachers whose performance is in any way problematic. Interns are often uncomfortable confronting ineffective practices, but they are not alone. Practicing leaders are often just as uncomfortable giving authentic feedback to teachers. It is easier to say that all is well, especially if a teacher's performance is not too worrisome, than to provide feedback that might include suggestions to strengthen instruction or signal that changes are needed. Many administrators concentrate on the procedural steps they are required to complete in the evaluation process rather than addressing the content and messages that they discuss with teachers. Some teachers are overlooked because they are "doing fine," with the leader providing no specific data. Others are overlooked because they have significant problems that have been overlooked for so long that the leader does not know where to begin to address them. In either case, little or no data are used, and feedback is generally ignored or ineffective.

Changes in teacher evaluation systems have been central to nearly every state's efforts to improve the quality of teaching and learning in America's public schools over the last decade.[5] Most of these initiatives have focused on how different forms of data—including data from administrators' classroom observations of teachers and data on student learning derived from standardized tests—can be combined in composite assessments of teachers' performance. Policy changes that focus on how classroom observations are to be used in teacher evaluations have dealt principally with defining the criteria to be used in observations, the rubrics that will be used to assess these criteria, and the training administrators will receive in techniques for observing teachers and generating ratings that are reliable across different observers and teachers. Teachers and administrators have told us that the rubrics administrators are required to use in New York State, with as many as ninety indicators of performance, are so cumbersome that both administrators and teachers have become preoccupied with evaluation ratings, leaving little time for serious discussions of performance or the ways it might be improved.

For all the attention recently paid to changing teacher evaluations, there has been little attention to what is, in theory, the linchpin in the entire evaluation process: the process by which administrators engage teachers in discussions of their performance. One of our main objectives in developing school leader simulations has been to address this gap in the preparation of school administrators. Starting with the Jerry Michaelson scenario, we have developed several simulations that enact the process by which school administrators engage teachers in performance discussions, sometimes framing the teacher's performance as thoroughly problematic (like Michaelson) and sometimes focusing on teachers whose performance is strong in some respects and problematic in others.

There would not be much need to model the feedback process at all if the sole or primary purpose of such discussions were to communicate ratings or summative assessments of teachers' performance. But we are convinced that the primary purpose of performance discussions should be diagnostic and developmental: to explore and reach agreement on what a teacher has done, could do, and will do to enhance student learning. Much of the literature on performance evaluation, mentoring, counseling, clinical supervision, and cognitive coaching suggests that there is a natural tension between the summative and formative functions of performance evaluation, especially in situations where evaluators have formal authority over those being evaluated.[6] Some observers maintain that the two functions are inherently incompatible and should be kept separate. We disagree. We maintain that the functions are potentially complementary and even necessary to each other's success.

Employees are bound to interpret any comments that come from their supervisors about their performance at least partly as summative and judgmental, but our own experiences as administrators (Leela George and Diane Canino-Rispoli) as well as interviews and surveys that the other author (Joe Shedd) and his graduate assistants have conducted with administrators and teachers convince us that administrators and teachers can still make evaluation feedback conferences serve formative and developmental purposes—if both parties are committed to doing so. In fact, we doubt that conferences that are treated exclusively or even primarily as summative are of much use at all. We agree with one author who argues that, "An evaluation has no meaning if it is not interpreted, questioned, discussed, and reflected on, ultimately leading to making different and more effective [teaching] decisions."

We turn now to how we have tried to build this perspective into the design and execution of the performance feedback simulations we employ in our program, starting with Jerry Michaelson, and to some of the questions about performance feedback and simulations our efforts have raised.

WHAT CONSTITUTES AN "EFFECTIVE" FEEDBACK CONFERENCE, AND HOW CAN SIMULATIONS BE DESIGNED TO MODEL ONE?

One of the authors (Joe Shedd) and one of our graduate assistants (Danielle Brain) conducted a preliminary study to see if we could describe what constitutes an effective evaluation feedback conference. The question deserves attention in its own right, but we also wanted to see if we could identify aspects of feedback conferences that could be observed, both in actual conferences and in our clinical simulations, so we could draw our leadership candidates' attention to how they conduct conferences with teachers like Jerry Michaelson. Although our immediate purpose was to see what teachers think makes conferences effective, we drew on analyses of our candidates' eight years of experience conducting feedback conferences with Michaelson, several sets of interviews with both teachers and administrators, and the literature cited in this chapter to explore the question from a variety of perspectives.[7] We developed an eighty-two-item survey that we administered to teachers, asking each of them to describe how their evaluator had conducted their most recent evaluation feedback conference and how effective or ineffective they thought that conference had been. At the time of this writing (fall 2020), we have administered this survey to a limited number of teachers (thirty-eight) in five randomly selected districts.[8] The results provided us preliminary but statistically strong evidence that certain evaluator behaviors are highly correlated with perceptions of a conference's effectiveness.[9] We identified items that were highly correlated with our two measures of effectiveness and then used factor analysis and tests of reliability to group nineteen of these items into five groups in figure 7.2, each item referring to how an evaluator conducts a conference.

Although the items associated with most of these factors (specifically, the second through fifth factors) are framed in terms of objective behaviors that are easily observed, we recognize that those associated with the first factor are more general, contextual, and subjective and probably cannot be assessed without a measure of judgment ("demonstrating understanding," "showing awareness," "offering useful perspectives," and "giving careful attention"). The teachers we have interviewed and surveyed think these considerations are important, but we don't yet know how easy or difficult it will be to use

FIGURE 7.2 Effective feedback conference behaviors

Demonstrating awareness of teacher's circumstances

a. Demonstrates an understanding of the curriculum and instructional challenges the teacher faces
b. Shows awareness of what the teacher has done to meet the challenges they face
c. Offers or shows openness to different vantage points on situations the teacher faces
d. Shows that they have given the teacher's evaluation careful attention

Communicating one's own concerns and expectations to the teacher

a. Provides concrete examples of any concerns they raise
b. Explains reasoning for their own conclusions
c. Conveys which concerns should receive highest priority
d. Clarifies what the teacher needs to do to address identified concerns

Facilitating the teacher taking ownership and personal responsibility for their evaluation

a. Prompts the teacher to lead the discussion
b. Urges the teacher to identify goals or concerns to address
c. Encourages the teacher to suggest options for addressing identified concerns
d. Defers to the teacher or asserts their own perspective, depending upon how willing the teacher is to take the lead

Building trust and collaboration between the evaluator and teacher

a. Discusses ways of building on the teacher's strengths and prior growth
b. Encourages the teacher to express their opinions, even if they differ from the evaluator's own
c. Uses open-ended questions that invite discussion
d. Uses strategies like paraphrasing or nonverbal cues to convey attention to the teacher's opinions

Providing for follow-up on concerns raised in the feedback discussion

a. Makes suggestions for specific things the teacher might do to improve teaching
b. Encourages the teacher to try new things, even if that might mean making mistakes
c. Makes sure the parties agree on steps the teacher will take as a result of the conference
d. Discusses specific things the evaluator will do to support the teacher's efforts to improve

them to document how our simulation participants manage their feedback conferences. That is a healthy reminder that some important considerations may not be easy to capture or observe in a clinical simulation.

Our list of effective evaluation conference behaviors became our preliminary definition of skills we hope our simulations will help our ECs develop over a series of feedback simulations. We turned our list into the scoring chart in figure 7.3 and used it for the first time in the spring of 2020 (just before the pandemic ended face-to-face instruction) as a basis for ECs' self-reflections on how they conducted their discussions with Jerry Michaelson.

FIGURE 7.3 Evaluation conference behaviors rubric

Demonstrating awareness of teacher's circumstances	Evidence			Communicating own concerns and expectations	Evidence			Facilitating teacher taking ownership and personal responsibility for the evaluation	Evidence			Building trust and collaboration	Evidence			Providing for follow-up	Evidence		
The evaluator	**Substantial**	**Moderate**	**Little/None**	**The evaluator**	**Substantial**	**Moderate**	**Little/None**	**The evaluator**	**Substantial**	**Moderate**	**Little/Nnone**	**The evaluator**	**Substantial**	**Moderate**	**Little/None**	**The evaluator**	**Substantial**	**Moderate**	**Little/None**
Demonstrates an understanding of the curriculum and instructional challenges the teacher faces				Provides concrete examples of any concerns they raise				Prompts the teacher to lead the discussion				Discusses ways of building on the teacher's strengths and prior growth				Makes suggestions for specific things the teacher might do to improve teaching			
Shows awareness of what the teacher has done to meet the challenges they face				Explains reasoning for his or her own conclusions				Urges the teacher to identify goals or concerns to address				Encourages the teacher to express their opinions, even if they differ from the evaluator's own				Encourages the teacher to try new things, even if that might mean making mistakes			
Offers or shows openness to different vantage points on situations the teacher faces				Conveys which concerns should receive highest priority				Encourages the teacher to suggest options for addressing identified concerns				Uses open-ended questions that invite discussion				Makes sure the parties agree on steps the teacher will take as a result of the conference			
Shows that they have given the teacher's evaluation careful attention				Clarifies what the teacher needs to do to address identified concerns				Defers to the teacher or asserts his or her own perspective, depending on how willing the teacher is to take the lead				Uses strategies like paraphrasing or using nonverbal cues to convey attention to the teacher's opinions				Discusses specific things the evaluator will do to support the teacher's efforts to improve			
Comments:																			

Our ECs' self-assessments provide preliminary grounds for believing that the checklist items are both observable and useful for prompting self-reflection and for distinguishing how ECs felt about different aspects of their performance. They tend to be most satisfied with their ability to build trust and collaboration with Jerry Michaelson and least confident about their ability to get him to take ownership and accept personal responsibility for the evaluation discussion. They differ most widely in their assessments of how well they made provision for following up on their conference with Michaelson. Most initially thought they had communicated their own concerns clearly to Michaelson, but after viewing video recordings of their exchanges and observing others' exchanges, they were less certain they had been as clear as they first thought.

HOW CAN WE DESIGN SIMULATIONS LIKE JERRY MICHAELSON TO REFLECT THE INTERACTIVE NATURE OF ADMINISTRATORS' AND TEACHERS' EXCHANGES?

Conducting an effective evaluation conference is not a simple matter of following a checklist because each person's approach is likely to be contingent on the other's. The more a teacher is prepared to accept responsibility for critiquing and finding ways of improving their own performance, the less assertive and the more facilitative an evaluator can afford to be. Conversely, the more resistant a teacher is to critiquing and considering ways of improving their performance, the more assertive an evaluator must be. The more effective the evaluator is in managing the conference, the more likely it is that the teacher will be receptive to the invitation to engage in a serious dialogue about their performance. But some teachers are likely to resist, regardless of how effective the evaluator's effort might seem.

How, then, can we encourage evaluators to adjust to teachers' willingness or reluctance to scrutinize their own performance, and how can simulations be designed to allow for such different possibilities? How can simulations be structured to represent these interactive and contingent dynamics? Our first step was to add a twentieth element to our list of effective behaviors, adding a new element to our factor on facilitating teacher ownership: "Defers to the teacher or asserts [the evaluator's] own perspective, depending on how willing the teacher is to take the lead."[10,11] But this observation begs the more fundamental reason for incorporating interactivity into the simulation design: the basic purpose of the evaluation conference is to get the teacher to actually change how they teach. How can we prepare a standardized teacher to be ready to accommodate an evaluator's concerns only if the evaluator manages their conversation well enough?

If we were content simply to use simulations to expose our ECs to situations and get them to consider how they might address them, there would be no reason to be concerned about whether ECs were successful in getting the standardized teachers to change their behavior. Since our purposes were broader than exposure, we had to contend with the fact that our instructions to SIs to stay in character actually limited their ability to adjust their behavior, regardless of how effective or ineffective an EC's approach might be. Over time, our ECs got the message that the SI was not going to change, no matter how well or poorly they conducted the conversation.

We began to realize that the expectation that SIs would not change their behaviors over the course of a simulation had become a problem in our evaluation conference simulations: if our ECs knew actors were not going to change their behavior, how could we expect them to try to get them to change? We began to explore different ways of introducing the possibility of SIs changing their stance into our simulations. The first step was to develop a pair of Jerry Michaelson simulations—one structured as an initial evaluation conference and the second as a follow-up conference. Because of how we had designed the first simulation, it was clear that even a skillful evaluator would not be able to make significant progress in getting Michaelson to change in a single conference. Even an evaluator who is skillful at communicating their own concerns would almost certainly have to arrange for some period of additional observation, documentation, and follow-up discussion once Michaelson understood the evaluator's concerns. Although it was logical for our ECs to suggest that they would observe Michaelson for an additional period of time and then meet again to discuss their observations, we did not want their performance discussion to stop there. Doing so would allow the EC and Michaelson to avoid the underlying concerns. We restructured the simulation, therefore, in two parts, with both parties understanding that there would be an initial meeting and then a follow-up meeting. We did not want our ECs to end their only conference with Michaelson simply by saying, "We'll meet again to discuss this further," and we did not want them to let Michaelson off the hook. We wanted our ECs to understand that if issues are not fully discussed, they cannot be resolved, and improvement is unlikely to occur.

Reviewing and discussing additional data with the SI are now important parts of this simulation. For the second meeting, our ECs are given a summary of several sets of observation notes from walk-through visits to Michaelson's classroom. We know that when teachers have significant issues, discussing improvement is not a one-shot deal; ongoing feedback and monitoring of progress are essential. The walk-through data that are provided for part two of the Michaelson simulation includes specific evidence from four classroom visits and some additional information. Figure 7.4 provides a sample of that evidence.

FIGURE 7.4 Jerry Michaelson simulation "walk-through" notes

Walk-Through Notes

Visit 1 (Honors History, Grade 10)

- Teacher standing at the board reading notes that are written on the board
- Some students copying the notes but you observe two students talking to each other and not listening to the teacher, two students with their heads down on their desks, one student texting on his phone and one student drumming on his desk with a pencil, singing, wearing earphones
- The teacher tells the student to stop singing and to listen. The teacher tells him he will be sent to the office if he doesn't stop. The student grunts, stop singing, but still continues to drum on his desk. Other students in the class don't react to this.

Visit 2 (Honors History, Grade 10)

- Most kids are quiet and facing the teacher but you note that only about five of them are copying the notes. A few students are doing homework from another class, two students are playing games on their phone, one student is reading a book, one girl is braiding another girl's hair, and one student is drawing a picture of a superhero. One student appears to be asleep.
- You walk around the room and softly speak to a few students about what they are learning, and they are not able to answer with any specificity. You also ask them if they ever have an opportunity to work in groups or engage in classroom discussion, and they say, 'Not in this class. We mostly copy notes.'

Visit 3 (AP History)

- Despite the fact that this is an AP class, you notice that the students are still copying notes from the board. The teacher is at his desk and tells you that this class is much more self-directed because they are AP kids. He doesn't feel a need to read the notes to them.
- The teacher tells the class that a unit test will be given at the end of the week and if they have their notes, they will be prepared for the test. He also tells the class that this unit test includes some of the content that will be a part of the AP exam.

Additional information

✓ You have also requested Mr. Michaelson's lesson plans, and he has sent you the directions from the AP teacher's guide.
✓ You have looked again at the AP test scores and the results from the History regents and find that Mr. Michaelson has the lowest scores on the Social Studies team.
✓ You have looked for previous evaluations of Mr. Michaelson's teaching and find that he has not been evaluated in five years.

We have since discovered that two-part simulations, while helpful, might not be sufficient. The bottom line with many of the simulations, especially those where a teacher is meant to be resistant, is that our ECs must sometimes decide to change course and take the conversation in a different direction. Although it is always appropriate for an evaluator to encourage teachers to take the lead in beginning a performance feedback discussion and to let teachers lead the entire discussion if they are willing to do so, evaluators must be prepared to decide whether and when they need to turn from a collaborative to more directive approach. This is difficult for many experienced administrators much less ECs, and it often results in the leader backing off or softening the feedback provided. We want to be sure that students understand and are able to draw this line between formative supervision and summative evaluation.

Now that we have refined our concept of what effective management of an evaluation conference might look like, we have begun to explore how we might construct simulations that challenge ECs to find ways of convincing teachers to change their behavior and/or attitudes. To do so, we must allow the SIs playing standardized teachers to agree to change their behaviors or attitudes in the course of the simulations, depending on how effectively the EC manages their exchange. Doing so will require us to specify the following design principles:

- The conditions under which SIs will be instructed to change their positions from resistance to cooperation (e.g., the behavioral triggers the participant must exhibit that would be preconditions for change),
- The steps or procedures SIs would follow before making any concessions, and
- The kind(s) of changes they would be instructed to agree to.

Opening the possibility that SIs might change their positions will require us to change our approach to simulations in important ways. First, as noted above, we will have to finalize what we consider "effective performance" on the part of ECs so we can specify the behaviors they must exhibit before an SI would be permitted to change their own behavior or attitudes. We will have to decide whether to define effectiveness in terms of a single set of behaviors or in terms of alternative criteria, any one of which might trigger an SI's willingness to change. Second, while we are used to specifying "triggers" for SIs, this application of the concept will be new, since we will have to instruct SIs how to respond to what an EC does. It will require SIs to exercise judgment to determine whether an EC had met the preconditions for changing a position. We need to consider how this new application changes our concept of standardization and what different kinds of training might be needed to effect the change. Finally, having finalized criteria for effectiveness, we will have to decide whether we will (1) alert ECs to these criteria ahead of time; (2) reveal those criteria to ECs after they complete one or more exercises; (3) let them discover those criteria for themselves, either on their own or through debriefing with each other; or (4) let ECs discover those criteria for themselves over a succession of simulations and debriefings. We are just beginning to explore these questions and have no experience on which to assess possible alternatives.

Exploring how to instruct SIs to change their behavior in response to how our ECs conduct conferences will allow us to focus on the big picture in terms of developing realistic simulations and aligning them to our course content. We will also have to rethink how much feedback we provide to individual ECs on their performance. Although participants do learn from each other and from general comments that faculty members make in debriefing sessions, we have not provided detailed feedback to individual candidates before. Ideally, this would be the next step, but it would add considerably to the time and logistical challenges of administering simulations since it would require us to watch up to twenty minutes of video for each EC (or forty minutes for a two-part simulation), compose detailed feedback, and meet separately with each EC. This is something that is important to address if we are looking at the simulations as a teaching tool. We do not want to inadvertently give the impression that strategies an EC may have used were effective if the video shows otherwise. This would still not be an evaluative conversation but rather a discussion of effective conferencing strategies.

HOW SHOULD THE DEBRIEFING PROCESS BE DESIGNED AND CONDUCTED?

Following a simulated conference, ECs are encouraged to reflect personally on the issues they have dealt with and the ways they have addressed them and then to share their reflections with each other. Unlike some of our sister preparation programs that arrange for ECs to meet immediately after they have completed their conferences, our program's debriefing sessions are always conducted one or two weeks later, after ECs have had an opportunity to review and reflect on video recordings of their conferences. In the debriefing after the pair of Jerry Michaelson conferences, ECs learn how differently they have conceptualized the challenge they faced. Most of our ECs and all of our faculty members consider this debriefing the most important part of the process. We have not developed a single debrief protocol, but we have some standard prompts that we use when discussing the simulations. These questions include how candidates defined goals for the conversation, what success they had in meeting them, what strengths they think they demonstrated, what areas for continued personal growth they would identify, and what advantages or disadvantages they perceive in how other students approached the same simulation.

Beyond these commonalities, each of the authors tends to structure debriefing sessions differently. Diane has participants identify portions of their video recordings to show and discuss in a debriefing session, Leela reviews student videos herself and identifies portions of exchanges she will use to raise particular questions, and Joe reviews videos himself and selects whole exchanges to have the class view and discuss. Each of these debriefing strategies is arguably effective in different ways. Having ECs select a portion of their simulation videos to share with the class and request feedback individualizes the process gives candidates control of the discussion and ensures that issues of concern to each of them are addressed. Having the instructor select either portions or whole episodes for the class to review provides opportunities to highlight examples or strategies that may be different and that many ECs might not have considered. Showing instructor-selected segments also allows the EC to recognize that different approaches may have particular strengths and that no one approach may be best in all respects. The common element that all of our approaches share is almost certainly the most important part of the debriefing process: candidates watch the video, reflect in writing about effective and ineffective strategies, and share their reflections and questions with each other.

Our experiences with debriefing sessions raise other questions: do the functions or utility of debriefing sessions change over time after participants have engaged in a sequence of simulations? Our experience is that their reflections during debriefing sessions grow increasingly sophisticated—shifting, for example, from whether they set goals for themselves prior to their conferences to how differences in the goals that they set may have affected the course of their discussions. Do debriefing sessions serve different functions for different audiences (such as preservice administrators and practicing administrators)?[12] By providing time and space for debriefing and reflection, we have seen leadership candidates develop a variety of strategies for engaging in difficult conversations.

HOW DOES USING SIMULATIONS ACROSS AN ENTIRE PREPARATION PROGRAM AFFECT CANDIDATES' DEVELOPMENT?

Table 7.1, referenced above, provides examples of the types of simulations we use in various courses throughout our educational leadership program, including verbal triggers that we want SIs to use and our ECs to encounter to represent situations they are likely to confront in practice. In developing the simulations, we were conscious of making these realistic and relevant with clear connections to the daily practice of school leaders.

Developing multiple simulations and considering how they will be sequenced across our different courses now represents a powerful feature of our leadership program. Our initial efforts to assess the effectiveness of our leadership simulations used focus-group interviews and brief paper-and-pencil surveys to identify participants' reactions to the simulation process. Colleagues at the SUNY-Albany Evaluation Consortium, who served as evaluators for our initial development project, documented evidence that the simulations were effective in four respects:

1. Developing ECs' ability to critically analyze difficult situations, not only after the fact but while they are in progress,
2. Enhancing ECs' confidence in their ability to conduct potentially emotionally charged discussions in challenging situations,
3. Developing ECs' ability to establish and maintain focus on their own goals for difficult discussions, and
4. Developing ECs' ability to build trust and listen carefully to the perspectives of those they are talking with.

Our evaluators concluded that all four of these effects were produced not by any one simulation but by our repeated use of simulations across our different courses. They documented the ways in which ECs' emotions changed over time as they completed multiple simulations. Toward the beginning of their programs, EC reflections stressed their anxiety: "I'm not a combative person, and I got flustered when we got to the point where he was going to have me force him to participate," or "I was not confident enough in my purpose statement, which opened it up for the teacher to come up with another excuse, and I was not prepared for the teacher to reject all of my suggestions." Later in the program, ECs were more likely to share that they were effective and felt confident about the skills they had developed: "I felt that I was leading the conversation when I was asking the questions," "I felt like I was gaining ground with the teacher as I started to understand her concerns by actively listening," and "I think my strategies were effective because the teacher continued to communicate despite her resistance and was even willing to compromise by the end of the conversation. I think she needed to feel more control over the situation and wanted to feel validated/affirmed." Furthermore, ECs who were engaged in their internships at the end of their programs were much more likely to express enthusiasm and excitement about the simulation experience than the fear or dread they expressed at earlier stages of the program.

We agree with our evaluators.[13] Being able to think critically, develop personal confidence, keep focused on one's own goals, and listen carefully to others—all while engaged in difficult conversations—are not skills or dispositions that can be developed effectively in one exercise and thereafter retained. They must be developed, reinforced, nurtured, and practiced over and over. This, we think, is the real significance of our decision to make simulations an ongoing thread across all our courses and a repeated part of our ECs' experience.

In doing so, we have had to address several key questions: Can our list of effective feedback conference behaviors be used and expanded to document our ECs' growth over a succession of simulations, or will that list of behaviors have to be adjusted for each simulation? How and in what ways do they change? If some of our ECs struggle with how to communicate their own (sometimes critical) assessments clearly while others find it difficult to listen respectfully to those with whom they disagree, how can we nurture and document their ability to balance such different considerations? Is growth transferable across different kinds of situations (e.g., in interactions with parents or other kinds of situations with teachers), or is growth independent and nontransferrable across different contexts? Is there a logic to how simulations should be sequenced to promote particular kinds of learning and growth, or does growth simply come with increasing experience with simulations, regardless of how they are sequenced? We are just beginning to explore these questions.

The bottom line is that we want to see how our ECs deal with resistance. We want to determine, by the end of the simulation, whether ECs have found a way of getting Jerry Michaelson and standardized stakeholders in other simulations to adjust their thinking and behavior, or if not, how they have addressed the SI's reluctance to do so. This raises, again, the question of whether simulations can realistically capture the interactive nature of difficult interpersonal situations in which each party's decisions and behaviors must necessarily reflect those of the other. It raises, too, another question with which we are only beginning to grapple—namely, the question of summative assessment.

SHOULD SIMULATIONS BE USED TO ASSESS CANDIDATE SKILLS?

We have set out to develop a definition of what constitutes an effective way of conducting an evaluation feedback conference, to specify what we hope our ECs will learn from our simulations, to structure the formative feedback we provide to them, and to ensure that those objectives are reflected in how we design and administer the simulations. The next logical question is whether and how we might use that definition to provide our students with a summative assessment of their performance. Should we, for example, use one or more simulations to assess whether our ECs can demonstrate some level of effectiveness in managing feedback conferences, before we permit them to move on to the administrative internship that is the final step in their preparation programs?[14] We already know that we would never make such use of simulations unless an EC has had an opportunity to engage in several formative simulations prior to a final summative one. We are already satisfied that we were right not to rush to make summative use of simulations until we had extensive experience using them for instructional and formative purposes. And we are convinced that we and our SOE colleagues would not have had the opportunity to develop the rich potential of simulations as instructional tools if we had been too quick or eager to use them for summative purposes.

Still, it is worth considering whether—with over ten years of experience using a variety of simulations in our educational leadership programs and with progress in defining what feedback conference behaviors might be considered effective—it may be time to consider using them for summative purposes. If the conferencing skills we want our ECs to develop really are as fundamental to their eventual effectiveness as school leaders as we have come to believe, can we really justify *not* using simulations to assess whether they have mastered them?

But it is also worth considering whether adding a summative function to our simulation agenda might undermine the instructional and formative functions it already serves so well. It may be that we should use our effectiveness criteria to assess simulations themselves and the overall success of our preparation programs but should let simulations continue to serve an exclusively developmental function for our individual students. It is also possible that we could make hybrid formative/summative use of one of our simulations, not evaluating the effectiveness of how a candidate manages a feedback conference but evaluating how thoughtfully they critique their own performance.[15]

DO SIMULATIONS REPRESENT A POSSIBLE "SIGNATURE PEDAGOGY" FOR THE PREPARATION OF EDUCATIONAL LEADERS OR PERHAPS FOR THE PREPARATION OF ALL EDUCATORS?

We have come to believe that our use of simulations in our educational leadership program may represent more than a new and promising pedagogy. We think we may have begun to craft a "signature pedagogy" for the preparation of school leaders. As chapters 1 and 2 of this volume describe, Lee Shulman has argued that each well-established profession tends to have a set of distinctive forms of teaching and learning "that organize the fundamental ways in which future practitioners are educated for their new professions."[16] Shulman notes that case dialogue methods in law, clinical hospital rounds in medicine, and design studio dialogues in engineering and architecture are pervasive characteristics of professional training in those fields. They require students to engage with complex issues under circumstances of uncertainty, to grapple with basic contradictions and balance competing values that are inherent in their field, and to account publicly for their decisions to both their instructors and peers. They require students to integrate ways of thinking, ways of performing, and ways of acting with integrity that are considered basic to their professions. Because they combine elements of uncertainty, visibility, accountability, and (in some cases) real-world consequences for the kinds of stakeholders students will engage with in their professional practice, they invariably invoke both excitement and anxiety and provide opportunities for growing self-confidence as students master challenges that might initially seem paralyzing.

Our use of simulations in the preparation of educational leaders has nearly all of these characteristics. They are now employed throughout our entire program and require students to apply skills and habits of clarity, respectfulness, and attention to data to a wide variety of situations that, on the surface, might seem unique to the subjects of particular courses. ECs' gradual mastery of these common elements frees ECs from "hav[ing] to think about them" and instead "think with them."[17] And the routine of sharing personal analyses of one's own performance in debriefing sessions with instructors and peers, after viewing the videos of one's conference with a standardized stakeholder, overcomes what Shulman notes is the passivity, invisibility, anonymity, and lack of accountability that is typical of most higher education classrooms.[18] The emotional potential for both anxiety and satisfaction—and ultimately, self-confidence—that our simulations provide is undoubtedly one of the reasons the experiences and the lessons students derive from them are so memorable.

The parallel between our use of simulations and the use of signature pedagogies in other fields is not perfect, but even the exceptions are instructive. Our simulations do not have the real-world impact on actual stakeholders that signature pedagogies in some professions (like clinical rounds in medicine and design studio interactions in engineering and architecture) have. But that exception underscores the importance of simulating the real-world experience of engaging in difficult conversations that leadership students rarely have opportunities to experience until their culminating internships and then only haphazardly. If conducting difficult and ultimately productive conversations with stakeholders is a fundamental part of what it means to be a school leader, it is imperative that leadership preparation programs find ways of cultivating the knowledge, skills, and dispositions that are required to conduct them effectively.

The contrast between our use of simulations and the use of simulations in medicine is instructive in another respect. Although our colleague Benjamin Dotger drew inspiration from the use that the medical professions have made of simulations in the preparation of physicians and nurses, he has insisted—correctly, we believe—that medicine's near-exclusive use of simulations as tools for summative assessment, rather than formative development, would be inappropriate in the development of educational professionals. Indeed, it is instructive that Shulman cites clinical rounds, not simulations, as the core signature pedagogy in the preparation of physicians. But if simulations are to be the linchpin in a signature pedagogy for leadership candidates, we are still left with the questions we posed and left unanswered in our previous section: Should we use a simulation or some combination of simulations as summative assessments at the culmination of an educational leader's preservice preparation once he or she has had extensive experience engaging with them as formative experiences at earlier stages? Would knowing that there is a summative simulation at the end of their program give leadership candidates an additional incentive to take earlier formative simulations seriously? These questions and exceptions, as well as the many parallels our experience with simulations have with signature pedagogies in other fields, underscore the broader significance of our efforts to develop simulations in the preparation of educational leaders.

Might these same observations on simulations as signature pedagogies in educational leadership apply to the preparation of other educators? The other chapters in this volume provide ample evidence that preparing teachers and counselors to conduct difficult one-on-one conversations is an important part of professional preparation for all educators. We leave it to our colleagues and readers to decide whether it might be of sufficient importance in other programs to justify the amount of attention we have devoted to simulations in our leadership program. Clearly, our decision to embed simulations in nearly all of our program's courses and to extend them from the very beginning to the very end of each student's program allows our candidates to develop facility and confidence in their ability to conduct difficult conferences that would be less possible if we were to use them less often.

But there is one aspect of our experience that is almost certainly relevant to the use of simulations in the preparation of all educators and of professionals in other fields. Conducting difficult conversations is not an end in itself but a means to an end. It is not sufficient for school leaders or other educators to learn how to say the right things, either in professional practice or in simulations designed to mirror that practice. *The object of such conversations is to change something.* Every difficult conversation in education represents an opportunity to enhance children's chances to learn and promote goals that serve that purpose. That means, first, that simulations should be designed and implemented in ways that teach educators-in-training to set goals for their conversations, to communicate their purposes as clearly as possible, and to monitor their progress toward those goals while they are conducting each conversation. It means, second, that they cannot expect those they are talking with to listen to them if they are not prepared to listen to them in return. The point is not just to be polite and show others respect but to acknowledge that one might actually learn something from the other person, however inexpertly or aggressively they might frame what they have to say. That means that we must prepare the SIs who play such "others" to resist or accede to our ECs' overtures, depending on how clearly they present their own positions and how well they listen to those whose attitudes or behavior they are seeking to change. We know of no other pedagogy so well suited to teaching these lessons as simulations.

SECTION III
CROSS-PROGRAM PERSPECTIVES ON CLINICAL SIMULATIONS

CHAPTER 8

A Cross-Program Analysis of Disability, Difference, and Inclusion in Multiple Simulations for Educator Candidates

CHRISTINE ASHBY AND MEGAN E. CARTIER

During a meeting of the clinical simulations study group, five faculty members are seated around a conference table with their eyes on the video playing at the front of the room. They are watching and taking notes about an interaction between an educator candidate (EC) in physical education and an actor playing a standardized individual (SI)—the parent of a student with a visual impairment. At one point, one faculty member places her hand over her mouth and grimaces in apparent discomfort at the actions of the EC while the remaining four group members continue to watch or take notes with no change of expression. A little later, a different faculty member picks up her pencil and starts furiously writing in response to a comment by the EC. This happens several more times as the footage continues to roll, with different colleagues around the table reacting to different verbal and nonverbal cues.

When the video ends and the postviewing discussion ensues, Christy (first author) is bursting to share: "Did any of you notice that every time the parent mentioned specifics of the student's disability, the candidate visibly pulled back and squirmed a little?" Around the room, eyes go down to scan notes and heads shake back and forth. An animated discussion breaks out, filled with exclamations like, "I can't believe I didn't notice that," "That wasn't something I was watching for," and "What did you think when he said . . . .?"

That series of what simulation study group members came to call "wince moments" and the discussion that followed were the inspiration for this chapter. That day sparked discussion of the potential for simulations to prompt consideration of issues and challenges our candidates experience *across* programs rather than just *within* them. The group discussed the benefit of watching these videos collaboratively, with faculty bringing their differing pedagogical training and theoretical framing to the analysis—work that continues, both formally and informally, in various configurations.

Excited to extend this cross-program exploration in an even more systematic way, Christy reached out to this chapter's second author, doctoral student Megan E. Cartier. Megan, like Christy, teaches in the inclusive elementary and special education undergraduate program in the Syracuse University School of Education (SOE) but has also taught a course on differentiation taken by students in our 7–12 and K–12 certification programs. Megan agreed to join Christy for this analysis of how simulations can be used to explore disability, difference, and inclusion across multiple programs.

In the pages that follow, we offer a brief review of the context for the study and then present an overview of the literature related to the use of simulations in education, with a specific focus on disability. Next, we examine data from disability-focused simulations from several disciplinary contexts in SOE, looking carefully at three crosscutting themes that emerged. We conclude with a discussion of key findings and then discuss implications for simulation development and the use of simulations across academic programs.

BACKGROUND AND RELATED LITERATURE

SOE's tagline—"Leading through inquiry, inclusion, and action"—frames inclusion as one of three hallmarks of an education degree at Syracuse. The mission statement takes this even further: "[T]o prepare thoughtful and socially just leaders who bridge scholarship and practice. Through collaborative partnerships and *multifaceted inclusive approaches* [emphasis added], we enhance student learning and success, physical activity and health, and mental health and wellbeing across communities." Our core commitments expressly name inclusive practices, aiming "To graduate highly skilled and knowledgeable practitioners, teachers, administrators, counselors, scholars, and other professionals who are leaders in their respective fields and are committed to inclusion in policy and practice."

It is perhaps unsurprising, then, that several faculty members have developed simulations for candidates that focus on issues of disability, difference, and inclusive education. These interactions have been developed and implemented in programs such as English education, physical education, and science education, in addition to the inclusive elementary and special education program in which both of us primarily work. Although the use of simulations as a signature pedagogy in SOE has been covered extensively in earlier chapters in this book, in this chapter we draw attention to the potential for simulations to highlight tensions and gaps in our programs and to create opportunities for faculty to talk about how to better enact our shared commitments. Several metaquestions guide our work, including the following: What can we learn about our candidates, our education preparation programs, and even ourselves in relation to understandings of disability, difference and inclusive education when we look across programs and across simulations? What are the implications for our program and for the integration of simulations as an element of teacher development? How do we avoid essentializing disability in the development of simulation protocols? How do we use the data from simulated interactions to talk across programs?

Relevance of Clinical Simulations

SOE's use of clinical simulations as a signature pedagogy allows education candidates across multiple disciplines to engage in situations relevant to their professional practice.[1] Through participation in simulated encounters, ECs encounter various challenges they are likely to experience in their own classrooms. They are able to reflect on and address their responses to the prompts and triggers intentionally embedded within a particular simulation protocol. From an instructor standpoint, simulations present our faculty with opportunities to think critically about the broader implications of our collective commitment to preparing students to enter the profession.

Generally, simulations give us a way to engage students and faculty in productive discourse around disability and difference across our programs. Specifically, simulations present opportunities to support our commitment to preparing educators who are, regardless of program or discipline, committed to meeting the needs of all students, including those students with complex learning and support needs.[2] Indeed, the chance to think critically about adapting lessons and modifying curricula in a simulated environment presents a unique opportunity for our ECs to operationalize their understanding of and commitment to inclusive education and provides faculty with insight into misconceptions and underdeveloped thoughts held by our ECs. But simulations also allow for faculty and program coordinators to look across programs to consider the ways core commitments and strategies get taken up and enacted across disciplines. For us, that core commitment under consideration here is inclusive education.

Grounding in Inclusive Education

All of the simulations referenced in this chapter focus on the education of K–12 students with disabilities in inclusive settings. Although there are multiple definitions and interpretations of the meaning and scope of *inclusion*, educators in the United States, including us, must anchor their work in an understanding of federal law. Least restrictive environment is one of the six major principles of the Individuals with Disabilities Education Improvement Act (IDEIA) and provides that, to the maximum extent appropriate, students with disabilities in public and private schools are educated with nondisabled peers.[3] LRE further stipulates that the removal of children with disabilities from the general education setting should occur only when education in regular classrooms with supplementary aids and supports cannot be achieved satisfactorily. The general education classroom is where consideration of placements for students with disabilities should begin.

The federal metric for "full inclusion" is participation by students with disabilities in general education for at least 80 percent of the day, but we expect our education candidates to plan for all students to be included in such instruction at all times. Inclusive education means all students receive access to general education curricula and are included in general education spaces. In a truly inclusive classroom, the general education teacher, inclusive education teacher, and all related service providers actively and routinely collaborate to create and design lessons that meet a variety of student learning needs. Although discussion about inclusive education typically centers around including students with disabilities, when inclusive education solely focuses on disability, it excludes all other marginalized groups and doesn't recognize the intersectional identities many of our children experience. The ultimate goal of inclusive education is for students to learn and work together in partnership regardless of race, class, ethnicity, religion, gender, or disability.

Inclusive education at SU is further grounded in a disability studies in education (DSE) framework. We seek to instill within our candidates a sense that recognizing difference as a natural human variation provides a deeper understanding of the complexities underpinning inclusion. A subdiscipline of the larger field of disability studies, DSE recognizes disability as a social construct that centers the ways in which individuals with disabilities experience education. To this end, DSE scholars raise questions such as "What constitutes a disability? According to whom, and based upon what evidence? Where and how should students identified as dis/abled be taught? And, what are possibilities for research on education and disability without the automatic default of special education?"[4] These questions represent the overall mission of DSE scholars, promote an understanding of disability as a social construct, and challenge deficit models of disability as they pertain to education that are grounded in narrow conceptions of medicine and psychology.

The Problem of Simulating Disability

As authors of this chapter, we are keenly aware of the potential connection some may see between clinical simulations as described in this book and common approaches used by others to simulate disability. Disability simulations in which an able-bodied individual impersonates a person with a disability (typically through physical mechanisms such as blindfolds, wheelchairs, and other devices generally associated with a physical disability) are often used in disability awareness training sessions. However, these particular events are inherently problematic and disrespectful to people with disabilities. "The focus on difficulties, problems, and the disabled person's supposed inabilities and inadequacies is both inaccurate and depressing and gives rise to some damaging stereotypes and misconceptions."[5] Disability simulations are often used with the expressed intention of informing able-bodied people about what it is like to have a disability. The very idea of taking on any aspect of a perceived disability wholly undermines the lived experiences of people with disabilities and ignores the systemic oppression and ableism that individuals with disabilities have to navigate. Such an experience may also problematically leave the able-bodied or neurotypical individual with a lasting image of disability as a deficit, ignoring the fact that many individuals with disabilities locate their identity within their disability and draw strength and power from the assistive devices they routinely use.

Rather than simulating the experience of disability, simulations at Syracuse provide opportunities for meaningful encounters that allow our ECs to practice aspects of serving students with disabilities, such as parent-teacher conferences, meetings with paraprofessionals, and interactions with administrators. We steadfastly refuse to design simulations for standardized students with disabilities and work diligently to ensure that our protocols do not essentialize difference. To do so is in direct opposition to our beliefs.

DESIGNING FOR DISABILITY, DIFFERENCE, AND INCLUSION

Simulations can enhance the development of educators, both future ones and current practitioners. However, in order to achieve the end goal of enhanced learning experiences, simulation protocols must be meticulously developed. Here we turn our attention to the actual process of designing simulations focused on disability, difference, and inclusion. Our colleague Benjamin Dotger has spent considerable time designing clinical simulations to be used in many different educational contexts. Doing so, he aligns the protocols closely with the pioneering work of Howard S. Barrows by adhering to Barrows's core tenets (prevalence, clinical impact, social impact, and instructional importance) to undergird decisions about how to craft interaction protocols and how to sequence them.[6] Readers are encouraged to review previous chapters within this text for a deeper grounding in Barrows's work. Ben speaks about the importance of authenticity in the development of each simulation, stating, "I'm trying to make these simulation experiences feel, sound, and reflect issues, ideas, and problems that are as close to real as possible."[7] Building from these basic design principles, we move in the next section to share more details about the five different simulations yielding data highlighted in this chapter.

One of the simulations (Lori Danson) was originally designed for Study of Teaching, a course for undergraduates in our 7–12 and K–12 education majors. The genesis for this protocol involving a proactive parent of an autistic child came from a suggestion of an individual hired as a standardized actor for a different simulation. This parent approached Ben and suggested creating a protocol centering on personal experience with their child's new teacher. This protocol was later modified with the support of two faculty colleagues to transform the protocol into one for English-language arts candidates (Lori Blake). This revised, subject-specific protocol was intended for ECs further along in their teacher preparation program—those who were simultaneously enrolled in an English methods course and the first of two student teaching placements. The faculty responsible for developing the Lori Blake simulation—Kelly Chandler-Olcott, Marcelle Haddix, and Benjamin Dotger—explained that they wanted their students to discuss their approach to curricular adaptation and student specific supports. The focus was not on disability per se but on how the ECs understood and articulated their role in adapting content and pedagogy in light of a diverse student body.

The Elizabeth Meyers simulation was developed by Christy and Ben for use with inclusive elementary education students engaged in their full-time student teaching placements. This simulation was designed to address a challenge many of our ECs face—how to collaborate with adults who may be older, have more experience in the class, and articulate a different belief system than theirs about educating students with disabilities, thus addressing Barrows's tenets of prevalence and social impact. The Meyers interaction protocol has also been used with candidates in our secondary and K–12 programs, such as mathematics education and art education.

The Brad Winston simulation was developed for use in an adapted physical education course where the codesigners wanted students to consider language and the means to adapt lessons for students with disabilities in physical education. These faculty, Michael Norris and Luis Columna, wanted to push candidates to think of inclusion as an action and think strategically about what they were going to do to make it possible for every child to be included. This interaction protocol does not start from a current conflict but instead features a concerned parent reaching out to the teacher regarding strategies for including his daughter, whose visual impairment was caused by a household-based injury several years earlier. Faculty designed this simulation to focus on an acquired visual impairment because they assumed the ECs would be more comfortable discussing accommodations and supports for a student who had typical visual acuity prior to an accident. This protocol was later adapted by Ben Dotger and Sharon Dotger for use with secondary science candidates in the Josh Churchill simulation. Although visual impairment is a fairly low-incidence disability, the experience of talking with a concerned parent about how an educator will address their child's specific needs is a common occurrence.

Table 8.1 outlines the simulation name, the cohort of ECs for whom it was designed, the context of the SI directly engaging with the ECs, and a summary of the verbal triggers issued by the SI during the simulated interaction.

TABLE 8.1 Protocols included in the disability, difference, and inclusion data set

Protocol	Educator Candidates (ECs)	Standardized Individual (SI) and Context	Summary of Instructions for SIs and Key Triggers
Lori Blake	English 7–12	Lori Blake is the parent of a 15-year-old student with autism. The parent-initiated interaction with a teacher focuses on the inclusion of the student in a high school English class.	• Share a desire for an early pattern of communication between home and school. • Present a general overview of the student's successes and struggles. • Ask the teacher about knowledge of autism, supports for social and academics, and social inclusion. • Share your concerns over peer interactions. • Present yourself as an advocate.
Josh Churchill	Science 7–12	Josh Churchill is the parent of a high school student with visual impairment. The parent-initiated conversation with a teacher focuses on the inclusion of the student in a chemistry class.	• Share the context of the home accident and the student's resulting vision loss. • Ask the teacher about experiences working with students with physical disabilities. • Ask what supports the teacher envisions. • Note your concerns for the student's safety.
Lori Danson	Inclusive Elementary and Special Education 1–6 Multiple 7–12 and K–12 programs	Lori Danson is the parent of a 10-year-old student with autism. The parent-initiated meeting with a teacher focuses on the inclusion of the student in a third-grade class.	• Express a desire for clear communications between school and home. • Overview the student's successes and struggles. • Ask the teacher about knowledge of autism, supports for social and academics, and social inclusion. • Express your concerns over peer interactions. • Parent as a student advocate in light of past challenges.

TABLE 8.1 *(Continued)*

Protocol	Educator Candidates (ECs)	Standardized Individual (SI) and Context	Summary of Instructions for SIs and Key Triggers
Elizabeth Meyers	Inclusive Elementary and Special Education 1–6 Multiple 7–12 and K–12 programs	Elizabeth Meyers is a veteran paraprofessional. The teacher-initiated "getting to know you" conversation is between a novice teacher and a veteran paraprofessional.	• Emphasize your years of experience with the "most challenging students." • Claim knowledge of what is best for kids and their comfort. • Express a desire to remove students with disabilities from the general education classroom to work with them privately. • Ask the teacher to "paint a picture" of the inclusive classroom.
Brad Winston	Physical Education K–12	Brad Winston is the parent of a student with a visual impairment. The parent-initiated conversation with a teacher focuses on the inclusion of the student with a visual impairment in a physical education class.	• Share the context of the home accident and the student's resulting vision loss. • Ask the teacher about experiences working with students with physical disabilities. • Ask what supports the teacher envisions. • Note your concerns for safety.

METHOD OF ANALYSIS

All interactions from implementation of these five simulations were video-recorded and then transcribed verbatim, yielding a rich set of fifty-one transcripts from consenting candidates for our crosscutting qualitative analysis of the five simulations. Working from the transcripts, we replaced the actual names of all ECs with pseudonyms to protect anonymity. We uploaded all transcripts to Dedoose, an online qualitative software program that allows multiple researchers to work within the same data set to code and organize the data in multiple and shifting ways.

Both researchers reviewed a subset of the transcripts and developed initial codes. We then shared and discussed our codes to determine an initial coding framework. Each of us independently applied that framework to an additional six transcripts, identifying additional codes as needed. After meeting again to compare our coding and refine our framework, we developed a final list of codes that we applied to the entire data set.

After this first full round of coding, we identified patterns and themes across the data set, which we pulled out for further analysis and a second round of coding. For example, several of the transcripts addressed the ways our ECs described disability and difference. Once those were coded in Dedoose, we could select all segments in which that code was applied and look at them together. This allowed for a finer-grain analysis of the differing ways disability was described and defined.

CROSSCUTTING THEMES

For this chapter, we focus on three main themes that were prevalent across all of the data sets, reflecting (1) how ECs talk about (and don't talk about) difference and disability, (2) how they define and enact inclusion, and (3) how they articulate their understanding of classroom roles. Following our discussion of these themes, we consider their implications for the development of future simulations and for the use of simulations to foster communications among faculty across programs.

Talking (and Not Talking) About Difference and Disability

One of the goals for using simulations is to help our ECs become more comfortable talking with parents and colleagues about disability and difference in ways that are productive and respectful. Unfortunately, disability is still a subject many people are uncomfortable discussing openly. Pervasive ableist attitudes and stigma surrounding disability may lead some ECs to talk around the topic rather than address disability directly.[8] *Ableism* is defined as the "devaluation of disability" resulting in "societal attitudes that uncritically assert that it is better for a child to walk than roll, speak than sign, read print than read Braille, spell independently than use a spell-check, and hang out with nondisabled kids as opposed to other disabled kids."[9] In other words, ableism assumes that a disabled identity is inherently less preferable than a nondisabled one. Simulations can provide a safer space to get more comfortable talking about disability and difference, but they also make visible the unspoken assumptions and biases our ECs carry with them. As we analyzed five data sets across multiple programs, we were able to see similarities and differences in the language used by our ECs, which may or may not mirror language practices in our disciplines and programs.

When discussing disability, many ECs employed euphemisms such as *special needs*, *special*, and *differently abled*. This was especially evident in the Elizabeth Meyers interaction, although examples of these euphemisms were present across all data sets. When we reviewed the protocols for the

Meyers simulation, the term *special needs* was used by the standardized professional, so our ECs may have been simply mimicking the language they were faced with. Sometimes, standardized individuals are instructed to use particular trigger words or phrases to elicit a response in line with the goals of the simulation experience. For example, designers may be interested in how candidates respond to particular key terms. In this protocol, for example, the SIs were explicitly trained to integrate a particular phrase ("It is sometimes easier if I pull my kids out of class and get them away from everyone else so we can really bond and focus on our own work") because the designers were focused on candidate responses to challenges to inclusion. At other times, the language choices made by the SIs were their own and may reflect personal biases or experiences.

Conversely, most ECs in the science and physical education programs engaging in the Brad Winston and Josh Churchill simulations tended to use person-first terms such as "student with a visual impairment" or "student with a physical disability." The language was more matter-of-fact rather than generalized. At first, we weren't sure what to make of this. Was this, once again, a function of the language in the protocol itself, or did it nod to something larger about our programs? There is considerable focus in the inclusive elementary and special education program on models of disability, with particular attention to the limitations of medicalized models that pay limited attention to the influence of social context and interaction. Faculty also discuss the problem of label-based or deficit-based approaches to working with students, where problems are identified and remediations implemented. Courses across multiple programs stress the socially constructed nature of ability and the role of teachers in altering environments rather than trying to fix something "broken" in students. There is a focus on changing systems rather than changing students. But could this lead to an unintended consequence? Had it unwittingly sent the message that disability isn't something to be talked about directly? In an attempt to shift the onus of responsibility from the student to the teacher, did that fail to set disability up as a potential attribute or source of pride?

The application of Universal Design for Learning (UDL) principles and strategies is fundamental to many classes across our teacher preparation programs as a way to ensure that supports and accommodations are built into the structure of the lessons from the start rather than added after the fact for specific students. UDL frameworks explicitly call for educators to reframe their ways of teaching by considering the different ways students learn and to help students reach their goals in authentic and meaningful ways. Mirko Chardin and Katie Novak go on to explain that the frameworks of UDL "call for educators to transfer power to students so they have options and choices for how to learn and how to share what they have learned."[10] What came through in the data, though, was another rationale that we weren't expecting. Some ECs described using UDL strategies to mitigate potential stigma and effectively mask disability. In other words, if a particular support or strategy was needed for one student, the candidates intended to make that available for all other students as well so it wouldn't "feel special" (Lisa), allowing them to ensure the student felt "just like everybody else" (Pepper). Although one of the clear benefits of universal design is that many students benefit from supports designed with specific students in mind, it was clear from many of the transcripts that disability was not constructed as a positive attribute or at least not something to draw attention to. Ableist assumptions about normative performance seemed to underscore many of these discussions.

We see further evidence of this ableism through the advancement or attention to strengths as a way to mitigate disability, again reinforcing the notion that disability can't in itself be regarded as a strength. This came through more in the language of the standardized parents, but it was interesting to note how this language was taken up by ECs. In both the Lori Blake and Lori Danson protocols, a parent of a child with autism initiated the conference with the ECs. The SI in each protocol was tasked with proactively advocating for their son, who is new to the district. During one such interaction in the Danson simulation, the SI remarked that her son was very adept at math. EC Marisol's response was, "That's what usually shows they're very bright." There was no follow-up to that statement. From there, both parties went on to discuss, at length, the areas in which the student struggled. In another interaction with the same protocol, the SI noted during a discussion about her autistic child's struggles with organizational skills that, despite these struggles, his exceptional knowledge of computers represented a positive. This need to offset struggles with strengths can send a subtle or not so subtle message that disability and difference render a student less worthy of respect and support and continues the practice of not talking about disability. The language in this simulation came directly from a local parent of a child with a disability, reflecting an authentic situation many caregivers experience—the need to talk up the positives about their child so they will be welcome in the class. From a programmatic standpoint, we need to consider the messages that our students are receiving through the simulated interaction and the ways they align with or challenge other discourses about ability and disability. In the next section, we move beyond the language our candidates used to describe students and the experience of disability to the ways in which they defined and discussed enacting inclusion.

Defining and Enacting Inclusion

As stated previously, the Elizabeth Meyers simulation involves a getting-acquainted conversation between the EC and a special education paraprofessional who will be providing support to several students with disabilities in the EC's classroom in the coming school year. In the protocol, SI Meyers is asked to describe her past experiences providing pull-out support to students with disabilities and to note the benefit of working with students requiring services in a separate, less stressful location. A previous study by Ben and Christy using the Meyers simulation found that despite significant coursework and fieldwork focusing on the importance of and strategies for inclusive education, our ECs were quick to defer to the "expertise" of the SI portraying a veteran paraprofessional. Findings included conditional support for inclusive education promoted by our ECs and the apparent ease with which they abdicated their responsibility and leadership, giving way to a less inclusive model of service delivery when faced with minor resistance from the SI.[11] So it was with trepidation that we approached this new data set involving the same Meyers interaction protocol—but different ECs—as one of the five simulations under consideration here.

One of the biggest takeaways from the second dip into this pool and the consideration of additional data sets focused on disability and inclusion was that ECs from different programs seemed to define and describe inclusion in different ways. Many ECs in inclusive elementary and special education—the only SOE program leading to dual certification in general education and students with disabilities—described inclusion as a feeling, a sense of belonging and community, and a respect for differences. Take, for example, Aaron talking with SI Meyers:

> I want to create an open environment where everyone feels like they can participate, where they're feeling like they are being paid attention to, like they're cared for and loved like every student should be. So I don't want to create . . . I don't want to push them off to the corner, or I don't want to separate them through another room. While I do think that the special needs that they have, they need to be addressed, I don't want to feel like I'm pushing them out because of them.

That feeling of care and love and belonging was evident in many transcripts, as was a focus on equality. For example:

> I really want to make it a classroom setting that allows for equality of education. I really want to stress that enough. The classroom—it's

> not only to just say all students are equal, but I wanted to make it that people hear it. I want kids to see it. These are the students: I want them to see the equality and hear the equality, and I want them to know that they all have the same opportunity. I don't want any question about that. (John)

"All students are equal." That sounds lovely on the surface, but an overemphasis on sameness and equality can once again mask individuality and diversity of experience and needs.[12] Just as we discourage ECs from espousing colorblind ideologies when discussing racial diversity in education, we were surprised by the emphasis on sameness and equality when discussing disability.[13] When we say, "All kids are special" or "I don't see color," we deny students the recognition of what makes them unique; it becomes a form of erasure. That can mean erasure of identity but also a failure to recognize systems of power and privilege that relegate particular identities to the margins. When we fail to recognize difference, we also fail to recognize the ways in which able-bodiedness and whiteness get held up and normalized at every turn. Perhaps what the ECs meant was equity, as the candidate above is referring to opportunity, but this still merits attention across all of our programs.

Conversely, an EC engaging with the standardized parent of an autistic child in the Lori Danson simulation described a focus on recognizing difference, but difference within community:

> I just would want to stress to the class that everyone's different. Everyone has a different way of expressing themselves, and we are a classroom community, so if something does happen like that, I want the kids to know not to freak out, not to scream, but if something's a problem, to come quietly speak to me so I don't make a big deal out of the situation. (Jean)

Equality, belonging, community—those words were threaded throughout candidates' responses. They also frequently commented on the importance of feeling safe and protected. Inclusion was an ethos, a world view, a sense of connection and comfort, but this was often described in very passive terms. As instructors teaching in the inclusive elementary and special education program, we were thrilled by our students' emphasis on the importance of feelings of belonging and community.[14] However, we were eager to hear more examples of how that positioning was operationalized and the specific teacher actions that might engender such feelings of connection.

Many ECs in the 7–12 and K–12 programs—English education, science education, physical education—described inclusion in more active terms than their peers in the inclusive elementary and special education program. Rather than being something that you feel, inclusion is something that you do. They described principles of universal design or specialized equipment to ensure access. Recall that both the Brad Winston and Josh Churchill protocols revolve around a parent of a student with an acquired visual impairment. The Winston protocol involves a parent concerned about his daughter's participation in physical education, while the Churchill protocol involves an upcoming class in chemistry. One candidate in physical education responded to the SI's prompt in this way:

> Mr. Winston: That's important to me. I was wondering how you would deal with her specifically, individually, because she doesn't see very well.
>
> Mark: Yeah, of course. It would just be not only unfair to her, but if any student that had some issue that wouldn't be able to participate, I would definitely make sure that every event or every activity that we do includes everyone.
>
> Mr. Winston: That's good because she desperately—And I want her to be included.

Although subtle, we noticed a shift from "I want the student to feel included" to "I would definitely make sure that every event or every activity that we do includes everyone." This reflects a differing onus of responsibility from the student to the teacher.

Working from a starting point of UDL, Annabelle added specific examples during the Churchill encounter, including the integration of manipulatives that both support an identified student's learning while also benefiting others in the chemistry class:

> Annabelle: [W]hat I have found is when you have one student that needs something, it actually generally helps the rest of the student body. Using more manipulatives, so she actually is helping everybody else. It makes me think outside of the box for the class, and it's pushing me a little bit further to help her. And then it'll actually, usually in turn, help everybody else. Because everybody enjoys manipulatives or any little hands-on things. But I've found that it generally helps everybody out, so thank you so much.

Gabriel discussed specified specialized equipment that could be beneficial for a student with a visual impairment in physical education:

> So it'll help everyone adapt to the bat. So we can have a bigger size bat as well. And then obviously, I'm not sure if she has a problem with depth perception. I would imagine that is an issue. Using a tee or something of that nature to have the ball propped there for her to hit, as well as the other students, would be a great tool to work with. But I mean, really just working with her.

Annabella and Gabriel spoke less about what the student might feel and more about what they, as the responsible educators, might do. In other words, inclusion was an action. The ECs in the Brad Winston and Josh Churchill simulations frequently discussed adaptive equipment in their discussion of needed supports. We posit that this makes sense given that a codesigner of the Winston simulation is an expert on adapted physical education and that many of the ECs had participated or were participating in an applied outreach and research project that provided specialized play equipment to children with autism and taught their families how to use that equipment.

Other ECs articulated inclusion as both a philosophy and a set of actions or practices. For example, inclusive elementary and special education candidate Angel described her commitment to inclusion and engagement to standardized parent Lori Danson:

> We want to work hard with him. We want him to have the same opportunities as all the other students. I want him to be able to show the knowledge that he has. He's intelligent; it's obvious. And I can't wait to just form a relationship with him. I'm very excited.

Here, we see Angel articulate a belief in the student's competence and right to equity of opportunity, but she partnered that with an implied action—relationship building. Also responding to the Danson parent, Jean described inclusion as a personal identity: "I am an inclusive teacher." She went on to add that she wanted the student in the room as much as possible:

> People might learn in different ways and different forms, but everyone has the ability to learn. And that's what I want to stress to you also because I want Brian in my classroom as much as possible, and I want to accommodate for his needs without it being too obvious

> for the rest of the classroom at all and so he can take part in everyday activities, which is really what I strive for in my class.

Although not an unconditional commitment to inclusion, given that she added the phrase "as much as possible," there is clear assumption of responsibility related to accommodation and support. We did find it telling, however, that an EC who described herself as "inclusive teacher" still leaves the door open for pull-out support, which begs the question of who decides what is possible. Whose job is that? Where is the dividing line between possible and not?

Other ECs were more vocal in their support for segregated activities or at least their lack of resistance to segregated approaches. This took two different forms. One mirrored our findings from the first study with the Elizabeth Meyers simulation. ECs demonstrated deference to the paraprofessional when she articulated a desire to work with the students in a pull-out model. Take, for example, Sarah's assertion that "But any time you go into big games, they're most likely not going to be able to stay with the class, and then you can pull them aside and do, honestly, whatever you want with them" or Ellen's reassurance to Ms. Meyers she can feel free to take them out "if things get too difficult for them." This deference was especially evident in the following quote from Keith: "[I]f I can get the lesson across to them at least first and then you need to take them out and do whatever aside you need to do with them, that works great, too. Of course, if you need to take them out at any time period, do whatever you have to do." What started as an attempt to establish ownership morphed immediately to total abdication.

But this acceptance of or even support for segregation was also a common thread across the data sets where the scenario introduced concerns about safety. A good example of this concern came from Laura, a candidate in physical education, when talking to the standardized parent in the Brad Winston simulation:

> I say definitely keep her secluded from sports that require anything throwing balls, things like that. So I feel like when it comes to situations like that, we can definitely set her aside and do something with her that works. Or we can do it slowly, maybe rolling the ball on the floor and then later seeding to throwing the ball to the front of her and then maybe overhead. So I feel like we'll definitely work with how she works with us. So we'll see how she cooperates with certain sports. So after that, we'll definitely modify it.

Whether it involved fears of bullying or unkind treatment by other kids in English class or worries of being injured by chemicals in a science lab, concerns about safety and comfort often seemed to drive the need for particular accommodations or service delivery models. Such a focus on safety and protection has deep roots in the history of disability as disabled people have often been constructed as objects of pity or charity—as individuals to be helped by the nondisabled. Not only does this paternalism reinforce able-bodied privilege and normativity, but it has also denied many disabled people the dignity of risk. Students are placed in segregated classrooms "for their own protection" or denied access to age-appropriate activities.

In some instances—the Brad Winston and Josh Churchill simulations, for example—this focus on safety was explicitly named in the protocol, and our candidates simply followed that conversational thread. In other cases, candidates introduced the topic of safety and protection from harm more organically. We explore this topic further in our discussion of design implications. But first we share our final crosscutting theme—understanding and articulating adult roles in the classroom.

Understanding and Articulating Adult Roles in the Classroom

Through analysis of the transcripts for all the interviews conducted, the authors began to notice a recurring theme among almost all ECs—a difficulty in articulating their role and authority in the classroom. Although noticeably more present in the Elizabeth Meyers data set, we did note similar trends in the Lori Danson, Brad Winston, Josh Churchill, and Lori Blake data sets as well. Our ECs did not appear to have precise language to define their roles in the classroom setting, particularly when multiple providers were involved. In almost all of the encounters, our ECs deferred to the other adult in the interview by saying things like, "Well, I don't want to step on your toes here because you have the experience" (Aaron) and "I'm giving you the benefit of the doubt on that one because you're the professional in this field" (Keith). Deference to others is addressed in another section of this chapter but bears repeating here as well. Built into several of the interaction protocols were demographics to include an older and more experienced actor portraying the paraprofessional or parent.

Unsurprisingly, there was a lot of deference to the paraprofessional in the Elizabeth Meyers simulation. What was surprising, though, was candidates' lack of authority and understanding of their role as the primary educator in the classroom. Megan's experiences as a graduate teaching assistant in multiple preservice teacher courses suggest that additional work might need to be done around helping candidates establish roles in shared classrooms. In Differentiation for Inclusive Education, a course designed for inclusive elementary education majors, ECs were encouraged to create ways for students with disabilities to relinquish their reliance on paraprofessionals by building in more natural peer support. Discussion took place about the desirability of all of the adults in the room having a well-defined task, such as running a station, so the paraprofessional could become an active participant in the classroom community for all students rather than simply be tethered to a student or students with disabilities. These are positive messages that we support, but the focus still seems to be more about severing the ties between a paraprofessional and a child and less about teacher candidates owning their role as the lead instructor.

Another common theme that emerged from across the data sets was that of ownership of the students. Despite the various classes our ECs take on the way to certification that talk about inclusion, diversity, and equity, our ECs still hold tightly to the "yours/mine" binary when it comes to talking about different student populations. This is most noticeable in the Elizabeth Meyers data set—as we would expect it to be. The simulation calls for the paraprofessional to be "a little overprotective" and "the top advocate" for the students she would work with. Statements such as "I want my students to feel comfortable" and "I don't want my students to feel frustrated or upset" are embedded in the SI's interaction protocol for enactment with ECs. Therefore, it was disappointing but not surprising to us when ECs once again deferred to the paraprofessional and subscribed to the same "yours/mine" binary regarding students.

Many of our candidates struggled to articulate their authority and positionality in the classroom, and this is potentially problematic for several reasons. First, it signals to the other adults (coteachers, paraprofessionals, parents) that our ECs lack the knowledge and training that should accompany their degree. Second, it fails to illustrate how, as general or special educators, they will protect the rights of all students, including students with disabilities, English-language learners, and other marginalized groups within their classrooms. We redirect your attention back to the beginning of this chapter where we state the importance of inclusion as a hallmark of a degree in education from Syracuse University. If we adhere to this fundamental belief in inclusion across all education courses, then our ECs must be given the tools to illustrate their commitment to inclusion—starting with their ability to effectively communicate their authority as certified educators with the requisite knowledge to lead.

One EC was the exception, however. This particular individual, Ezra, was a candidate in our K–12 art education program. Throughout her experience with the paraprofessional in the Elizabeth Meyers simulation, Ezra set a clear tone for inclusion in her classroom:

> What we will definitely be doing is working on actually, interestingly enough, a little bit of the opposite of what you've been doing. Instead of taking the students out of the classroom, we're going to fade your responsibility in the sense that instead of working really close physically with a student, at first you'll start the beginning of the year, you'll get to know the students, but after time goes on, you're actually gonna start to pull away and work with the classroom as a whole.

Ezra skillfully navigated many of the challenges embedded within the interaction protocol, demonstrating clear understanding that she is the expert in the classroom. She was clearly intent on disrupting the typical "yours/mine" binary and instead promoted the idea of "ours."

What we love about Ezra's participation in this simulation extends beyond the obvious—her demonstrated understanding of adult roles in the classroom and her commitment to inclusive practices. We also love how this EC seemed to understand the importance of including all of the adults in her classroom in meaningful ways. Later in the video, she acknowledged the paraprofessional's pursuit of a degree in special education and her extensive experience working with students with disabilities. She encouraged the paraprofessional to share lesson ideas:

> You're getting a certification. If you're learning something in the class and you're like, "Oh, I think this is a really cool idea," we can totally work together too. You write up a lesson plan and maybe in a couple of weeks, we can do this with the class. I don't view you as just, "Here is Student A. I'm stuck with Student A all day, and I have to only accommodate their specific needs constantly."

We know from research and experience that teacher candidates often struggle with other adults in the room. Instead of communicating with them and providing meaningful tasks for them to engage in, the ECs default to assigning others secretarial tasks such as copying papers and running errands, or they just ignore the adults altogether, leaving them to work with designated students with little direction. Understanding the roles within the classroom as well as having open lines of communication among the adults in the room are skills that we must ensure our ECs are equipped with.

Megan reflects on her experience as a teaching assistant in a different course, Adapting Instruction for Diverse Student Needs, required for candidates in both secondary education (such as science education) and the K–12 disciplines (such as art and physical education) and taught by a faculty member that specializes in inclusive special education. The course offered a robust history of disability and engaged in discussions around ableism and ways to meet the needs of all learners, but there was limited discussion about the roles of other adults in the classroom. Nearly all of the candidates participating in this course were concurrently enrolled in a significant field placement, and Megan recalls that they often came to class with questions about who the extra adults were in the room and how they might be integrated into upcoming instruction. Given that this course (at least at Syracuse University) is one of the only classes that candidates in numerous programs are required to take to satisfy their state requirement for coursework focused on students with disabilities, SOE content area faculty may be missing a prime opportunity to promote an understanding of what roles might be played in a classroom setting, by whom, and using what collaborative models. This is an example of how we could use the data from simulations to facilitate and inform cross-program discussion. Although the special education faculty may be especially attuned to the use of multiple adults to support the inclusion of students with disabilities, content area faculty may be far better equipped to respond to the curricular demands of the simulation. This type of cross-program interrogation can only strengthen our teacher education programs.

IMPLICATIONS FOR SIMULATION DESIGN

This cross-discipline study has significant implications for future simulation designs. Several areas emerged prominently. One, we need to look carefully at the language used to describe students in the protocols. Simulations present a means for ECs to develop clear language around disability instead of using euphemisms that take power away from individuals with disabilities. It was clear that our ECs picked up and in many cases emulated that language in their responses from the interaction protocols. When the standardized paraprofessional in the Elizabeth Meyers simulation used the language "special needs" to describe the students she worked with, our ECs utilized that language as well. We want to parse out how much of their language use results from the language in the protocol and how much reflects their own internalized assumptions about disability and difference. We need to continue to be intentional about our language choices when writing interaction protocols. Sometimes we may be looking for our ECs to actively push back against particular language patterns, but we want to be careful not to unintentionally reinforce outdated language. We also need to train the SIs carefully when there are specific language choices we wish to interrogate or evoke.

Second, when we were nearly done writing this chapter and reviewed all of the protocols again to describe them here, we noticed a trend in areas of disability addressed. The protocols that include specific reference to a disability category focused on autism and visual impairment. But in both instances, the students were described as having fairly minor support needs. These were not students requiring significant modification to content expectations or utilization of assistive technology for communication, for example. In other words, these students might not challenge our students' expectations or assumptions regarding inclusion in general education classrooms or push them to radically rethink instructional expectations. The Elizabeth Meyers protocol alludes to the presence of students with more complex support needs, since there is a paraprofessional assigned to the classroom, but provides no detail about student needs. And we saw repeatedly that our students readily abdicated instructional authority and responsibility to this paraprofessional when presented with minor resistance. It is clear from our review that we need to provide our students with more opportunities to practice thinking about and articulating specifically how they will meet the needs of students with more complex support needs, including how they will work with others to do so.

A third observation from our review of the protocols was how often safety and protection concerns were woven in. This could reinforce a pervasive stereotype about disability that positions students in the role of nondisabled helper and protector.[15] Concern about students with disabilities being picked on seemed to revolve around pity for the students and was used to justify pull-out approaches. The reasoning seemed to be that teachers need to protect these students from harm and students therefore should be removed from the setting, leaving the setting unchanged and the ableist attitudes unchallenged. Perhaps this stemmed from the language used in the protocol, such as "I don't want my students to be picked on" and "They already have so much to deal with." Our candidates are very likely to face this discourse of overprotection in their future work, and therefore, it is helpful for them to practice responding. However, we want to be sure that other simulations put forth different discourses around disability, including those that reflect disability rights and justice perspectives more squarely.

Finally, we also need to consider and clearly articulate the overall goals of each simulation, particularly those that will be implemented by instructors other than the original designers. Is disability the focus or an example used to articulate a curricular decision? Are we interested in philosophies of teaching and learning or the specific strategies ECs can draw on to enact a desired outcome? If we want ECs to describe their principles of enactment, we may need to alter the language in the protocols to ask for more targeted examples. It is also important to consider where the students are in their responsive programs when they engage with that simulation. What background knowledge is necessary for students to be successful? And how do we define success? What are we hoping to learn from our review of the data? Documenting answers to all of these questions explicitly would help guide the design and implementation of the simulation protocols, as well as inform more cross-program analysis.

IMPLICATIONS OF TALKING ACROSS PROGRAMS

Clinical simulations allow us a window into how our ECs make sense of the content we are teaching and the ways in which that content gets operationalized. Although that is important within programs, this also creates space for the possibility of conversations across programs, particularly in areas that are central to the overall mission of the college. Cross-program conversations about simulations thus represent a way to hold ourselves and our programs accountable for the principles we espouse throughout SOE. We already have evidence that simulations can lead to program revision. Ben and Christy's initial study of the Elizabeth Meyers simulation revealed that candidates headed for elementary schools were underprepared to respond to pedagogical challenges, despite considerable emphasis in the program on inclusive principles and practices.[16] That so many ECs deferred to the expertise and experience of the simulated paraprofessional led faculty to embed greater attention to addressing resistance to inclusion specifically. This current reexamination of data across several disability-focused simulations highlights continued work to do in this area. It is clear, for instance, that we need to better equip ECs to talk clearly and directly about disability as difference, not as a deficiency or some all-defining characteristic but as an attribute that can be a source of pride and simultaneously be accompanied by challenges that need to be addressed and supported. Curricular revisions to reinforce this message may be best accomplished across programs given that many of our courses enroll multiple majors and that many of our faculty serve more than one program.

We also need to give our candidates additional practice articulating examples of how they would enact their educational commitments. What specific teacher actions are necessary to realize their vision of the ideal classroom? Who are the students these ECs envision filling those seats, and what are their responsibilities to them? What specific supports and strategies are necessary to address the full range of diversity present in their classrooms?

It was also clear from this crosscutting analysis that students struggle to articulate their roles and responsibilities when they are not the only adult in the room. Classrooms that include students with disabilities, particularly those with more complex support needs, often draw on the resources of multiple professionals and paraprofessionals. Beyond explicit instruction in models of adult collaboration, our ECs may need additional opportunities to practice planning for and engaging with coteachers and paraprofessionals. That type of conversation is an ideal subject matter for future simulation development.

CONCLUSION

Simulations enhance candidates' development by allowing them to engage critically in scenarios relevant to their professional practice. Across disciplines, ECs participate in simulated encounters to develop new skills or strengthen existing ones through communication situated around potential challenges they may encounter in the field. In this chapter, we have tried to highlight specific tensions and gaps in our curricula and therefore create opportunities for faculty to critically examine the broader implications of our collective commitment to preparing ECs to enter the profession. As you explore the use of simulations in your own organizations, you should consider your crosscutting core commitments. What are the hallmarks of an education degree at your institution? What sets your program apart from others? What are the taglines on your website? Those are the areas ripe for investigation across programs. Those are the issues that you and your candidates should be wrestling with. How can you work together to write simulations that address those core commitments in a variety of meaningful and intentional ways and then use that data to further your individual and collective programmatic aims?

As we consider adding to our repertoire of simulation protocols to discuss disability and difference, we are drawn to a current challenge facing SOE and our field. How do we embed attention to culturally sustaining and antiracist pedagogies into our program in meaningful ways that build on our historic traditions but better account for the experiences of students of color? How do we bring more intersectional approaches to bear on our work? And how do we do this together?

It's time to start writing new interaction protocols.

CHAPTER 9

Collaborating to Support the Design, Implementation, and Investigation of Clinical Simulations

KELLY CHANDLER-OLCOTT

It's mid-February, and seven faculty in the clinical simulations study group are gathered in a conference room with a computer screen mounted in the corner. Today's attendees represent several different departments in the Syracuse University School of Education (SOE), including Teaching & Leadership, Counseling & Human Services, Higher Education, and my own unit, Reading & Language Arts. The group, which also includes a number of other members who couldn't be present at the gathering, has been meeting monthly since October, making this our fifth session.

Today's agenda is focused on discussing video clips and accompanying transcripts from a simulation in the school counseling master's program that Melissa Luke and Benjamin Dotger, cofacilitator of the study group with me, designed together. It is meant to develop and assess the competence of educator candidates (ECs) around navigating a relationship with a standardized individual (SI) named Ashley Wilson, a parent who suspects that her high school–aged son, who has been experiencing bullying in school, may be gay. For this meeting, Melissa has selected excerpts from three different candidates' conversations with trained actors playing Ms. Wilson for us to view. To frame our work, she explains that the simulation takes place in a course that candidates take in their first semester when they've had some exposure to research but minimal skills training or clinical fieldwork. It thus provides an early sense of how individuals will manage complexities associated with confidentiality, developing trust with clients, considering multiple perspectives, and determining potential courses for action.

Our postviewing conversation takes up these questions, but it also considers some broader issues. We discuss the benefits of integrating simulations into early courses. We propose and edit some coding categories that might be used to analyze simulation performance across programs, such as the degree to which candidates either make statements or ask questions of the SI. And we acknowledge the potential payoffs—and pitfalls—of using a series of simulations to assess candidate growth. Not for the first time, our investment in the discussion leads us to run into overtime without realizing it, causing us to chuckle a bit before we scatter for other obligations.

The purpose of this chapter is to describe how the study group of teacher, school leader, and counselor educators described in this vignette coalesced around shared professional interests in simulations in educator preparation. I write primarily from my perspectives as SOE's then–associate dean for research and cofacilitator of the group, although I have also experienced simulations in the context of the English education program in which I teach. In the pages that follow, I provide a short history of the collective work related to simulations at Syracuse, describe how my colleagues and I have benefited from these collaborations, and make some recommendations about how faculty who prepare educators and other professionals might organize themselves to reap similar benefits. I draw on a range of data sources, including meeting minutes and agendas, simulation documents, internal surveys, and my own notes to tell our story.

A BRIEF HISTORY OF OUR COLLECTIVE WORK

As described in chapter 1 of this volume, Benjamin Dotger provided the intellectual spark for clinical simulations at Syracuse with a line of inquiry that first explored preservice teacher candidates' simulated interactions with parents.[1] As he recounted during our first study group meeting, he began drawing other SOE faculty into this work when he realized that he was "going to need a lot more minds than just my own" to understand and harness the potential for simulations in educator preparation. His initial collaborations tended to unfold on a small scale, however, as he recruited a colleague or two at a time to work on discrete, discipline-specific scenarios such as a music teacher's encounter with a disgruntled parent about an audition outcome or a novice special educator's interpersonal negotiations with an older, more experienced paraprofessional.[2] This approach offered numerous faculty valuable experience with a stable but customizable approach to designing and implementing simulations, but the fulcrum for the work was always Ben, with limited opportunities for faculty to interact across program areas about their learning.

Coming Together Across Program Areas

In the summer of 2016, however, that pattern changed when Ben used funding from an Arthur Vining Davis Foundation grant to convene nearly a dozen colleagues from teacher education and school counseling, including me, for several daylong summer sessions on expanding simulations in secondary education. Only some of the invitees had been previously involved with simulation design or implementation. Most of us were unaware of one another's work, and none of us had talked with each other about our undertakings. To support such cross-project interaction as well as address participant variability in experience and exposure, those summer sessions featured the following:

- Discussion of several texts offering theoretical grounding for clinical simulations, including a paper by Lee Shulman on signature pedagogies across the professions and another by Pam Grossman, Karen Hammerness, and Morva McDonald on reimagining teacher education around core practices;
- Analysis of video clips and transcripts from selected simulations with Syracuse teacher candidates in introductory education courses;
- A presentation by Ben about medical educator Howard Barrows's design tenets for simulations; and
- Workshop time to make progress on individual and group simulation projects.[3]

During the workshop time, faculty who were new to simulations brainstormed possible scenarios with Ben that might suit their program goals. Others who had already been involved with simulation implementation, like me, met in pairs and trios with program partners to construct plans for data analysis and publication.

During a debriefing session at the end of the final day, praise for the sessions and ideas for future work flowed freely. My English education teammate Marcelle Haddix, for instance, shared how much she valued discussing common readings about simulations' theoretical underpinnings, arguing that sustained time spent together to build a scholarly knowledge base on educator preparation was "supportive, not burdensome," despite the scheduling crunch many of us felt. Melissa Luke agreed, commenting on how "healing it had been to have an intellectual conversation" following a year focused on many draining tasks related to strategic planning and accreditation. The whiteboard filled with suggestions about integrating simulations into our assessment systems, seeking stipends to support faculty and graduate student work on simulation projects, and adopting some common tools and procedures for coding video data, among others.

I noted this palpable energy with particular interest because I had just completed my first year as associate dean. During the individual interviews I conducted with all faculty members shortly after my appointment, more than a dozen colleagues recounted involvement of one kind or another in a simulation project. Later, when I surveyed faculty about possible topics for study groups and other professional development, clinical simulations represented the top interest among respondents, with 92 percent indicating "yes" or "maybe" when asked if they wanted to explore the topic further. These patterns convinced me that simulations could be a generative site for collaborative inquiry, not just a topic that individuals explored once, in turn, with Ben.

Forming the Study Group

To test that theory, Ben agreed to colead a study group on clinical simulations with me, and we invited all of SOE's more than fifty full-time faculty to participate. Beginning in October 2016, the group met monthly, typically on Fridays, over the next three years, with twenty-two faculty members attending at least one meeting during that span. Some colleagues came to a session or two and decided to focus on other priorities, two attended but then left for positions at other institutions, and a few had persistent conflicts with meetings but remained connected to the enterprise by reading minutes and chatting with members in other contexts. A core group of about ten came regularly, although the list on a given day varied depending on teaching conflicts, travel schedules, and family commitments.

Meeting agendas featured activities similar to the summer sessions: we explored common readings (see figure 9.1 for some recommendations),

FIGURE 9.1 Recommended readings

Theoretical Groundings and Principles

Barab, Sasha, and Jonathan Plucker. "Smart People or Smart Contexts? Cognition, Ability, and Talent Development in an Age of Situated Approaches to Knowing and Learning." *Educational Psychologist* 37, no. 3 (2002): 165–182. doi: 10.1207/S15326985EP3703_3.

Dotger, Benjamin. "Core Pedagogy: Individual Uncertainty, Shared Practice, Formative Ethos." *Journal of Teacher Education* 66, no. 3 (2015): 216–226. doi: 10.1177/0022487115570093.

Grossman, Pam, Karen Hammerness, and Morva McDonald. "Redefining Teaching, Re-imagining Teacher Education." *Teachers and Teaching: Theory and Practice* 15, no. 2 (2009): 273–289. doi: 10.1080/13540600902875340.

Korthagen, Fred, and Jos Kessels. "Linking Theory and Practice: Changing the Pedagogy of Teacher Education." *Educational Researcher* 28, no. 4 (1999): 4–17. doi: 10.3102/0013189X028004004.

Shulman, Lee. "Signature Pedagogies in the Professions." *Daedalus* 134, no. 3 (2005): 52–59.

Examples

Craig, Shelley, Lauren McInroy, Marion Bogo, and Michelle Thompson. "Enhancing Competence in Health Social Work Education Through Simulation-Based Learning: Strategies from a Case Study of a Family Session." *Journal of Social Work Education* 53 (2017): S47–S58. doi: 10.1080/10437797.2017.1288597.

Dotger, Benjamin, and Christine Ashby. "Exposing Conditional Inclusive Ideologies Through Simulated Interactions." *Teacher Education and Special Education* 33, no. 2 (2010): 114–130. doi: 10.1177/0888406409357541.

Mueller, Tracy, Amy Massafra, Jason Robinson, and Lori Peterson. "Simulated Individualized Program Meetings: Valuable Pedagogy Within a Preservice Special Educator Program." *Teacher Education and Special Education* 42, no. 3 (2019): 1–18. doi: 10.1177/0888406418788920.

Self, Elizabeth A., and Barbara S. Stengel. *Toward Anti-Oppressive Teaching: Designing and Using Simulated Encounters*. Cambridge, MA: Harvard Education Press, 2020.

Shaughnessy, Megan, Timothy Boerst, and Susanna Owens Farmer. "Complementary Assessments of Prospective Teachers' Skill with Eliciting Student Thinking." *Journal of Mathematics Teacher Education* 22, no. 6 (2019): 607–638. doi: 10.1007/s10857-018-9402-x.

examined video and transcript data from extant simulations, and discussed challenges we faced in designing new ones. Partway through the first year, we decided that working on this edited volume together would also be generative, so we added roughing out a table of contents and possible chapter outlines to our agendas as well. Later, we scheduled several book-focused writing retreats with schedules like the one shown in table 9.1.

TABLE 9.1 Sample agenda for book planning retreat

Time Estimate	Activity
9:00–9:30 a.m.	Breakfast, welcome, and overview of the day
9:30–9:45 a.m.	Scanning of the minutes from the last meeting into Google Docs Recording of questions and comments from current attendees
9:45–10:15 a.m.	Discussion of preliminary notes about chapter parameters Time to talk to another contributor about how you're envisioning the scope of your chapter
10:15–10:30 a.m.	Break
10:30–11:30 a.m.	Writing time for teams or individuals: Generate at least a paragraph summary of a proposed chapter by the end of the session
11:30 a.m.–12:00 p.m.	Round 1 paragraph sharing: Take notes about group feedback in Google Docs
12:00–12:30 p.m.	Lunch
12:30–1:00 p.m.	Round 2 paragraph sharing: Take notes about group feedback in Google Docs
1:00–1:45 p.m.	Writing and planning time for teams or individuals: Write yourself a note to document your personal plan to continue your work at the end of the session
1:45–2:00 p.m.	Whole-group discussion of next steps

Over time, we developed a number of tools and processes to support the group's functioning. Almost immediately, we realized that we needed an accessible digital space to store resources such as candidate and actor interaction protocols, readings, meeting minutes, and draft proposals for publications. We also needed a mechanism to communicate between meetings, especially since our affiliations with departments housed in multiple buildings limited incidental contact for some members. To these ends, we set up an organization within Blackboard, the online management system nearly all of us use in our teaching, and enrolled everyone who expressed any interest in the group or attended a session. Casting such a wide net meant that folks on the group's periphery would still receive notifications unless they asked to be removed from the roster. This approach created transparency and visibility about ongoing activities as well as held the door open to greater involvement in the future for individuals with shifting interests and commitments.

Early in the group's history, Ben and I met separately in between meetings to rough out open-ended meeting plans, often using a whiteboard to sketch activities in sequence and estimate time frames. We photographed those whiteboard notes on our cell phones and then took turns transforming them into a more organized agenda intended to respect members' time and honor their interests. As the group matured, however, we began to integrate planning for the next session—work that promoted continuity and coherence—into the end of the previous one, so that members themselves could suggest the group's next steps. These moves strengthened collective buy-in and reduced preparation time in between meetings for us as facilitators.

Planning and communication within the group were both enhanced by our adoption, early in our second year, of a system for taking running minutes in a groupwide Google Docs document. Prior to our embrace of this approach, both Ben and I made handwritten notes that we used to construct agendas in between sessions or as a reference during discussions if someone wanted to clarify a previously raised idea. The notes were not circulated within the group, though, and it wasn't always easy for either of us to locate needed information. To address this issue, we adopted a collaborative practice used by school leaders in a nearby district where several of us, including me, had a longstanding partnership: we designated an individual to be the lead recorder while others followed along on a digital device. Everyone could then contribute simultaneously to a single, continuously expanding document with bolded, dated headings to indicate the shift from one meeting to the next. We linked this document to a permanent announcement in our Blackboard organization so members could locate it easily without searching their Google drives. Members typically reread and commented on the last set of notes to launch a new meeting, which served to reintegrate individuals who had missed a meeting and helped all of us to reset the conversation after a month had elapsed.

Also useful to the group's functioning was the development, over time, of some predictable processes for viewing and discussing candidate video clips. Individual simulations tend to be fairly short (those we implemented in English methods lasted between nine and thirteen minutes), but even a thirteen-minute video eats up considerable meeting time when viewed in its entirety. As an alternative, we considered adopting the debriefing procedures that Ben typically uses in classes featuring simulations, where candidates select one-minute clips for sharing and discussion with peers. As inclusive education faculty member Christy Ashby pointed out, though, the interdisciplinary nature of the study group meant that we were often viewing scenarios out of our field. We also lacked the shared context candidates had from being in class together and enacting the same simulation. For this reason, we chose to strike a middle ground. Only rarely did we view entire simulation videos. Instead, we typically considered five- to eight-minute chunks selected by a member of the design and implementation team for the simulation, who briefly described the candidate and actor interaction protocols and oriented the rest of us to the clip. As we viewed, we had printed copies of the protocols for reference, along with the transcript of the full interaction if it was available. This approach balanced access to the data with time for the rich conversation about its meanings that members valued most.

As these examples show, we experimented with working processes to serve the group's particular needs and refined our approaches over time. Some of those approaches, like our collective notetaking, were generic enough to be useful for any kind of study group, while others, like our clip-viewing norms, were more grounded in our specific focus on videotaped simulations. In the next section, I discuss the benefits of this collective work for members.

HOW OUR COLLECTIVE WORK HAS BENEFITED US

As I reviewed varied artifacts from the life of the study group, I considered the same question again and again: why did people keep coming back? More specifically, I wondered what led members to allocate time to a voluntary, informal collective despite many other commitments. In this section, I describe the benefits of exploring simulations collaboratively, as an interdisciplinary group, including considering multiple perspectives, engaging new community members, and constructing an expanded sense of what is "sim-able."

Considering Multiple Perspectives

Both survey data and meeting minutes confirmed that the value of considering multiple perspectives on the simulation design process in general and specific simulation efforts more specifically was a key factor in individuals' decisions to join the study group. During our first few meetings, we were most concerned with simulations' potential to reveal gaps in candidates' knowledge and skills that other instructional activities, such as conventional written assignments, class discussions, or even in-class role-playing, did not reliably uncover. Partway through our first year together, the group was further united by a commitment to considering a common question: "In what ways do our students attend to difference in simulations across the disciplines?" Of particular interest was how that theme of difference was enacted variably across programs, in line with disciplinary norms and expectations while still reflecting what science educator Sharon Dotger called SOE's long-held "principles and values" related to inclusion and equity.

Irrespective of topic, members attended to simulation data differently. Even when presented with the same sources—say, a video clip and an accompanying transcript—some preferred to view first and then read while others favored the opposite. Some individuals focused on language, and others on physical cues such as eye contact and body positioning. Exploring such differences sometimes led members to new insights about themselves as researchers. For example, Christy pointed out multiple examples of potential discomfort expressed nonverbally by one candidate whenever the topic of violence came up in the Ashley Wilson simulation from school counseling. I had not noticed this pattern, leading me to record a personal aside in the margin of the minutes after listening to Christy's point: "I have a print bias. Being in this group gets me to pay attention to the visual and nonverbal." Surfacing such differences led us to consider an approach for collective analysis involving multiple viewings of selected clips combined with brief bursts of informal writing, in order to capture varied perspectives prior to discussion.

In other cases, multiple perspectives shared within the group were grounded in disciplinary differences, not process-related ones. For instance, members responded variably to clips and transcripts from the Brad Winston simulation (one that required physical education candidates to discuss curricular adaptations with the parent of an elementary student with a visual impairment) based on their experiences as teacher educators and researchers. Ben Dotger, whose early work focused on parents and families, noted that candidates were learning to ask respectful questions of students' caregivers. Inclusive educator Christy Ashby concentrated on the "assumptions about disability" that could be inferred from candidate talk. And Joe Shedd, faculty in educational leadership, raised questions about how repeated simulations, with reflections in between, might help candidates to construct stronger professional identities over time. No one individual would have seen all of those aspects of the simulation unassisted, but collaborative conversation over common data revealed them fairly efficiently. Group members could then toggle between applying disciplinary and cross-disciplinary lenses to how those issues might be addressed by simulations in their own programs.

Engaging New Community Members

The simulation study group also benefited members and SOE as a whole because it invited and then leveraged participation by scholars who were new to our community. On multiple occasions, the study group connected newly hired colleagues to existing simulation work in ways that eased their transition to SOE and helped to socialize them into work as faculty at a research-intensive institution. Once they established themselves in the group, their contributions enriched participation for everyone.

In some cases, the study group helped new faculty join an ongoing research initiative while putting their own spin on the work. For example, when Duane Graysay was hired as an assistant professor, he had access to several existing simulations designed by Joanna Masingila and Ben Dotger for implementation within a mathematics methods course. Conversations in and around the study group helped Duane connect an interest in mathematical conjectures and generalizations sparked by teaching college calculus to the development of preservice candidates' capacity to support such sense-making by adolescents. He sought and received seed money to design new simulations on this topic from an SOE internal grants program, work that is reported in chapter 3 and that also led to several proposals to external funders.

Contributions by new faculty also enhanced simulation work by established scholars. One instance was when Leela George, a former school administrator, joined the educational leadership faculty. Leela first experienced simulations as a doctoral student in the School of Education and saw them as powerful enough to warrant inclusion in the majority of required courses in the leadership certificate program. She served as a catalyst for speeding up the analysis efforts described in chapter 7 that her leadership colleagues Joe Shedd and Diane Canino-Rispoli had begun but didn't yet have the bandwidth to complete swiftly. She also brought a perspective deeply grounded in recent school experience to conversations in the study group that had previously been more anchored in university-based research on educator preparation.

When Sherrie Bruner was hired as new faculty in counseling and human services, she was curious about clinical simulations and, like Leela, saw study-group membership as a way to link with other researchers in a new context. Several years before Sherrie's arrival, counseling faculty member Melissa Luke implemented several simulations on counseling LGBTIQ+ students, including the one described in the opening of this chapter, but new leadership roles within the university and her professional organization slowed her data analysis. When one of Melissa's frequent thought partners, Derek Seward, became department chair, his time for scholarship was reduced, and his formal obligation to mentor new colleagues like Sherrie was increased. When all three began attending study-group meetings together, their strengths and needs became complementary: Derek and Sherrie benefited from Melissa's prior experience with simulations, Melissa benefited from fresh eyes on her data, Melissa and Derek benefited from Sherrie's energy and relative freedom from administrative duties, and Sherrie benefited from mentorship by senior colleagues in the context of shared work.

It might be argued that a study group of any kind, on any topic, might facilitate transition into a new community for new faculty hires. I would not dispute that assertion, but I would add that simulations as we enact them at Syracuse are particularly generative in this regard because they create and capture data of varying kinds that are accessible to newcomers. The same protocol documents that guide participation by candidates and actors orient new researchers to the context. Postinteraction data such as debriefing discussion transcripts and written reflections help to illuminate candidates' thinking about their experience without requiring extensive explanatory narration by established group members—narration that takes time and might steer how everyone makes sense of the data in ways that close down interpretive possibilities. These features of our model facilitate new faculty members' entry into the community and increase the chances that they will benefit from the experience as well as contribute to others' learning.

Constructing a Collective Sense of What Is "Sim-Able"

Study-group participation also helped members consider new simulation possibilities. Our discussions helped us refine and expand our ideas about what phenomena might be what we came to call "sim-able" and what phenomena might not. These conversations supported our design of more sophisticated simulations over time, as well as our recognition that some aspects of candidate learning were better developed and/or assessed by other approaches.

As members shared their experiences, our ideas expanded, for example, about standardized individuals with whom candidates could interact in real-world scenarios. Early simulation work at Syracuse focused on communication with parents, but the list of SI roles quickly lengthened to include paraprofessionals, teacher colleagues, school administrators, community volunteers, science museum patrons, and adolescent students played by adults with particularly young appearances. As of yet, however, none of us has figured out the ethical and logistical complexities associated with live simulations involving elementary-age or younger children, so our simulations don't involve such direct interactions.

In addition to expanding members' view of potential SI roles in their respective fields, study-group discussions prompted consideration of other ways to stretch simulation boundaries. Several colleagues modeled the possibilities of what Melissa Luke called "nested simulations"—distinct but related encounters that build on each other over time and allow for reflection and/or targeted inquiry in between them. As described more fully in chapter 6, Melissa's series of three simulations required counseling candidates to interact with both a standardized parent and a standardized high school student from the same family while exploring bullying and sexual orientation. Another example of nested simulations, which comes from the Educational Leadership program, features a pair of postobservation simulations with the same standardized teacher. This design was intended to mimic the rhythm of instructional supervision in K–12 contexts, where leaders often meet more than once with their supervisees. It was also intended to head off what Joe Shedd described as candidates' tendency to avoid difficult subjects such as individual teachers' need to improve practice by proposing to discuss them at a later time. These examples helped simulation designers in other contexts to think with more concreteness about constructing multipart simulations to achieve more depth of understanding for learners.

The two-part supervision examples in the leadership program also offered another innovation for members to take up in their own designing: the use of supplemental materials, beyond the basic orienting document, to guide candidates' decision-making within a simulation. Leela and Joe's leadership candidates, for instance, are required to review and use mock test score data from the standardized supervisee's classroom to inform their recommendations for instructional improvement. Similarly, several simulations in mathematics education provide candidates with examples of student work to help them identify individuals' misconceptions during extra-help sessions.

Both examples have been useful as my colleagues Marcelle Haddix, Zaline Roy-Campbell, Ben Dotger, and I revise and strengthen a simulation requiring secondary English candidates to plan for coteaching with Sam Garner, an English as a new language specialist assigned to several fictional eleventh-grade classes. Analysis of data from our initial implementation revealed that candidates struggled to identify specific ways they might collaborate with Ms. Garner to adapt instruction for English learners' needs. It was not clear, however, whether the difficulties were due to candidates' lack of knowledge about language-related adaptations, their fuzziness about the American literature curriculum, or both. Since our instructional goals in the simulation focus on collaboration and differentiation and not on curriculum familiarity per se, our next iteration of the simulation—inspired by our colleagues' use of documents to supplement the interaction protocols—will have both ECs and SIs working from the same yearlong curriculum map stipulating unit foci and core texts. (An update on what the revised protocols yield in terms of clarity will be generated when we implement the revised simulation in an upcoming version of the English methods course.) This example demonstrates the value of study-group membership in offering multiple models for problem solving as well as the flexibility and generativity of the simulation design process in general.

WHAT WE RECOMMEND TO OTHERS INTERESTED IN A COLLECTIVE APPROACH

In this section, I make recommendations about how faculty collectives might organize themselves productively to design, implement, and research clinical simulations as part of professional preparation. These recommendations are intended to supplement suggestions shared in earlier sections, such as the usefulness of adopting an online communication system for the group. Several ideas have been tested over time by my colleagues and me. In other cases, they represent ideas we wish we had implemented earlier in our process or that we continue to refine.

Submit a Collective Institutional Review Board (IRB) Application

Prior to the launch of the study group, Ben sought institutional review board (IRB) oversight for each project separately, with each partner or group of collaborators as coinvestigators. This approach meant that data from a simulation exploring adapted physical education for a student with a visual impairment, for instance, could be accessed only by Ben and our two colleagues in physical education, Michael Norris and Luis Columna (see chapter 4). Once the group established shared analysis of video and transcript data as a priority, it became apparent that a different approach was required—one that would allow colleagues from disciplines as varied as school leadership and special education to examine and offer perspectives on candidate performance in such a scenario.

To permit cross-disciplinary analyses, Ben eventually submitted an IRB application with a broad focus on simulations and educator preparation that included all faculty members of the study group as co-principal investigators (co-PIs). The document was constructed with a forward-looking view, expecting that new hires with an interest in joining the collective could be added quickly, with a simple amendment. It stipulated that all members could analyze video data, deidentified transcripts, and candidate reflections from course-based simulations in our counselor, leader, and teacher education preparation programs. Use of simulations for other purposes by other investigators—for example, special education doctoral student Justin Freedman's simulation for undergraduates seeking disability-related accommodations from their instructors—continued to receive separate IRB review, as would any simulation-focused study that drew on additional data sources or pursued purposes other than understanding the role of simulations in candidate development.[4]

If you are launching collaborative work focused on simulations, I recommend submitting an IRB application sooner rather than later, even if your initial goals are more focused on instruction than on research. Navigating this process together will help make members' expectations explicit and transparent, which is always helpful, and you'll be able to avoid the awkward situations that we sometimes had (before our collective application was approved) of having to exclude members from some portions of our meetings and not others because they lacked proper clearance to see certain kinds of data. Simulations are equally useful for research and instruction, often creating a synergy between the two, so it's useful to think about group members' purposes and stances from the beginning—a process that is supported by the submission of a joint application for review.

Create a Searchable Database of Simulations

Another snag that we encountered during our first year as a study group was related to making members aware of what data were available for collective review. Members knew what simulations had been developed for their own programs or for particular projects on which they partnered, but that information was not aggregated. The best example of the need for a master list arose after the group established an interest in examining simulations across programs that required candidates to explore issues of difference (see chapter 8 for more on this, authored by Christine Ashby and Megan E. Cartier). We learned quickly that it was neither efficient nor exhaustive to rely on Ben's memory to generate a list of simulations that might fit this focus.

TABLE 9.2 Sample entry from a master spreadsheet

Simulation Name	Standardized Individual (SI)	Program	Brief Context
Ashley Wilson	Parent (mother)	School counseling	A physical assault reported by a high school student; a question of sexual identity

Consequently, we created a master spreadsheet summarizing the name of the simulation (usually the last name of the standardized individual), the SI type (such as parent, student, or colleague), the program(s) where the simulation is implemented (such as secondary/K–12 programs, school leadership, or elementary science), and a brief summary of the context. Table 9.2 illustrates what the entry for the school counseling simulation described at the beginning of this chapter looks like. Such entries make it easier for members to identify simulations they might use as models for new designs, to avoid scenarios that might be duplicative of simulations in other courses, and to assemble a collection of simulations on a common topic or theme.

As you are developing your master list, I suggest having a discussion explicitly focused on tagging conventions for your simulations to make it easier for multiple people to maneuver within the data set. Topical tagging can offer useful affordances for searching and sorting, particularly given how labor-intensive and expensive video transcription can be. You may find it helpful to have faculty involved with the simulations tag them while working with them instructionally, both to flag topics of interest for others and to help prioritize what should be transcribed, in part or in full, and in what order. For example, the current Syracuse master list describes the Sam Garner simulation mentioned earlier as "Getting acquainted with an ESL coteacher," but my own tagging of it as a English language arts subject specialist would include key words such as *language diversity*, *inclusion*, *adaptations*, *coplanning*, and *multimodality* that might indicate additional connections to other simulations on the master list.

Along similar lines, I suggest having a discussion early on in your group's process about transcription conventions that will serve multiple members' needs and about data storage strategies that will permit particular materials to be retrieved once members have established which simulations serve their purposes. Ideally, group members should be able to call up a range of data related to a specified simulation, identify multiple simulations on a common topic or theme, or call up a particular data source (e.g., group debriefing transcripts versus individual candidates' written reflections).

Anticipate Candidate Responses

A final suggestion is one that our group has only begun to explore ourselves. The idea to anticipate and record candidates' potential responses to key elements of a simulation surfaced during a meeting when Michael Norris and Luis Columna, the physical education faculty members most closely associated with the simulation under review, could not be present. On that day, we found ourselves asking questions about their intent and expectations for candidate performance that were difficult to answer. As the discussion continued, several of us confessed that we might not have been able to answer such questions thoroughly for simulations of our own. We realized that SOE's typical simulation design process, described most fully in Ben's book "*I Had No Idea": Clinical Simulations for Teacher Development*, placed more emphasis on creating documents to guide participation for candidates and actors playing standardized individuals than it did on explicitly documenting faculty members' design principles or goals for candidate learning.[5]

For this reason, some group members have begun to document anticipated student responses, both desirable and undesirable, prior to implementation. I recommend that you do the same with your own simulations, perhaps by asking yourself questions like these: Given what students have had for courses and fieldwork to date, what resources do they have to draw on? How are they likely to respond? What responses might indicate candidates are developing appropriately versus raise concern? Your answers have the potential to

- make your design principles and intentions explicit;
- surface areas of consensus and disagreement, promoting calibration within a design team;
- launch discussion about how candidate performance aligns with design intentions; and
- suggest priorities for assessment, if the simulation is used for that purpose.

Figure 9.2 includes a sample set of my notes anticipating candidate responses to the Lori Blake simulation, which involves English teacher candidates in a parent-initiated meeting with Ms. Blake about her son Daniel, a student with autism who is about to begin ninth grade. The notes helped me to clarify my own hopes and expectations for the simulation and also make that thinking visible—and thus open to feedback and revision—from my research partners interested in English-language arts pedagogy as well as the full membership of the study group.

FIGURE 9.2 Anticipated responses to the Lori Blake simulation

I expect candidates may draw on ideas about:
• Partnering respectfully with parents as experts on their own children (from readings and simulations in the Study of Teaching class) • Social constructions of disability (from readings and assignments in the Adapting Instruction for Diverse Student Needs class) • Differentiation and multiple forms of representation (from readings and tutoring placement in the Literacy Across the Curriculum class and from readings and assignments in Adapting Instruction for Diverse Student Needs class)

I will be encouraged if candidates:	*I will be concerned if candidates:*
• Invite the standardized parent to tell them about her son Daniel's strengths, not just his needs • Offer instructional suggestions that support peer interactions for Daniel • Claim responsibility for Daniel as a learner and express enthusiasm for getting to know him	• Ask no or few questions of the standardized parent about her son Daniel's profile and interests • Offer instructional suggestions that will isolate or separate Daniel from his peers • Suggest with their language choices or instructional suggestions that they see Daniel as "someone else's" responsibility

CONCLUDING THOUGHTS

In the early stages of planning this book, several of us proposed that administering an informal online survey to all study-group members might help to capture key aspects of our perspectives on and experiences with simulations at Syracuse. We drafted and revised the questions collaboratively, through a series of face-to-face discussions and email exchanges. One of the items we settled on asked members to share what they valued about simulations, which generated the following response from my Reading & Language Arts colleague Zaline Roy-Campbell:

> [Simulations] provide an opportunity for students to engage in potential interactions they may encounter in their professional field in a nonthreatening environment where they can critique and reflect on their practice. They can compare and discuss their experiences with their peers and consider ways they might improve on their practice for the future.

As I write, it has been more than three years since the faculty study group on clinical simulations began to meet regularly. Some of the membership has shifted over that time, as have some of our typical activities (e.g., we now spend more time on writing together than we did early on, when we focused more on professional reading and discussion). What has not changed is our collective commitment to simulations as a beneficial tool for both research and pedagogy. Having reviewed the various artifacts, including but not limited to those member surveys, about the collective itself, I've come to realize that Zaline's description of what makes simulations valuable for candidates can be just as easily applied, with minor editing tweaks, to what has made being a part of a simulation-focused study group valuable for us as faculty.

Notes

CHAPTER 1 Clinical Simulations in Educator Preparation

1. Marilyn Cochran-Smith, Ana Maria Villegas, Linda Abrams, Laura Chavez-Moreno, Tammy Mills, and Rebecca Stern, "Critiquing Teacher Preparation Research: An Overview of the Field, Part 2," *Journal of Teacher Education* 66, no. 2 (2015): 109–121, doi: 10.1177/0022487114558268; Sheila Valencia, Susan Martin, Nancy Place, and Pam Grossman, "Complex Interactions in Student Teaching: Lost Opportunities for Learning," *Journal of Teacher Education* 60, no. 3 (2009): 304–332, doi: 10.1177/0022487109336543; Kristien Zenkov and Kristine Pytash, *Clinical Experiences in Teacher Education: Critical, Project-Based Interactions in Diverse Classrooms* (New York: Routledge, 2018).
2. Karen Hauer et al., "A National Study of Medical Student Clinical Skills Assessment," *Academic Medicine* 80 (2005): S25–S29.
3. Benjamin Dotger, Elisa Dekaney, and John Coggiola, "In the Limelight: Utilizing Clinical Simulations to Enhance Music Teacher Education," *Research Studies in Music Education* 41, no. 1 (2018): 99–116, doi: 10.1177/1321103X18773102; Benjamin Dotger, Sharon Dotger, Joanna Masingila, Jeffrey Rozelle, Mary Bearkland, and Ashley Binnert, "The Right 'Fit': Exploring Science Teacher Candidates' Approaches to Natural Selection in a Clinical Simulation," *Research in Science Education* 48, no. 3 (2018): 637–661, doi: 10.1007/s11165-016-9582-2; Osman Cil and Benjamin Dotger, "The Manifestation of Emotional Geographies on Preservice Teachers' Actions During a Clinically Simulated Interaction," *Teaching and Teacher Education* 67 (2017): 237–245, doi: 10.1016/j.tate.2017.05.018; April Coughlin and Benjamin Dotger, "How Can I Help: Practicing Familial Support Through Simulation," *Teacher Education Quarterly* 43, no. 4 (2016): 77–96, doi: https://www.jstor.org/stable/teaceducquar.43.4.77; Benjamin Dotger and Christine Ashby, "Exposing Conditional Inclusive Ideologies Through Simulated Interactions," *Teacher Education and Special Education* 33, no. 2 (2010): 114–130, doi: 10.1177/0888406409357541.

4. Lee Shulman, "The Signature Pedagogies of the Professions of Law, Medicine, Engineering, and the Clergy: Potential Lessons for the Education of Teachers," *Teacher Education for Effective Teaching and Learning* (Irvine, CA: National Research Council's Center for Education, 2005).
5. Megan Shaughnessy and Timothy Boerst, "Uncovering the Skills That Preservice Teachers Bring to Teacher Education: The Practice of Eliciting a Student's Thinking," *Journal of Teacher Education* 69, no. 1 (2018), 40–55, doi: 10.1177/00224871 17702574; Justin Freedman, Benjamin Dotger, and Yosung Song, "Encountering Ableism in the Moment: How Post-Secondary Students Discuss Accommodations with Faculty Members," *Critical Education* 11, no. 16 (2020): 21–37; Justin Freedman, Casey Woodfield, and Benjamin Dotger, "Using Simulated Meetings to Practice Advocating for Disability-Related Accommodations," *Journal of Postsecondary Education and Disability* 33, no. 4 (2020): 387–394.
6. Harold S. Barrows, *Simulated (Standardized) Patients and Other Human Simulations: A Comprehensive Guide to Their Training and Use in Teaching and Evaluation* (Chapel Hill, NC: Health Sciences Consortium, 1987); Harold S. Barrows, "An Overview of the Uses of Standardized Patients for Teaching and Evaluating Clinical Skills," *Academic Medicine* 68, no. 6 (1993): 443–453, doi: 10.1097/00001888-199306000-00002; Harold S. Barrows, *Problem-Based Learning Applied to Medical Education* (Springfield: Southern Illinois University Press, 2000); Harold S. Barrows and Stephen Abrahamson, "The Programmed Patient: A Technique for Appraising Student Performance in Clinical Neurology," *Journal of Medical Education* 39 (1964): 802–805.
7. Such supplemental texts have included assignment examples, samples of student work, observation notes from classroom observations, district communications, and, once, a rubric to evaluate an audition for the school musical.
8. The COVID-19 pandemic shifted the implementation location of simulations, beginning in the summer of 2020. During the pandemic, multiple-candidate cohorts utilized a video-based platform to engage with SIs and to guide faculty in simulation debriefings. Postpandemic, we envision the implementation of simulations through both in-person and live, video-based platforms.
9. Shulman, "Signature Pedagogies."
10. Shulman, "Signature Pedagogies," n.p.
11. Kelly Chandler-Olcott, Sharon Dotger, Heather Waymouth, Michael Crosby, Molly Lahr, Keith Newvine, and Kathleen Hinchman, "Teacher Candidates Learn to Enact Curriculum in a Partnership-Sponsored Literacy Enrichment Program for Youth," *New Educator* 14, no. 3 (2018): 192–211, doi: 10.1080/1547688X.2017.1407852; Kelly Chandler-Olcott, Sharon Dotger, Kathleen Hinchman, Heather Waymouth, and Keith Newvine, "Collaborative Design to Support Digital Literacies Across the Curriculum," in *Design Based Research in Education: Theory and Applications*, ed. Zoi A. Philippakos, Emily Howell, and Anthony Pellegrino (New York: Guilford, 2021); Sharon Dotger, "Methodological Understandings from Elementary Science Lesson Study

Facilitation and Research," *Journal of Science Teacher Education* 26, no. 4 (2015): 349–369, doi: 10.1007/s10972-015-9427-2; Sharon Dotger and Vicki McQuitty, "Describing Teachers' Operative Systems: A Case Study," *Elementary School Journal* 115, no. 1 (2014): 73–96, doi: 10.1086/676945.

12. Pam Grossman, *Teaching Core Practices in Teacher Education* (Cambridge, MA: Harvard Education Press, 2019), 3; see also Kenneth Zeichner, "The Turn Once Again Toward Practice-Based Teacher Education," *Journal of Teacher Education* 63, no. 5 (2012): 376–382, doi: 10.1177/0022487112445789.
13. Christine Ashby, "Disability Studies and Inclusive Teacher Preparation: A Socially Just Path for Teacher Education," *Research and Practice for Persons with Severe Disabilities* 37, no. 2 (2012): 88–99, doi: 10.2511/027494812802573611; Christine Ashby and Megan Cosier, *Enacting Change from Within: Disability Studies Meets Teaching and Teacher Education* (New York: Peter Lang Publishers, 2016); Douglas Biklen, *Schooling Without Labels: Parents, Educators, and Inclusive Education* (Philadelphia: Temple University Press, 1992); Julie Causton-Theoharis, George Theoharis, Thomas Bull, Meghan Cosier, and Kathy Dempf-Aldrich, "Schools of Promise: A School District-University Partnership Centered on School Reform," *Remedial and Special Education* 32, no. 3 (2011): 192–205, doi: 10.1177/0741932510366163; Kelly Chandler-Olcott, *A Good Fit for All Kids: Collaborating to Teach Writing in Diverse, Inclusive Settings* (Cambridge, MA: Harvard Education Press, 2019); Kelly Chandler-Olcott and Paula Kluth, "Why Everyone Benefits from Including Students with Autism in Literacy Classrooms," *The Reading Teacher* 62, no. 7 (2009): 548–557, doi: 10.1598/RT.62.7.1; Beth A. Ferri and David J. Connor, "Tools of Exclusion: Race, Disability, and (Re)Segregated Education," *Teachers College Record* 107, no. 3 (2005): 453–474, doi: 10/1111/j.1467-9620.2005.00483x.
14. Elizabeth A. Self and Barbara S. Stengel, *Toward Anti-Oppressive Teaching: Designing and Using Simulated Encounters* (Cambridge, MA: Harvard Education Press, 2020).
15. Osman Cil, "Teacher Identities as Decision-Makers and Facilitators: An Investigation of Pre-Service Teacher Performances and Reflections Within a Clinical Simulation" (PhD diss., Syracuse University, 2014); Justin E. Freedman, "Is That Okay with You? Examining a Simulated Discussion About Accommodations Between University Students Identified as Having a Disability and a Standardized Faculty Member" (PhD diss., Syracuse University, 2018); John Mungai Njoroge, "Examining Mathematical Knowledge for Teaching: An Exploratory Study of Prospective Teachers' Transition of Knowledge to Practice in Clinical Simulations" (PhD diss., Syracuse University, 2017).
16. Benjamin Dotger, *"I Had No Idea!" Clinical Simulations for Teacher Development* (Charlotte, NC: Information Age Publishing, 2013); Benjamin Dotger, *Beyond Tears, Tirades, and Tantrums: Clinical Simulations for School Leader Development* (Charlotte, NC: Information Age Publishing, 2014).
17. Shulman, "Signature Pedagogies."

CHAPTER 2 The Conceptual Underpinnings of Clinical Simulations

1. Lee S. Shulman, "The Signature Pedagogies of the Professions of Law, Medicine, Engineering, and the Clergy: Potential Lessons for the Education of Teachers," *Teacher Education for Effective Teaching and Learning* (Irvine, CA: National Research Council's Center for Education, 2005).
2. Howard Barrows and Stephen Abrahamson, "The Programmed Patient: A Technique for Appraising Student Performance in Clinical Neurology," *Journal of Medical Education* 39 (1964): 802–805; Harold S. Barrows, *Simulated (Standardized) Patients and Other Human Simulations: A Comprehensive Guide to Their Training and Use in Teaching and Evaluation* (Chapel Hill, NC: Health Sciences Consortium, 1987).
3. Barrows, *Simulated (Standardized) Patients*; Benjamin Dotger, "Core Pedagogy: Individual Uncertainty, Shared Practice, Formative Ehos," *Journal of Teacher Education* 66, no. 3 (2015): 215–226, doi: 10.1177/0022487115570093.
4. John Brown, Allan Collins, and Paul Duguid, "Situated Cognition and the Culture of Learning," *Educational Researcher* 18 (1989): 32–42, doi: 10.3102/0013189X018001032.
5. Brown, Collins, and Duguid, "Situated Cognition," 33.
6. Brown, Collins, and Duguid, "Situated Cognition," 34.
7. Brown, Collins, and Duguid, "Situated Cognition."
8. Brown, Collins, and Duguid, "Situated Cognition," 34.
9. Benjamin Dotger, Elisa Dekaney, and John Coggiola, "In the Limelight: Utilizing Clinical Simulations to Enhance Music Teacher Education," *Research Studies in Music Education* 41, no. 1 (2018): 99–116, doi: 10.1177/1321103X18773102.
10. Shulman, "Signature Pedagogies."
11. Benjamin Dotger, Kevin Heffernan, and Tiago Barreira, "My Heart Is Racing! Physiological Responses Within and Across a Clinical Simulation Learning Environment" (working paper, Faculty of School of Education and Falk College, Syracuse University, 2020).
12. Jean Piaget, *Logic and Psychology* (Manchester, UK: Manchester University Press, 1959).
13. Shulman, "Signature Pedagogies."
14. Shulman, "Signature Pedagogies."
15. Sasha Barab and Jonathan Plucker, "Smart People or Smart Contexts? Cognition, Ability, and Talent Development in an Age of Situated Approaches to Knowing and Learning," *Educational Psychologist* 37, no. 3 (2002): 165–182, doi: 10.1207/S15326985EP3703_3.
16. Lisa Johnson and Alan Reiman, "Beginning Teacher Disposition: Examining the Moral/Ethical Domain," *Teaching and Teacher Education* 23 (2007): 677, doi: 10.1016/j.tate.2006.12.006.
17. Benjamin Dotger and Christine Ashby, "Exposing Conditional Inclusive Ideologies Through Simulated Interactions," *Teacher Education and Special Education* 33, no. 2 (2010): 114–130, doi: 10.1177/0888406409357541.

18. Readers might consult Jean Lave and Etienne Wenger's *Situated Learning: Legitimate Peripheral Participation* (Cambridge: Cambridge University Press, 1991) and Wenger's *Communities of Practice: Learning, Meaning, and Identity* (Cambridge: Cambridge University Press, 2000) for rich descriptions of how distinct groups utilize collaboration in teaching and learning environments.

CHAPTER 3 Simulations in Secondary Mathematics Teacher Education: The Role of Debriefings in Providing Opportunities to Develop Knowledge for Teaching

1. The development, implementation, and data collection for the Word Problem simulations referenced in this chapter were funded by a National Science Foundation Discovery Research K–12 (DR-K12) exploratory grant (award #1118772). The development, implementation, and data collection for the Numerical Approach to Generalizing and the Figural Approach to Generalizing simulations were funded by a Syracuse University School of Education Internal Seed Grant. The authors wish to acknowledge Benjamin Dotger for collaborating and mentoring to construct and implement all of the simulations described in this chapter. We also thank Sharon Dotger and Mary Bearkland for their contributions to the Word Problem simulation and Lynea Snyder for her contributions to constructing the Generalizing simulations reported in this chapter.
2. In the implementation of the simulation, not all simulated individuals (SIs) were represented by female actors and therefore did not always introduce themselves using female names. However, in the interests of clear writing, we have chosen to refer to the SIs as female and to substitute female pronouns in place of male pronouns in candidates' statements throughout the chapter.
3. James W. Stigler and James Hiebert, *The Teaching Gap: Best Ideas from the World's Teachers for Improving Education in the Classroom* (New York: Free Press, 1999).
4. National Council of Teachers of Mathematics (NCTM), *Principles to Actions: Ensuring Mathematical Success for All* (Reston, VA: NCTM, 2014).
5. "edTPA," Stanford Center for Assessment, Learning, and Equity, Stanford University, 2019, https://scale.stanford.edu/teaching/edtpa.
6. Eric Banilower et al., *Lessons from a Decade of Mathematics and Science Reform* (Chapel Hill, NC: Horizon Research, 2006).
7. Fran Arbaugh et al., *We Reason and We Prove for ALL Mathematics: Building Students' Critical Thinking, Grades 6–12* (Thousand Oaks, CA: Corwin Press, 2019).
8. NCTM, *Principles to Actions.*
9. Anders Jonsson and Lotte Leden, "The Ambiguous Influence of High-Stakes Testing on Science Teaching in Sweden," *International Journal of Science Education* 41, no. 14 (2019): 1926–1943, doi:10.1080/09500693.2019.1647474.

10. Mike Rose, "School Reform Fails the Test," *The American Scholar* (Winter 2015): 18–30.
11. Benjamin Dotger et al., "Exploring Iconic Interpretation and Mathematics Teacher Development Through Clinical Simulations," *Journal of Mathematics Teacher Education* 18 (2014): 577–601, doi: 10.1007/s10857-014-9290-7; Meghan Shaughnessy et al., "Simulating Teaching: New Possibilities for Assessing Teaching Practices," *Proceedings of the 37th Annual Meeting of the North American Chapter of the International Group for the Psychology of Mathematics Education*, ed. Tonya G. Bartell et al. (East Lansing: Michigan State University, 2015). 924–927; Corey Webel and Kimberly A. Connor, "Using Simulated Teaching Experiences to Perturb Preservice Teachers' Mathematics Questioning Practices," *Mathematics Teacher Educator* 6, no. 1 (2017): 9–26, doi: 10.5951/mathteaceduc.6.1.0009.
12. Arbaugh, *We Reason and We Prove*; Shaughnessy et al., "Simulating Teaching."
13. Patricio Herbst et al., "Using Comics-Based Representations of Teaching, and Technology, to Bring Practice to Teacher Education Courses," *ZDM Mathematics Education* 43 (2011): 91–103, doi: 10.1007/s11858-010-0290-5; Webel and Connor, "Using Simulated Experiences"; Meghan Shaughnessy and Timothy A. Boerst, "Uncovering the Skills That Preservice Teachers Bring to Teacher Education: The Practice of Eliciting a Student's Thinking," *Journal of Teacher Education* 69, no. 1 (2018): 40–55, doi: 10.1177/0022487117702574.
14. Lee S. Shulman, "Those Who Understand: A Conception of Teacher Knowledge," *American Educator* 10, no. 1 (1986): 9–15, 43–44.
15. Deborah. L. Ball and Hyman Bass, "Toward a Practice-Based Theory of Mathematical Knowledge for Teaching," *Proceedings of the 2002 Annual Meeting of the Canadian Mathematics Education Study Group*, ed. Elaine Simmt and Brent Davis (Edmonton: CMESG/GCEDM, 2002): 3–14; Heather C. Hill and Deborah L. Ball, "Learning Mathematics for Teaching: Results from California's Mathematics Professional Development Institutes," *Journal for Research in Mathematics Education* 35, no. 5 (2004): 330–351, doi: 10.2307/30034819.
16. Deborah L. Ball, Mark H. Thames, and Geoffrey Phelps, "Content Knowledge for Teaching: What Makes It So Special?," *Journal of Teacher Education* 59, no. 5 (2008): 389–407, doi: 10.1177/0022487108324554.
17. Deborah A. Zopf, "Mathematical Knowledge for Teaching Teachers: The Mathematical Work of and Knowledge Entailed by Teacher Education" (PhD diss., University of Michigan, 2010), https://deepblue.lib.umich.edu/bitstream/handle/2027.42/77702/dzopf_1.pdf; see also Alison Castro-Superfine and Wenjuan Li, "Exploring the Mathematical Knowledge Needed for Teaching Teachers," *Journal of Teacher Education* 65, no. 4 (2014): 303–314, doi: 10.1177/0022487114534265; and Ball and Bass, "Toward a Practice-Based Theory."
18. Conference Board of the Mathematical Sciences, *The Mathematical Education of Teachers II* (Washington, DC: American Mathematical Society, 2012), 7.

19. Carrie W. Lee, "Rehearsals of Ambitious Teaching in Immersive Classroom Simulation Activities," in *Proceedings of the 40th Annual Meeting of the North American Chapter of the International Group for the Psychology of Mathematics Education*, ed. Thomas E. Hodges, George J. Roy, and Andrew M. Tyminski (Greenville: University of South Carolina and Clemson University, 2018), 763–766.
20. Dotger et al., "Exploring Iconic Interpretation."
21. Corey Webel et al., "Simulations as a Tool for Practicing Questioning," in *ICME-13 Monographs: Mathematics Teachers Engaging with Representations of Practice*, ed. Orly Buchbinder and Sebastian Kuntze (Dordrecht: Springer, 2018), 95–112, doi: 10.1007/978-3-319-70594-1_6.
22. Dotger et al., "Exploring Iconic Interpretation."
23. Webel et al., "Simulations for Practicing Questioning."
24. Lee, "Rehearsals of Ambitious Teaching."
25. Dotger et al., "Exploring Iconic Interpretation."
26. John Clement et al., "Translation Difficulties in Learning Mathematics," *American Mathematical Monthly* 88, no. 4 (1981): 288.
27. Ferdinand D. Rivera, "Generalizing as a Mathematical Way of Knowing: Understanding Figural Generalization," *The Mathematics Teacher* 101, no. 1 (2007): 69–75, doi: 10.5951/MT.101.1.0069; Ferdinand D. Rivera and Joanne Rossi Becker, "Middle School Children's Cognitive Perceptions of Constructive and Deconstructive Generalizations Involving Linear Figural Patterns," *ZDM Mathematics Education* 40, no. 1 (2008): 65–82, doi: 10.1007/s11858-007-0062-z.
28. Joanne Rossi Becker and Ferdinand Rivera, "Generalization Strategies of Beginning High School Algebra Students," in *Proceedings of the 29th Conference of the International Group for the Psychology of Mathematics Education*, vol. 4, ed. Helen L. Chick and Jill L. Vincent (Melbourne: PME, 2005), 121–128.
29. Rivera and Rossi Becker, "Middle School Children's Cognitive Perceptions of Constructive and Deconstructive Generalizations"; Rivera, "Generalizing as a Mathematical Way of Knowing"; Rossi Becker and Rivera, Generalization Strategies of Beginning High School Algebra Students"; Kay Stacey, "Finding and Using Patterns in Linear Generalising Problems," *Educational Studies in Mathematics* 20, no. 2 (1989): 147–164, doi: 10.1007/BF00579460; Lyn D. English and Elizabeth A. Warren, "Introducing the Variable Through Pattern Exploration," *The Mathematics Teacher* 91, no. 2 (1998): 166–170, http://www.nctm.org/publications/mt.aspx.
30. Duane Graysay acknowledges again, with gratitude, the work of Lynea Snyder, SUNY College of Environmental Science and Forestry, who was a crucial partner in creating the protocols for the Approaches to Generalizing simulations.
31. Throughout the manuscript, we use pseudonyms to refer to participants in the research. We selected pseudonyms to correspond with the genders of the participants.
32. Ball, Thames, and Phelps, "Content Knowledge for Teaching."

33. Ball, Thames, and Phelps, "Content Knowledge for Teaching," 401.
34. Ball, Thames, and Phelps, "Content Knowledge for Teaching," 401.
35. Ball, Thames, and Phelps, "Content Knowledge for Teaching."
36. Orit Zaslavsky and Roza Leikin, "Professional Development of Mathematics Teacher Educators: Growth in Practice," *Journal of Mathematics Teacher Education* 7, no. 1 (2004): 9.
37. Deborah L. Ball and David Cohen, "Developing Practice, Developing Practitioners," *Teaching as the Learning Profession*, ed. Linda Darling-Hammond and Gary Sykes (San Francisco: Jossey-Bass, 1999), 3–32.
38. Edward A. Silver et al., "Where Is the Mathematics? Examining Teachers' Mathematical Learning Opportunities in Practice-Based Professional Learning Tasks," *Journal of Mathematics Teacher Education* 10, no. 4–6 (2007): 276.
39. Orit Zaslavsky, "Meeting the Challenges of Mathematics Teacher Education Through Design and Use of Tasks That Facilitate Teacher Learning," in *The International Handbook of Mathematics Teacher Education: The Mathematics Teacher Educator as a Developing Professional*, vol. 4, ed. Barbara Jaworski and Terry L. Wood (Rotterdam: Sense Publishers, 2008), 93–114.
40. Zopf, "Mathematical Knowledge for Teaching Teachers."

CHAPTER 4 "How Can She Participate?" Examining Inclusion in Physical Education Through Simulation

1. Terese Wilhelmsen and Marit Sørensen, "Inclusion of Children with Disabilities in Physical Education: A Systematic Review of Literature from 2009 to 2015," *Adapted Physical Activity Quarterly* 34, no. 3 (2017): 311–337, doi: 10.1123/apaq.2016-0017.
2. "Statistics About Youth and Children with Vision Loss," American Federation for the Blind, https://www.afb.org/research-and-initiatives/statistics/statistics-blind-children#gender19.
3. Martin Block and Iva Obrusnikova, "Inclusion in Physical Educaton: A Review of the Literature from 1995–2005," *Adapted Physical Activity Quarterly* 24, no. 2 (2007): 103–124, doi: 10.1123/apaq.24.2.103; Nancy Spencer-Cavaliere and E. Jane Watkinson, "Inclusion Understood from the Perspectives of Children with Disability," *Adapted Physical Activity Quarterly* 27, no. 4 (2010): 275–293, doi: 10.1123/apaq.27.4.275; Justin Haegele, "Inclusion Illusion: Questioning the Inclusiveness of Integrated Physical Education," *Quest* 71, no. 4 (2019): 387–397, doi: 10.1080/00336297.2019.1602547.
4. Justin Haegele and Lauren Lieberman, "The Current Experiences of Physical Education Teachers at Schools for Blind Students in the United States," *Journal of Visual Impairment & Blindness* 110, no. 5 (2016): 323–334; Kara Perkins et al., "Parents' Perceptions of Physical Activity for Their Children with Visual Impairments," *Journal of Visual Impairment & Blindness* 107, no. 2 (2013):

131–142, doi: 10.1177/0145482X1310700206; Moira Stuart, Lauren Lieberman and Karen Hand, "Beliefs About Physical Activity among Children Who Are Visually Impaired and Their Parents," *Journal of Visual Impairment & Blindness* 100, no. 4 (2006): 223–234, doi: 10.1177/0145482X0610000405.

5. Samuel Hodge et al., "Comparison of Practicum Types in Changing Preservice Teachers' Attitudes and Perceived Competence," *Adapted Physical Activity Quarterly* 19, no. 2 (2002): 155–171, doi: 10.1123/apaq.19.2.155; Bethany Hersman and Samuel Hodge, "High School Physical Educators' Beliefs About Teaching Differently Abled Students in an Urban Public School District," *Education and Urban Society* 42, no. 6 (2010): 730–757, doi: 10.1177/0013124510371038.
6. Haegele and Lieberman, "The Current Experiences," 323.
7. Hodge et al., "Comparison of Practicum Types," 155.
8. Hyun-Kyoung Oh et al., "Pre Service Physical Education Teachers' Attributes Related to Teaching a Student Labeled ADHD," *Teaching and Teacher Education* 26, no. 4 (2010): 885–890, doi: 10.1016/j.tate.2009.10.027.
9. Kara Perkins et al., "Parents' Perceptions," 131.
10. Christine Ashby, "Disability Studies and Inclusive Teacher Preparation: A Socially Just Path for Teacher Education," *Research and Practice for Persons with Severe Disabilities* 37, no. 2 (2012): 88–99, doi: 10.2511/027494812802573611; Christine Ashby, "The Trouble with Normal: The Struggle for Meaningful Access for Middle School Students with Developmental Disabilities," *Disability and Society* 25, no. 3 (2010): 345–358, doi: 10.1080/09687591003701249.
11. Fernanda Orsati and Christine Ashby, "'My Mission': Life Stories of Mothers of Individuals Who Type to Communicate," *Considering Disability* 1, nos. 3–4 (2016); Katherine Runswick-Cole, "'The Tribunal Was the Most Stressful Thing: More Stressful Than My Son's Diagnosis or Behaviour': The Experiences of Families Who Go to the Special Educational Needs and Disability Tribunal (SENDisT)," *Disability & Society* 22, no. 3, (2007): 315–328, doi: 10.1080/09687590701259674.
12. Harold S. Barrows, *Simulated (Standardized) Patients and Other Human Simulations: A Comprehensive Guide to Their Training and Use in Teaching and Evaluation* (Chapel Hill, NC: Health Sciences Consortium, 1987).
13. Kara Perkins et al., "Parents' Perceptions of Physical Activity Experiences for Their Families and Children with Visual Impairments," *British Journal of Visual Impairment* 35, no. 2 (2017): 88–102, doi: 10.1177/0264619617691081.
14. Pat Bazeley and Kristi Jackson, *Qualitative Data Analysis with Nvivo*, 2nd ed. (Los Angeles: Sage, 2013).
15. "SHAPE America: National Standards for K–12 Physical Education," Society of Health and Physical Educators, Reston, VA, 2013, https://www.shapeamerica.org.
16. Kara Perkins et al., "Parents' Perceptions," 88.

CHAPTER 5 Designing Simulations for Building Scientific Explanations with Elementary Teacher Candidates

1. Benjamin Dotger and Sharon Dotger, "ELEM-SIM: Elementary Science Simulations to Advance Undergraduate Teacher Preparation," National Science Foundation, Improving Undergraduate STEM Education: Education and Human Resources, IUSE, EHR, NSF 15-585.
2. Benjamin Dotger et al., "The Right 'Fit': Exploring Science Teacher Candidates' Approaches to Natural Selection in a Clinical Simulation," *Research in Science Education* 48, no. 3 (2018): 637–661, doi: 10.1007/s11165-016-9582-2; Benjamin Dotger et al., "Exploring Iconic Interpretation and Mathematics Teacher Development Through Clinical Simulations," *Journal of Mathematics Teacher Education* 18 (2014): 577–601, doi: 10.1007/s10857-014-9290-7; Sharon Dotger, Benjamin Dotger, and John Tillotson, "Examining How Pre-service Teachers Navigate Simulated Parent-Teacher Conversations on Evolution and Intelligent Design," *Science Education* 94 (2010): 552–570, doi: 10.1002/sce.20375; NGSS Lead States, *Next Generation Science Standards: For States, by States* (Washington, DC: National Academies Press, 2013); National Research Council, *A Framework for K–12 Science Education: Practices, Crosscutting Concepts, and Core Ideas* (Washington, DC: National Academies Press, 2012).
3. Courtney L. Plumley, *2018 NSSME+: Status of Elementary School Science* (Chapel Hill, NC: Horizon Research, 2019).
4. William Tate, "Science Education as a Civil Right: Urban Schools and Opportunity-to-Learn Considerations," *Journal of Research in Science Teaching* 38, no. 9 (2001): 1015–1028, doi: 10.1002/tea.1045.
5. Daniel Morales-Doyle, "Justice-Centered Science Pedagogy: A Catalyst for Academic Achievement and Social Transformation," *Science Education* 101 (2017): 1034–1060, doi: 10.1002/sce.21305.
6. Phillip L. Bell et al., "Exploring the Science Framework: Engaging Learners in Scientific Practices Related to Obtaining, Evaluating, and Communicating Information," *Science Scope* 36, no. 3 (2012): 17–22, doi: 10.1.1.393.8990.
7. Erin M. Furtak and William Penuel, "Coming to Terms: Addressing the Persistence of 'Hands-on" and Other Reform Terminology in the Era of Science as Practice," *Science Education* 103 (2019): 167–186, doi: 10.1002/sce.21488.
8. National Research Council, *A Framework for K–12 Science Education*, 67.
9. Melissa Braaten and Mark Windschitl, "Working Toward a Stronger Conceptualization of Scientific Explanation for Science Education," *Science Education* 95, no. 4 (2011): 639–669, doi: 10.1002/sce.20449.
10. Leema Berland et al., "Epistemologies in Practice: Making Scientific Practices Meaningful for Students," *Journal of Research in Science Teaching* 53, no. 7 (2016): 1082–1112, doi: 10.1002/tea.21257.
11. Mark Windschitl, Jessica Thompson, and Melissa Braaten, *Ambitious Science Teaching* (Cambridge, MA: Harvard Education Press, 2018).
12. Dotger et al., "The Right 'Fit'"; Dotger et al., "Exploring Iconic Interpretation"; Dotger, Dotger, and Tillotson, "Examining How Preservice Teachers Navigate."

13. Onondaga Nation, https://www.onondaganation.org.
14. Nanticoke Lenni-Lenape Tribal Nation, https://nlltribe.com/about-us/
15. Clint Carroll et al., "Using PhotoVoice to Promote Land Conservation and Indigenous Well-Being in Oklahoma," *EcoHealth* 15 (2018): 450–461, doi: 10.1007%2Fs10393-018-1330-9; Jeff Corntassel and Cheryl Bryce, "Practicing Sustainable Self-Determination: Indigenous Approaches to Cultural Restoration and Revitalization," *Brown Journal of World Affairs* 18, no. 11 (2012): 151–162, doi: https://www.jstor.org/stable/24590870.

CHAPTER 6 Using Nested Simulations to Assess School Counselor Learning

1. Lisa Schelbe, Helen E. Petracchi, and Addie Weaver, "Benefits and Challenges of Service-Learning in Baccalaureate Social Work Programs," *Journal of Teaching in Social Work* 34, no. 5 (2014): 480–495, doi: 10.1080/08841233.2014.954689.
2. Peitao Zhu, "Experiential Growth Group in Counselor Education: A Review of Its Pedagogy, Research, and Ethical Dilemmas," *Journal for Specialists in Group Work* 43, no. 2 (2018): 144–165; doi: 10.1080/01933922.2018.1451581; Michael Mariska, "The Client Role in a Pre-Practicum Counseling Skills Course," *Journal of Counselor Preparation and Supervision* 7, no. 1 (2015): 1–28, doi: 10.7729/71.1067.
3. Mariska, "The Client Role."
4. Malcolm Knowles, *Andragogy in Action* (San Francisco: Jossey-Bass, 1984).
5. Katie Kozak, Melissa Luke, and Benjamin Dotger, "Thanks for Coming in, Ms. Wilson: A Grounded Theory of School Counselor Professional Identity Development," *Excelsior*, n.d.
6. Kozak, Luke, and Dotger, "Thanks for Coming In."
7. Eva Hava Peisachovich et al., "Proposing a Model to Embed a Simulated-Person Methodology Program Within Higher Education," *Innovations in Education and Teaching International* 56, no. 1 (2019): 46–56, doi: 10.1080/14703297.2017.1399808.
8. Kozak, Luke, and Dotger, "Thanks for Coming In."
9. Shelley L. Craig et al., "Enhancing Competence in Health Social Work Education Through Simulation-Based Learning: Strategies from a Case Study of a Family Session," *Journal of Social Work Education* 53 (2017): S47–S58, doi: 10.1080/10437797.2017.1288597; Christianne Fowler and Kaprea Hoquee, "Using Geriatric Standardized Patients and Technology to Teach Counseling and Health Science Students How to Work Interprofessionally," *Adultspan Journal* 15, no. 1 (2016): 25–37, doi: 10.1002/adsp.12017.
10. Council for the Accreditation of Counseling and Related Educational Programs (CACREP), "2016 CACREP Standards," 2015, https://www.cacrep.org/for-programs/2016-cacrep-standards; Manivong J. Ratts, *Multicultural and Social Justice Counseling Competencies: A Blueprint for the Profession* (Alexandria, VA: American Counseling Association, 2021).

11. Melissa Luke and Kris Goodrich, "LGBTQ Responsive School Counseling Supervision," *The Clinical Supervisor* 31, no. 1 (2012): 81–102, doi: 10.1080/07325223.2012.672391.
12. Melissa Luke and Janine M. Bernard, "The School Counseling Supervision Model: An Extension of the Discrimination Model," *Counselor Education and Supervision* 45, no. 4 (2006): 282–295, doi: 10.1002/j.1556-6978.2006.tb00004.x.
13. CACREP, "2016 CACREP Standards," 2015.
14. Norma L. Day-Vines et al., "Broaching the Subjects of Race, Ethnicity, and Culture During the Counseling Process," *Journal of Counseling & Development* 85, no. 4 (2007): 401–409, doi: 10.1002/j.1556-6678.2007.tb00608.x.
15. Toula Kourgiantakis et al., "Students' Conceptualization of Culture and Diversity with a Simulated Client," *Journal of Ethnic and Cultural Diversity in Social Work* (2020), https://doi.org/10.1080/15313204.2020.1839618; Jill C. Schreiber and Joseph D. Minarik, "Simulated Clients in a Group Practice Course: Engaging Facilitation and Embodying Diversity," *Journal of Social Work Education* 54, no. 2 (2018): 310–323, doi: 10.1080/10437797.2017.1404528; Micki Washburn, Danielle E. Parrish, and Patrick S. Bordnick, "Virtual Patient Simulations for Brief Assessment of Mental Health Disorders in Integrated Care Settings," *Social Work in Mental Health* 18, no. 2 (2020): 121–148, doi: 10.1080/15332985.2017.1336743; Micki Washburn and Shu Zhou, "Teaching Note—Technology-Enhanced Clinical Simulations: Tools for Practicing Clinical Skills in Online Social Work Programs," *Journal of Social Work Education* 54, no. 3 (2018): 554–560, doi: 10.1080/10437797.2017.1404519.

CHAPTER 7 Using Simulations to Prepare School Leaders to Conduct Difficult Conversations

1. The actor who plays the standardized individual (SI) in this simulation is sometimes male and sometimes female, but to simplify the discussion of this case here, we refer to the standardized teacher as male.
2. The first author was coordinator of all the university's leadership programs for twelve years, was principal investigator for the New York State–funded grant that supported the development and assessment of our initial simulations, and used simulations in his courses on organizational leadership and curriculum and instructional leadership. The second and third are the current and former coordinators of our certification program for school building and district leaders and are responsible the supervision and internship courses that have made the most frequent use of simulations. All of our efforts were conducted in cooperation with and under the guidance of our colleague, Benjamin Dotger, who first introduced us to the approach and wrote or coauthored most of our original simulations, including the Jerry Michaelson case that is the focus of this chapter.

3. Development of most of these simulations was funded by grants from the US Department of Education's Institute for Education Sciences, the National Science Foundation, and the Arthur Vining Davis Foundation. In addition, development of leadership simulations was supported by two Teacher/Leader Quality Partnership grants from the New York State Education Department.
4. Chris Argyris and Donald Schön, *Theory In Practice: Increasing Professional Effectiveness* (San Francisco: Jossey-Bass, 1974).
5. Since 2010, at least forty-two US states and the District of Columbia have passed legislation or issued major new regulations related to teacher evaluation. For more, see *Race to the Top at a Glance: Evaluations of Teacher Effectiveness: State Requirements for Classroom Observations* (Washington, DC: Reform Support Network, 2012).
6. Keith Acheson and Meredith Damien Gall, *Clinical Supervision and Teacher Development: Preservice and Inservice Applications*, 5th ed. (New York: John Wiley and Sons, 2003); Shelly Arneson, "Improving Teaching One Conversation at a Time," *Educational Leadership* 72, no. 7 (2015): 32–36; Jo Blase and Joseph Blase, "Micropolitical Strategies Used by Administrators and Teachers in Instructional Conferences," *Alberta Journal of Educational Research* 42, no. 2 (1996): 345–360; Arthur Costa and Robert Garmston, *Cognitive Coaching: A Foundation for Renaissance Schools*, 2nd ed. (Norwood, MA: Christopher-Gordan Publishers, 2002); Charlotte Danielson, "Framing Discussion About Teaching," *Educational Leadership* 72, no. 7 (2015): 38–41; Linda Darling-Hammond, Audrey Amrein, Edward Beardsley, and Jesse Rothstein, "Evaluating Teacher Evaluation," *Phi Delta Kappan* 93, no. 6 (2012): 8–15, doi: 10.1177/003172171209300603; Eric J. Feeney, "Quality Feedback: The Essential Ingredient for Teacher Success," *The Clearing House* (March–April 2007): 191–197; Robert Garmston, "Reflections on Cognitive Coaching," *Educational Leadership* 51, no. 2 (1993): 57; Edit Khachatryan, "Feedback on Teaching from Observations of Teaching: What Do Administrators Say and What Do Teachers Think About It?," *NASSP Bulletin* 99, no. 2 (2015): 164–188, doi: 10.1177/0192636515583716; Steven Kimball, "Analysis of Feedback, Enabling Conditions and Fairness Perceptions of Teachers in Three School Districts with New Standards-Based Evaluation Systems," *Journal of Personnel Evaluation in Education* 16 (2002): 241–268, doi: 10.1023/A:1021787806189; Deidre LeFevre and Viviane Robinson, "The Interpersonal Challenges of Instructional Leadership: Principals' Effectiveness in Conversations About Performance Issues," *Educational Administration Quarterly* 51, no. 1 (2015): 58–95, doi: 10.1177/0013161X13518218; Joseph Murphy, Philip Hallinger, and Ronald Heck, "Leading via Teacher Evaluation: The Case of the Missing Clothes?," *Educational Researcher* 42, no. 6 (2013): 349–354, doi: 10.3102/0013189X13499625; Shane Safir, "Learning to Listen," *Educational Leadership* 74, no. 8 (2007): 16–21; Bob Tschannen-Moran and Megan Tschannen-Moran, "The Coach and

the Evaluator," *Educational Leadership* 69, no. 2 (2011): 10–16; Melissa Tuytens and Geert Devos, "The Role of Feedback from the School Leader During Teacher Evaluation for Teacher and School Improvement," *Teachers and Teaching* 23, no. 1 (2017): 6–24, doi: 10.1080/13540602.2016.1203770.

7. Feeney, "Quality Feedback," 195.
8. We planned to administer the survey to teachers in many more districts, but only a few of the superintendents we approached were receptive to having their teachers answer questions about how their administrators conduct performance evaluations or feedback discussions. This is a reminder of how uncomfortable the topic of performance evaluation is in many (and we guess, most) school systems. We hope to streamline the survey and find ways of getting a larger and more representative sample of teachers to complete it.
9. We measured perceptions of effectiveness with two sets of items—one focusing on effectiveness in helping teachers improve their instruction and the other focusing on effectiveness in strengthening the teacher/evaluator relationship.
10. Item 3 was not included on the teacher survey used to generate the other items and factors on this list but was added later.
11. This item could not have been included in our teacher survey, since doing so would have required us to ask teachers if they themselves were open or resistant to scrutinizing their own performance. We wanted survey respondents to concentrate on characterizing the evaluator's approach, not their own. See Danielle Brain, "Teacher Evaluation Conferences: A Mixed Methods Study" (PhD diss, Syracuse University, 2020).
12. We have used some of our leadership simulations in professional development workshops for practicing administrators. Our experience serving this audience has been promising but too limited to draw any confident conclusions, so our attention in this chapter has been confined to the use of simulations in the preparation of administrator candidates.
13. We are indebted to our evaluators, Kathy Gullie and Dean Spaulding, for helping us crystallize and recognize the importance of these lessons.
14. We already require that candidates pass a group leadership exercise (GLE) before they are allowed to begin their internships. The GLE requires each candidate and a group of colleagues to work for three hours to solve a complex organizational problem and then develop individual analyses of how effectively they and their group negotiated the exercise, addressed the problem, and made personal contributions to the group's effort. Passing the exercise depends on the quality of a candidate's personal analysis, not on whether the faculty believes they and their group approached and solved the problem appropriately.
15. Note that this hybrid approach would be similar to our program's use of our group leadership exercise discussed in note 14 above.
16. Lee Shulman, "Signature Pedagogies in the Professions," *Daedalus* 34, no. 3 (Summer 2005): 52–59, 52.
17. Shulman, "Signature Pedagogies," 56.
18. Shulman, "Signature Pedagogies," 57.

CHAPTER 8 A Cross-Program Analysis of Disability, Difference, and Inclusion in Multiple Simulations for Educator Candidates

1. Lee Shulman, "The Signature Pedagogies of the Professions of Law, Medicine, Engineering, and the Clergy: Potential Lessons for the Education of Teachers," *Teacher Education for Effective Teaching and Learning* (Irvine, CA: National Research Council's Center for Education, 2005).
2. Christine Ashby, "Disability Studies and Inclusive Teacher Preparation: A Socially Just Path for Teacher Education," *Research and Practice for Persons with Severe Disabilities* 37, no. 2 (2012): 88–99, doi: 10.2511/027494812802573611.
3. Individuals with Disabilities Education Act, 20 USC 1412 § 61(a)(5)(A) (2004); Education for All Handicapped Children Act, Pub. L. 94-142 (1975).
4. David J. Connor, "Why Is Special Education So Afraid of Disability Studies? Analyzing Attacks of Disdain and Distortion from Leaders in the Field," *Journal of Curriculum Theorizing* 34, no. 1 (2019): 10.
5. Sally S. French, "Simulation Exercises in Disability Awareness Training: A Critique," *Disability, Handicap & Society* 7, no. 3 (1992): 257–266, doi: 10.1080/02674649266780261.
6. Harold S. Barrows, *Problem-Based Learning Applied to Medical Education* (Springfield: Southern Illinois University Press, 2000).
7. Benjamin Dotger, email message to authors, December 20, 2020.
8. Christine Ashby, "The Trouble with Normal: The Struggle for Meaningful Access for Middle School Students with Developmental Disabilities," *Disability and Society* 25, no. 3 (2010), 345–358, doi: 10.1080/09687591003701249; Thomas Hehir, "Eliminating Ableism in Education," *Harvard Educational Review* 72, no. 1 (2002): 1–33, doi: 10/17763/haer/72/1/03866528702g2105.
9. Thomas Hehir, "Eliminating Ableism."
10. Mirko Chardin and Katie Novak, *Equity by Design: Delivering on the Power and Promise of UDL* (Thousand Oaks, CA: Corwin Press. 2020), 3.
11. Benjamin Dotger and Christine Ashby, "Exposing Conditional Inclusive Ideologies Through Simulated Interactions," *Teacher Education and Special Education* 33, no. 2 (2010): 114–130, doi: 10.1177/0888406409357541.
12. Ashby, "The Trouble with Normal."
13. Ibram X. Kendi, *How to Be an Antiracist* (New York: Random House Publishing Group, 2019); Gloria Ladson-Billings and William Tate, "Towards a Critical Race Theory of Education," *Teachers College Record* 97 (1995): 47–68, doi: 10.1080/10282580701850413.
14. Norman Kunc, "The Need to Belong: Rediscovering Maslow's Hierarchy of Needs," in *Restructuring for Caring and Effective Education: An Administrative Guide to Creating Heterogeneous Schools*, ed. Richard A. Villa, Jacquelyn Thousand, William Stainback, and Susan Stainback (Baltimore: Paul H. Brookes Publishing, 1992), 25–39.
15. Joseph Shapiro, *No Pity: People with Disabilities Forging a New Civil Rights Movement* (New York: Three Rivers Press, 1993).
16. Dotger and Ashby, "Exposing Conditional Inclusive Ideologies."

CHAPTER 9 Collaborating to Support the Design, Implementation, and Investigation of Clinical Simulations

1. Benjamin Dotger, "'I Had No Idea': Developing Dispositional Awareness and Sensitivity Through a Cross-Professional Pedagogy," *Teaching and Teacher Education* 26, no. 4 (2010): 805–812, doi: 10.1016/j.tate.2009.10.017; Benjamin Dotger, Steve Harris, and Amber Hansel, "Emerging Authenticity: The Crafting of Simulated Parent-Teacher Candidate Conferences," *Teaching Education* 19, no. 4 (2008): 335–347, doi: 10.1080/10476210802438324; Benjamin Dotger, Steven Harris, Michael Maher, and Amber Hansel, "Exploring the Emotional Geographies of Parent-Teacher Candidate Interactions: An Emergent Signature Pedagogy," *The Teacher Educator* 46, no. 3 (2011): 208–230, doi: 10.1080/08878730.2011.581882; Benjamin Dotger and Mara Sapon-Shevin, "But What Do I Say? New Teachers Learn to Talk with Parents," *Educational Leadership* 66, no. 9 (2009), http://www.ascd.org/publications/educational-leadership/summer09/vol66/num09/But-What-Do-I-Say¢.aspx; Benjamin Dotger and Melissa Smith, "Where's the Line? Negotiating Simulated Experiences to Define Teacher Identity," *The New Educator* 5, no. 2 (2009): 161–180, doi: 10.1080/1547688X.2009.10399570.
2. Benjamin Dotger, Elisa Dekaney, and John Coggiola,"In the Limelight: Utilizing Clinical Simulations to Enhance Music Teacher Education," *Research Studies in Music Education* 41, no. 1 (2018): 99–116, doi: 10.1177/1321103X18773102; Benjamin Dotger and Christine Ashby, "Exposing Conditional Inclusive Ideologies Through Simulated Interactions," *Teacher Education and Special Education* 33, no. 2 (2010): 114–130, doi: 10.1177/0888406409357541.
3. Lee Shulman, "The Signature Pedagogies of the Professions of Law, Medicine, Engineering, and the Clergy: Potential Lessons for the Education of Teachers," paper delivered at the Math Science Partnerships (MSP) Workshop on Teacher Education for Effective Teaching and Learning, National Research Council's Center for Education, Irvine, CA, 2005; Pam Grossman, Karen Hammerness, and Morva McDonald, "Redefining Teaching, Re-imagining Teacher Education," *Teachers and Teaching: Theory and Practice* 15, no. 2 (2009): 273–289, doi: 10.1080/13540600902875340; Harold S. Barrows, *Simulated (Standardized) Patients and Other Human Simulations: A Comprehensive Guide to Their Training and Use in Teaching and Evaluation* (Chapel Hill, NC: Health Sciences Consortium, 1987).
4. Justin E. Freedman, "Is That Okay with You? Examining a Simulated Discussion About Accommodations Between University students Identified as Having a Disability and a Standardized Faculty Member" (PhD diss., Syracuse University, 2018).
5. Benjamin H. Dotger, *"I Had No Idea": Clinical Simulations for Teacher Development* (Charlotte, NC: Information Age Publishing, 2013).

Acknowledgments

We are grateful to the following for their support of this work:

- Clinical Simulations Study Group participants, for their interest and continuing engagement with simulations in and across their respective disciplines.
- SUNY Upstate Medical University colleagues, especially Steve Harris, for their long-standing generosity of Clinical Skills Center space and expertise in recruiting and training standardized individuals.
- The colleagues in our home departments of Teaching & Leadership and Reading & Language Arts, for their tireless work to make K–12 schools better places for all.
- The leadership of the Syracuse University School of Education, particularly our former dean Joanna Masingila, for backing our efforts from the beginning.
- Nancy Walser at Harvard Education Press, for helping us shape this book for the better from its conception, and Jayne Fargnoli, for shepherding it to completion.
- Our families, on both sides of the ravine, for love, laughter, and many campfires over the past year.

About the Editors and Contributors

Christine Ashby, PhD, is a professor in the Teaching & Leadership Department at Syracuse University. She coordinates the inclusive special education 1–6 and 7–12 master's programs and the inclusive elementary and special education undergraduate program. She is the director of the Center on Disability and Inclusion, principal investigator for the Syracuse Urban Inclusive Teacher Residency Program, and coprincipal investigator for the Mid-State Regional Partnership Center. Her teaching and research focus on inclusive education, with specific emphasis on supports for students with labels of autism and other developmental disabilities, disability studies, and inclusive teacher preparation.

Sharon L. Bruner, PhD, is a clinical assistant professor and Counselor Training Clinic director in the Educational Psychology and Counseling Department at the University of Tennessee, Knoxville. She is a licensed professional counselor and mental health service provider whose scholarship focuses on issues of persistence and retention of traditionally marginalized students in higher education. She utilizes a variety of qualitative methodologies to explore student experiences in higher education and the ways those experiences are impacted by their intersecting identities.

Megan E. Cartier, MEd, worked as a high school special education teacher for twelve years in central Kentucky before coming to Syracuse University, where she is now a doctoral candidate in special education. She has earned a certificate of advanced study in disability studies. Her research interests include inclusive education, Universal Design for Learning, inclusive higher education for individuals with intellectual and developmental disabilities, and postinclusive higher education outcomes for individuals who participate in and/or complete a postsecondary inclusive education program.

She is also interested in the continuity of special education services for children of military service members.

Diane Canino-Rispoli, CAS, served as a clinical professor and program coordinator in the certificate of advanced study (CAS) program in educational leadership at Syracuse University for over twenty years. Her experiences as an educational leader at both the building and district levels in the Syracuse City School District served as an important component of her teaching. In the district, she held a variety of leadership positions that included service as curriculum coordinator in English-language arts, building principal, administrator in human resources, and administrator for leadership development. As a practitioner, her experiences were primarily in urban settings, and her area of interest and expertise was providing growth-focused feedback to teachers through the evaluation process and instructional leadership. She has also been involved in the administration of several federal and state grants that were designed to reform leadership preparation programs and was part of a statewide committee of leaders that developed the New York State leadership assessments.

Kelly Chandler-Olcott, EdD, is Laura J. and L. Douglas Meredith Professor for Teaching Excellence in the Reading & Language Arts Department, and the interim dean of the School of Education, at Syracuse University. She teaches literacy methods courses to secondary and K–12 education majors and coordinates undergraduate and master's programs in English education. Her design-based research focuses on teaching literacy across the disciplines in diverse, inclusive classrooms, and she has coedited the *Journal of Adolescent & Adult Literacy* since 2015. Her awareness of the potential for clinical simulations in teacher education was heightened by cofacilitating a faculty study group on that topic for several years with Benjamin Dotger.

Luis Columna, PhD, is an associate professor in the Kinesiology Department at the University of Wisconsin at Madison. Prior to coming to Madison, he was an associate professor in the Exercise Science Department at Syracuse University. Throughout his doctoral studies, he taught adapted physical education in the Denton, Texas, public schools. He has published two books, numerous peer-reviewed journal articles, and book chapters. His research focuses on ways to increase the participation of families (especially those who identify as Hispanic) of children with disabilities into physical activity. He also focuses on ways to better prepare physical activity professionals and physical education teachers to work with diverse populations.

Benjamin Dotger, PhD, is a professor in the Teaching & Leadership Department at Syracuse University. He teaches education foundations courses to secondary and K–12 teacher candidates, coordinates the teaching and curriculum master's program, and directs clinical simulation design and implementation efforts between the School of Education and SUNY Upstate Medical University's Clinical Skills Center. His scholarship centers on the design and study of clinical simulations within and across educator preparation disciplines, with emphasis on identity formation, discipline-specific practices, and physiological responses. This work has been supported by numerous federal and private foundations, including the Spencer Foundation, the Arthur Vining Davis Foundations, the National Science Foundation, and the Institute for Educational Sciences.

Sharon Dotger, PhD, is an associate professor in the Teaching & Leadership Department at Syracuse University. She focuses her research on conditions for facilitating teacher learning for equitable science learning outcomes for all students. She is an experienced science educator within the elementary and secondary grade bands. She uses multiple forms of approximations of practice—simulations, mediated field experiences, and mock-up lessons in lesson study—to assist teachers, both preservice and in-service, in developing their core pedagogies for science teaching.

Leela J. George, EdD, is an associate teaching professor in the Teaching & Leadership Department and program coordinator of the educational leadership certificate program at Syracuse University. She is a graduate of St. Lawrence University, State University at Cortland, and Syracuse University. Before joining the SU faculty in 2017, she was a teacher and school leader in the region for thirty-three years, ending her career with seven years as the assistant superintendent for curriculum and instruction in the Auburn (New York) Enlarged City Schools. Additionally, she serves as the executive director for the Study Council at Syracuse University, which is a regional partnership of the university and local school districts.

Duane T. Graysay, PhD, is an assistant professor at Syracuse University, dually appointed in the Mathematics Department and the Teaching & Leadership Department. He coordinates undergraduate and master's programs in mathematics education and teaches undergraduate mathematics courses, methods courses for secondary mathematics education majors, and courses for graduate students in mathematics education. His research focuses on understanding the process of mathematical generalizing and on methods for supporting prospective teachers in developing ambitious teaching practices. His interest in clinical simulations is an extension of prior involvement in examining preservice teacher learning within simulated rehearsals.

Melissa M. Luke, PhD, is a provost faculty fellow at Syracuse University, associate dean for research in the School of Education, and Dean's Professor in the Counseling & Human Services Department. Her scholarship focuses on counselor preparation and practice to more effectively respond to the needs of underserved persons across global contexts. She has utilized simulations in content and clinical coursework. She has published extensively in the areas of counselor professional identity, clinical supervision, recently completing a grounded theory of school counselor trainees' professional identity development evidenced throughout a codeveloped series of interrelated, nested simulations.

Joanna O. Masingila, PhD, is the former dean of the School of Education at Syracuse University and Laura J. and L. Douglas Meredith Professor for Teaching Excellence dually appointed in the Teaching & Leadership Department and the Mathematics Department. Her research interests include teacher development, teacher educator development, mathematical knowledge for teaching teachers, and students' out-of-school mathematics practice. She has grown as a mathematics educator by working as a team with Benjamin Dotger, Sharon Dotger, and others in developing mathematics and science content clinical simulations with the support of a National Science Foundation grant.

Michael L. Norris, PhD, is an assistant professor for health and physical education in the Teaching & Leadership Department at Syracuse University. He teaches physical education methods courses to PreK–12 physical education majors and coordinates undergraduate programs in health and physical education, physical education, and the coaching minor. His expertise focuses on curriculum and assessment as well as physical education teacher education pedagogy. His contribution to this text stems from his awareness of the potential for clinical simulations in physical education teacher education pedagogy, and he was instrumental in providing input into the design, data collection, and analysis of clinical simulations with physical education majors that centered around adapted physical education for students in education foundations courses that included clinical simulations.

Joseph Shedd, PhD, is a graduate of the University of North Carolina at Chapel Hill and Cornell University. He has been in the Teaching & Leadership Department at Syracuse University since 1990, serving as chair from 1998 to 2008. He coordinated the leadership programs from 1995 to 1998 and from 2008 to 2017. His research and teaching have focused on organizational development and school improvement processes in public education, curriculum and instructional leadership, teacher evaluation, and collective bargaining in education. His current work focuses on the use of video-documented simulations to prepare school administrators to provide evaluation feedback to teachers. He has served as principal investigator for several federally funded initiatives to reform the preparation of school leaders. He retired from the active faculty and was appointed adjunct associate professor in August 2020 but continues his research on teacher evaluation and the use of simulations in leadership preparation.

Index

ableism, 136–38
adapted physical education (APE), 54–55
adult roles, articulating, 144–47
American Community Survey, 54
Arthur Vining Davis Foundation, 3, 155
Ashby, Christy, 26, 161
Ashley Wilson simulation, 24–25, 88–89, 161. *See also* counselor education; nested simulation
  applicability of, 99–101
awareness, demonstratig, 112

Ball, Deborah L., 36
Barab, Sasha, 26
Barrows, Harold S., 5, 30, 56, 132
Becker, Joanne Rossi, 39
book planning retreat, sample agenda for, 158
Brad Winston simulation, 133, 135, 142–43, 161
  analysis, 57–59
  assessment of skills, 59–60
  data collection, 57–59
  design/methodology, 55–59
  discussion, 63–66
  educator candidate demographics, 58
  findings, 59–63
  implications, 63–66
  inclusion through modification, 60–63
  overview, 57
  participants, 57–59
Brown, John, 19, 30

candidates
  active attendance, 46–47
  affordances of multiple representations, 43–44
  attending to student's thinking, 47
  comparing/contrasting student thinking, 47–49
  representation limitations, 44–45
Canino-Rispoli, Diane, 110, 162
Carnegie Foundation for the Advancement of Teaching, 8
Cartier, Megan E., 128
clinical simulation. *See* simulations
  conceptual underpinnings of, 15–30
  defining, 4–7
  embracing as pedagogy, 8–10
co–principal investigators (co-PIs), 166
collaboration, 153–54
  benefits of, 160–65
  brief history of, 154–60
  coming together, 155–56
  forming study group, 156–60
  recommendations for, 165–70
Collins, Allan, 19, 30
Collisions simulation, 75
Columna, Luis, 168
community members, engaging, 162–63
community, tenet, 28–30
concerns, communicating, 112
Conference Board of Mathematical Sciences, 36

Council for Accreditation of Counseling and Related Educational Programs (CACREP), 91
Council for the Accreditation of Counseling and Related Educational Programs (CACREP), 86–87
counselor education
  conceptual knowledge, 91–93
  connections with nested simulations, 90–99
  counseling skills, 94–97
  experiential pedagogies, 84–86
  intra-/interpersonal awareness, 93–94
  nested simulation design in, 86–89
  overview for, 87
  social justice advocacy, 97–99
cross-program perspective, simulation, 127–28
  crosscutting themes, 136–47
  disability simulations, 131–36
  implications for, 147–51
  related literature, 128–32

Davis, Arthur Vining, 9
debriefing process, designing, 118–19
difference. *See* disability
difficult conversations, conducting. *See* school leaders, preparing
disability
  designing simulations for, 132–35
  method of analysis, 135–36
  problem of simulating, 131–32
  talking (and not talking about), 136–38
  terms referring to, 136–38
disability studies in education (DSE), 130
disciplinary core ideas (DCI), 70, 73
disposition, defining, 26
Dotger, Benjamin, 38, 86
  caregiver communications elective, 2
  foundations course of, 1–2
Dotger, Sharon, 38, 161
Duguid, Paul, 19, 30
dynamic learning context, 52, 95, 100, 104, 114

education candidate (EC), 54, 68
  affecting development of, 120–21
  designing debriefing process, 118–19
  effectiveness criteria, 118–19
  Niagara Falls simulations, 76–78
  Shoreline Erosion, 78–80
educator
  disposition of, 26
educator candidate (EC), 4–5, 16, 32, 83, 104, 127, 153
  community, 28–30
  Elizabeth Meyers candidate, 26–28
  fully inclusive school environments, 18–19
  protocol provided to, 6
educators, identity of, 26–28
elementary science, status of, 68–70. *See also* science education, simulation
Elizabeth Meyers simulation, 26–27, 133, 135, 139
evaluation systems, changes in, 109–10
experiential pedagogies, 84–85
explanation, defining, 71–72

feedback
  behaviors, 112, 113
  effective feedback conference, 111–14
  providing, 109–11
Figural Approach to Generalizing simulation, 38–41
follow-up, providing, 112
Framework for K-12 Science Education, 70–72

George, Leela, 110, 162
Goodrich, Kris, 87
Graysay, Duane, 39
Greenberg, Susie, 39
Grossman, Pam, 9

Harris, Steven, 2
health teacher candidate, example, 23
Hiebert, James, 33

inclusion, defining/enacting, 139–44. *See also* disability
inclusive education, grounding in, 130–31
inclusive schooling, 10
Individuals with Disabilities Education Improvement Act (IDEIA), 130
Institute of Education Sciences, 3
institutional review board (IRB), 165–66

Jasper Johnson simulation, 17–18
Jennifer Boyton simulation, 17

Jerry Michaelson simulation, 103–5. *See also* school leaders, preparing
designing debriefing process, 118–19
designing simulations similar to, 114–18
walk-through notes, 116
Josh Churchill simulation, 133, 134, 141

knowledge of content and curriculum (KCC), 36
knowledge of content and students (KCS), 36
opportunities to develop, 45–49
knowledge of content and teaching (KCT), 36, 42
multiple representations, 43–45
opportunities to develop, 43

leadership, simulations used in, 106–7. *See also* school leaders, preparing
Lee, Carrie E., 37
Leikin, Roza, 50
LGBTIQ+, 87
"LGBTIQ+ Responsive School Counseling Supervision," 87
Lori Blake simulation, 132–33, 134, 169
Lori Danson simulation, 132–33, 134, 140
Luke, Melissa, 87, 162

Marissa Collins simulation, 20
Masingila, Joanna, 38
mathematical education simulation
affordances of, 37–38
constitution of, 37
designing and implementation of, 38–40
discussion, 49–51
findings, 43–49
methods, 40–42
reflections, 52
mathematical knowledge for teaching (MKT), 35–37
mathematical knowledge for teaching teachers (MKTT), 36
mathematics educators, 31–32
addressing issues faced by, 34–35
facilitating candidate reflections, 51
mathematical knowledge for teaching, 35–37
opportunities to develop MKTT, 49–50
problem faced by, 33
program overview for, 35
simulations for, 37–40
task creation, 50

McNally, Nellie, 39
Multicultural and Social Justice (MSJ), 87
Multicultural and Social Justice Counseling Competencies (MSJCC), 86
multifaceted inclusive approaches, 128–29
multiple perspectives, considering, 160–61
mythological scientific method, 70

National Council of Teachers of Mathematics (NCTM), 33
National Science Foundation, 3
National Science Foundation DR-K12, 17
nested simulation, 83–84
connections with counseling domain, 90–99
within counselor education, 84–86
design, 86–89
protocols, 88–89
Next Generation Science Standards (NGSS), 68
Niagara Falls simulation, 75–78
Norris, Michael, 168
Numerical Approach to Generalizing simulation, 38–41

performance expectation, 70
physical education (PE), 53–54
background/context, 54–55
discussion, 63–66
findings, 59–63
methodology, 55–59
Piaget theory, 22
Plucker, Jonathan, 26
preprofessionals, teaching, 8
professional preparation, 34, 124, 165

readings, recommending, 157
representations, limitations of, 44–45
responses, anticipating, 168–69
responsibility, ensuring, 112
Rivera, Ferdinand, 39
Roy-Campbell, Zaline, 169

school counselors, 18, 85–86, 90–93, 101
school leaders, preparing, 103–5
designing simulations, 114–18
overview, 105
performance feedback, 109–14
simulations as assessment, 118–22
simulations as signature pedagogy, 123–25
using simulations, 105–9

School of Education (SOE), 1–2, 16, 54, 104, 128, 153–54
science education, simulation, 67–68
  defining explanation, 71–72
  design implications, 80–82
  designing standards, 70–71
  recruiting children, 74
  simulation overview, 74–78
  standards/design criteria, 72–74
Self, Elizabeth A., 10
Seward, Derek, 163
Shadows simulation, 75
shared learning, 30, 86
Shedd, Joe, 162
Shoreline Erosion simulation, 78–80
Shulman, Lee, 4, 8, 123
signature pedagogy, 123–25
  community, 28–30
  tenets of, 28
  term, 8
Silver, Edward A., 50
sim-able, constructing collective sense of, 163–65
simulation initiatives, 6–7
  process overview, 7
simulations
  affecting candidate development, 120–21
  assessing candidate skills using, 122
  collaborations to support, 153–70
  comparing, 124
  creating searchable database of, 166–67
  designing, 16–21
  engaging in authentic practice using, 16–21
  forming educator identity using, 26–28
  inclusion in, 127–51
  key constructs of, 23–24
  live actors, 5–6, 12, 17–18, 37, 42, 52, 67, 83, 88, 106–8, 154, 163, 168
  mathematics educators, 31–52
  mathematics teacher education, 37–40
  nested, 83–101
  physical education inclusion, 53–66
  preparing school leaders using, 103–25
  programs-specific uses of., *See*
  relevance of, 129–30
  science education, 67–82
  as signature pedagogy, 123–25
  two-part, 117–18
  uncertainty and, 21–25
social justice, advocacy for, 97–99
Spencer Foundation, 3
standardized individual (SI), 5–6, 17, 31, 54, 73, 83, 106, 127, 153
  changing positions, 117–18
  interaction protocol provided to, 6
  Word Problem simulation, 39
standardized patients, 5
standardized, term, 6
Stengel, Barbara S., 10
Stigler, James W., 33
study group, forming, 156–60
SUNY Upstate Medical University, 2
Syracuse University. *See* School of Education (SOE)

take care of, phrase, 23
tasks, creating, 50
teacher education, 1, 11, 16
  mathematics, 31–52
  physical education, 53–66
  science education, 67–82
teacher preparation, 8, 108, 132, 136
technology, utilizing, 6–7
Tiling Squares problem, 40
triggers, 117–18
trust, building, 112

uncertainty, navigating, 21–25
Universal Design for Learning (UDL), 137–38
Upstate Medical University's Clinical Skills Center, 6

verbally aggressive standardized student, example, 23

Water Quality simulation, 75
Webel, Corey, 38
wince moments, 127–28
Word Problem simulation, 38–41

Yellowstone simulation, 75

Zaslavsky, Orit, 50
Zopf, Deborah A., 36